The Quran With Tafsir Ibn Kathir Part 13 of 30: Yusuf 053 To Ibrahim 052

The Quran With Tafsir Ibn Kathir
Part 13 of 30:
Yusuf 053 To
Ibrahim 052

With
Arabic Script, Transliteration of Arabic, Meaning in English
and Ibn Kathir's Abridged Tafsir (Explanation)

Muhammad Saed Abdul-Rahman
BSc, DipHE

© Muhammad Saed Abdul-Rahman,2012
ISBN 978-1-86179-864-0

All Rights reserved

British Library Cataloguing in Publication Data. A Catalogue record for this book is available from the British Library

Designed, Typeset and produced by:
MSA Publication Limited, 4 Bello Close, Herne Hill,
London SE24 9BW
United Kingdom

Cover design: Houriyah Abdul-Rahman

TABLE OF CONTENTS

- TABLE OF CONTENTS V
- **PRELUDE** XIII
  - OPENING SERMAN XIII
  - OUR MISSION XIV
  - BIOGRAPHY OF HAFIZ IBN KATHIR (701 H - 774 H) XIV
    - Ibn Kathir's Teachers xiv
    - Ibn Kathir's Students xv
    - Ibn Kathir's Books xv
    - Ibn Kathir's Death xvi
- **PREFACE** XVII
  - ABOUT THIS BOOK XVII
  - PERFORMING PROSTRATION WHILE READING THE QUR'AN XVII
- **PART 13 FULL ARABIC TEXT** 1
- **CHAPTER (SURAH) 12: YUSUF (JOSEPH), VERSES 053-111** 12
  - *Surah: 12 Ayah: 53* 12
    - Tafsir Ibn Kathir 12
  - *Surah: 12 Ayah: 54 & Ayah: 55* 13
    - Tafsir Ibn Kathir 13
    - Yusuf's Rank with the King of Egypt 13
  - *Surah: 12 Ayah: 56 & Ayah: 57* 14
    - Tafsir Ibn Kathir 14
    - Yusuf's Reign in Egypt 14
  - *Surah: 12 Ayah: 58, Ayah: 59, Ayah: 60, Ayah: 61 & Ayah: 62* 15
    - Tafsir Ibn Kathir 16
    - Yusuf's Brothers travel to Egypt 16
  - *Surah: 12 Ayah: 63 & Ayah: 64* 17
    - Tafsir Ibn Kathir 18
    - Yusuf's Brothers ask Ya`qub's Permission to send Their Brother Binyamin with Them to Egypt 18
  - *Surah: 12 Ayah: 65 & Ayah: 66* 18
    - Tafsir Ibn Kathir 19
    - They find Their Money returned to Their Bags 19
  - *Surah: 12 Ayah: 67 & Ayah: 68* 20
    - Tafsir Ibn Kathir 20
    - Ya`qub orders His Children to enter Egypt from Different Gates 20
  - *Surah: 12 Ayah: 69* 21
    - Tafsir Ibn Kathir 21
    - Yusuf comforts Binyamin 21
  - *Surah: 12 Ayah: 70, Ayah: 71 & Ayah: 72* 21

  Tafsir Ibn Kathir 22
    Yusuf had His Golden Bowl placed in Binyamin's Bag; a Plot to keep Him in Egypt 22
Surah: 12 Ayah: 73, Ayah: 74, Ayah: 75 & Ayah: 76. .... *22*
  Tafsir Ibn Kathir 23
Surah: 12 Ayah: 77 .... *24*
  Tafsir Ibn Kathir 25
    Yusuf's Brothers accuse Him of Theft! 25
Surah: 12 Ayah: 78 & Ayah: 79 .... *25*
  Tafsir Ibn Kathir 26
    Yusuf's Brothers offer taking One of Them instead of Binyamin as a Slave, Yusuf rejects the Offer 26
Surah: 12 Ayah: 80, Ayah: 81 & Ayah: 82 .... *26*
  Tafsir Ibn Kathir 27
    Yusuf's Brothers consult Each Other in Confidence; the Advice Their Eldest Brother gave Them 27
Surah: 12 Ayah: 83, Ayah: 84, Ayah: 85 & Ayah: 86 .... *28*
  Tafsir Ibn Kathir 29
    Allah's Prophet Ya`qub receives the Grievous News 29
Surah: 12 Ayah: 87 & Ayah: 88. .... *30*
  Tafsir Ibn Kathir 30
    Ya`qub orders His Children to inquire about Yusuf and His Brother 30
    Yusuf's Brothers stand before Him 31
Surah: 12 Ayah: 89, Ayah: 90, Ayah: 91 & Ayah: 92 .... *31*
  Tafsir Ibn Kathir 32
    Yusuf reveals His True Identity to His Brothers and forgives Them 32
Surah: 12 Ayah: 93, Ayah: 94 & Ayah: 95. .... *33*
  Tafsir Ibn Kathir 33
    Ya`qub finds the Scent of Yusuf in his Shirt! 33
Surah: 12 Ayah: 96, Ayah: 97 & Ayah: 98. .... *34*
  Tafsir Ibn Kathir 35
    Yahudha brings Yusuf's Shirt and Good News 35
    Yusuf's Brothers feel Sorry and Regretful 35
Surah: 12 Ayah: 99 & Ayah: 100. .... *35*
  Tafsir Ibn Kathir 36
    Yusuf welcomes His Parents; His Dream comes True 36
Surah: 12 Ayah: 101 .... *38*
  Tafsir Ibn Kathir 38
    Yusuf begs Allah to die as A Muslim 38
Surah: 12 Ayah: 102, Ayah: 103 & Ayah: 104 .... *39*
  Tafsir Ibn Kathir 39
    This Story is a Revelation from Allah 39
Surah: 12 Ayah: 105, Ayah: 106 & Ayah: 107 .... *40*
  Tafsir Ibn Kathir 41
    People neglect to ponder the Signs before Them 41

Table of Contents

Surah: 12 Ayah: 108 43
    Tafsir Ibn Kathir 43
        The Messenger's Way 43
Surah: 12 Ayah: 109 43
    Tafsir Ibn Kathir 44
        All of the Prophets are Humans and Men 44
        All Prophets were Humans not Angels 44
        Drawing Lessons from the Incidents of the Past 45
Surah: 12 Ayah: 110 45
    Tafsir Ibn Kathir 45
        Allah's Prophets are aided by Victory in Times of Distress and Need 45
Surah: 12 Ayah: 111 47
    Tafsir Ibn Kathir 48
        A Lesson for Men Who have Understanding 48

CHAPTER (SURAH) 13: AR-RAD (THE THUNDER), VERSES 001-043 48

Surah: 13 Ayah: 1 48
    Tafsir Ibn Kathir 49
        The Qur'an is Allah's Kalam (Speech) 49
Surah: 13 Ayah: 2 49
    Tafsir Ibn Kathir 50
        Clarifying Allah's Perfect Ability 50
        Al-Istawa', Rising above the Throne 50
        Allah subjected the Sun and the Moon to rotate continuously 50
Surah: 13 Ayah: 3 & Ayah: 4 51
    Tafsir Ibn Kathir 52
        Allah's Signs on the Earth 52
Surah: 13 Ayah: 5 53
    Tafsir Ibn Kathir 54
        Denying Resurrection after Death, is Strange 54
Surah: 13 Ayah: 6 54
    Tafsir Ibn Kathir 55
        The Disbelievers ask for the Punishment to be delivered now! 55
Surah: 13 Ayah: 7 56
    Tafsir Ibn Kathir 56
        The Idolators ask for a Miracle 56
Surah: 13 Ayah: 8 & Ayah: 9 57
    Tafsir Ibn Kathir 57
        Allah is All-Knower of Al-Ghayb (Unseen) 57
Surah: 13 Ayah: 10 & Ayah: 11 59
    Tafsir Ibn Kathir 60
        Allah's Knowledge encompasses all Things Apparent and Hidden 60
        The Guardian Angels 60
Surah: 13 Ayah: 12 & Ayah: 13 61

- Tafsir Ibn Kathir ... 62
  - Clouds, Thunder and Lightning are Signs of Allah's Power ... 62
  - Supplicating to Allah upon hearing Ar-Ra`d (Thunder) ... 63
- *Surah: 13 Ayah: 14* ... 65
  - Tafsir Ibn Kathir ... 65
    - A Parable for the Weakness of the False Gods of the Polytheists ... 65
- *Surah: 13 Ayah: 15* ... 66
  - Tafsir Ibn Kathir ... 66
    - Everything prostrates unto Allah ... 66
- *Surah: 13 Ayah: 16* ... 66
  - Tafsir Ibn Kathir ... 67
    - Affirming Tawhid ... 67
- *Surah: 13 Ayah: 17* ... 68
  - Tafsir Ibn Kathir ... 68
    - Two Parables proving that Truth remains and Falsehood perishes ... 68
    - The Qur'an and the Sunnah contain Parables that use Water and Fire ... 70
- *Surah: 13 Ayah: 18* ... 71
  - Tafsir Ibn Kathir ... 72
    - Blessed and Wretched Ones ... 72
- *Surah: 13 Ayah: 19* ... 72
  - Tafsir Ibn Kathir ... 73
    - The Believer and the Disbeliever are never Equal ... 73
- *Surah: 13 Ayah: 20, Ayah: 21, Ayah: 22, Ayah: 23 & Ayah: 24* ... 73
  - Tafsir Ibn Kathir ... 74
    - Qualities of the Blessed Ones, which will lead to Paradise ... 74
- *Surah: 13 Ayah: 25* ... 77
  - Tafsir Ibn Kathir ... 77
    - Characteristics of the Wretched Ones which will lead to the Curse and the Evil Home ... 77
- *Surah: 13 Ayah: 26* ... 78
  - Tafsir Ibn Kathir ... 78
    - Increase and Decrease in Provision is in Allah's Hand ... 78
- *Surah: 13 Ayah: 27, Ayah: 28 & Ayah: 29* ... 79
  - Tafsir Ibn Kathir ... 79
    - Disbelievers ask for Miracles, Allah's Response to Them ... 79
    - The Believer's Heart finds Comfort in the Remembrance of Allah ... 80
    - The Meaning of Tuba ... 81
- *Surah: 13 Ayah: 30* ... 82
  - Tafsir Ibn Kathir ... 82
    - Our Prophet was sent to recite and call to Allah's Revelation ... 82
- *Surah: 13 Ayah: 31* ... 83
  - Tafsir Ibn Kathir ... 84
    - Virtues of the Qur'an and the Denial of Disbelievers ... 84
- *Surah: 13 Ayah: 32* ... 86
  - Tafsir Ibn Kathir ... 86

Table of Contents

Surah: 13 Ayah: 33 87
    Tafsir Ibn Kathir 87
        There is no Similarity between Allah and False Deities in any Respect 87

Surah: 13 Ayah: 34 & Ayah: 35 89
    Tafsir Ibn Kathir 89
        Punishment of the Disbelievers and Reward of the Pious Believers 89

Surah: 13 Ayah: 36 & Ayah: 37 92
    Tafsir Ibn Kathir 92
        The Truthful Ones from among the People of the Scriptures rejoice at what Allah has revealed to Muhammad 92

Surah: 13 Ayah: 38 & Ayah: 39 94
    Tafsir Ibn Kathir 94
        All Prophets and Messengers were Humans 94
        No Prophet can bring a Miracle except by Allah's Leave 94
        Meaning of Allah blotting out what He wills and confirming what He wills of the Book ..95

Surah: 13 Ayah: 40 & Ayah: 41 96
    Tafsir Ibn Kathir 96
        Punishment is by Allah, and the Messenger's Job is only to convey the Message 96

Surah: 13 Ayah: 42 97
    Tafsir Ibn Kathir 97
        The Disbelievers plot, but the Believers gain the Good End 97

Surah: 13 Ayah: 43 98
    Tafsir Ibn Kathir 98
        Allah and those who have Knowledge of the Scripture are Sufficient as Witness to the Message of the Prophet 98

CHAPTER (SURAH) 14: IBRAHIM (ABRAHAM), VERSES 001-052 99

Surah: 14 Ayah: 1, Ayah: 2 & Ayah: 3 99
    Tafsir Ibn Kathir 100
        Describing the Qur'an and warning Those Who defy it 100

Surah: 14 Ayah: 4 101
    Tafsir Ibn Kathir 101
        Every Prophet was sent with the Language of His People; Guidance or Misguidance follows the Explanation 101

Surah: 14 Ayah: 5 102
    Tafsir Ibn Kathir 102
        Story of Musa and His People 102

Surah: 14 Ayah: 6, Ayah: 7 & Ayah: 8 103
    Tafsir Ibn Kathir 104

Surah: 14 Ayah: 9 105
    Tafsir Ibn Kathir 106
        Earlier Nations disbelieved in Their Prophets 106
        Meaning of, "They put Their Hands in Their Mouths 106

Surah: 14 Ayah: 10, Ayah: 11 & Ayah: 12 107

- Tafsir Ibn Kathir ... 108
  - The Argument between the Prophets and the Disbelievers ... 108
  - Disbelievers reject Prophethood because the Messengers were Humans! ... 108
- *Surah: 14 Ayah: 13, Ayah: 14, Ayah: 15, Ayah: 16 & Ayah: 17 ... 109*
  - Tafsir Ibn Kathir ... 110
  - Disbelieving Nations threaten Their Messengers with Expulsion ... 110
- *Surah: 14 Ayah: 18 ... 113*
  - Tafsir Ibn Kathir ... 114
  - A Parable for the Deeds of the Disbelievers ... 114
- *Surah: 14 Ayah: 19 & Ayah: 20 ... 114*
  - Tafsir Ibn Kathir ... 115
  - Proof that Resurrection occurs after Death ... 115
- *Surah: 14 Ayah: 21 ... 116*
  - Tafsir Ibn Kathir ... 116
  - Disbelieving Chiefs and Their Followers will dispute in the Fire ... 116
- *Surah: 14 Ayah: 22 & Ayah: 23 ... 117*
  - Tafsir Ibn Kathir ... 118
  - Shaytan disowns His Followers on the Day of Resurrection ... 118
- *Surah: 14 Ayah: 24, Ayah: 25 & Ayah: 26 ... 120*
  - Tafsir Ibn Kathir ... 120
  - The Parable of the Word of Islam and the Word of Kufr ... 120
- *Surah: 14 Ayah: 27 ... 122*
  - Tafsir Ibn Kathir ... 122
  - Allah keeps the Believers Firm in This Life and in the Hereafter with a Word that stands Firm ... 122
- *Surah: 14 Ayah: 28, Ayah: 29 & Ayah: 30 ... 126*
  - Tafsir Ibn Kathir ... 126
  - The Recompense of Those Who have changed the Blessings of Allah into Disbelief ... 126
- *Surah: 14 Ayah: 31 ... 127*
  - Tafsir Ibn Kathir ... 127
  - The Command for Prayer and Charity ... 127
- *Surah: 14 Ayah: 32, Ayah: 33 & Ayah: 34 ... 128*
  - Tafsir Ibn Kathir ... 129
  - Describing Some of Allah's Tremendous Favors ... 129
- *Surah: 14 Ayah: 35 & Ayah: 36 ... 130*
  - Tafsir Ibn Kathir ... 130
  - Ibrahim's Supplication to Allah when He brought Isma`il to Makkah ... 130
- *Surah: 14 Ayah: 37 ... 132*
  - Tafsir Ibn Kathir ... 132
- *Surah: 14 Ayah: 38, Ayah: 39, Ayah: 40 & Ayah: 41 ... 133*
  - Tafsir Ibn Kathir ... 133
- *Surah: 14 Ayah: 42 & Ayah: 43 ... 134*
  - Tafsir Ibn Kathir ... 135
  - Allah gives Respite to the Disbelievers and is never unaware of what They do ... 135

Table of Contents

Surah: 14 Ayah: 44, Ayah: 45 & Ayah: 46 ...... *135*
    Tafsir Ibn Kathir 136
        There will be no Respite after the Coming of the Torment 136

Surah: 14 Ayah: 47 & Ayah: 48 ...... *138*
    Tafsir Ibn Kathir 138
        Allah never breaks a Promise 138

Surah: 14 Ayah: 49, Ayah: 50 & Ayah: 51 ...... *140*
    Tafsir Ibn Kathir 140
        The Condition of the criminals on the Day of Resurrection 140

Surah: 14 Ayah: 52 ...... *142*
    Tafsir Ibn Kathir 142
        Allah states that this Qur'an is a Message for mankind, ... 142

PRELUDE

Opening Serman

Indeed, all praise is due to Allah. We praise Him and seek His help and forgiveness. We seek refuge with Allah from our soul's evil and our wrong doings. He whom Allah guides, no one can misguide; and he whom He misguides, no one can guide

I bear witness that there is no (true) god except Allah – alone without a partner, and I bear witness that Muhammad (peace and blessings of Allah be upon him) is His 'abd (servant) and messenger.

يَٰٓأَيُّهَا ٱلَّذِينَ ءَامَنُوا۟ ٱتَّقُوا۟ ٱللَّهَ حَقَّ تُقَاتِهِۦ وَلَا تَمُوتُنَّ إِلَّا وَأَنتُم مُّسْلِمُونَ ﴿١٠٢﴾

O you who believe! Fear Allâh (by doing all that He has ordered and by abstaining from all that He has forbidden) as He should be feared. (Obey Him, be thankful to Him, and remember Him always), and die not except in a state of Islâm (as Muslims (with complete submission to Allâh)).

يَٰٓأَيُّهَا ٱلنَّاسُ ٱتَّقُوا۟ رَبَّكُمُ ٱلَّذِى خَلَقَكُم مِّن نَّفْسٍ وَٰحِدَةٍ وَخَلَقَ مِنْهَا زَوْجَهَا وَبَثَّ مِنْهُمَا رِجَالًا كَثِيرًا وَنِسَآءً ۚ وَٱتَّقُوا۟ ٱللَّهَ ٱلَّذِى تَسَآءَلُونَ بِهِۦ وَٱلْأَرْحَامَ ۚ إِنَّ ٱللَّهَ كَانَ عَلَيْكُمْ رَقِيبًا ﴿١﴾

O mankind! Be dutiful to your Lord, Who created you from a single person (Adam), and from him (Adam) He created his wife (Hawwâ (Eve)) and from them both He created many men and women; and fear Allâh through Whom you demand (your mutual rights), and (do not cut the relations of) the wombs (kinship). Surely, Allâh is Ever an All-Watcher over you.

يُصْلِحْ لَكُمْ أَعْمَٰلَكُمْ وَيَغْفِرْ لَكُمْ ذُنُوبَكُمْ ۗ وَمَن يُطِعِ ٱللَّهَ وَرَسُولَهُۥ فَقَدْ فَازَ فَوْزًا عَظِيمًا ﴿٧١﴾

He will direct you to do righteous good deeds and will forgive you your sins. And whosoever obeys Allâh and His Messenger (peace be upon him), he has indeed achieved a great achievement (i.e. he will be saved from the Hell-fire and will be admitted to Paradise).

Indeed, the best speech is Allah's Book and the best guidance is Muhammad's () guidance. The worst affairs (of religion) are those innovated (by people), for every such innovation is an act of misguidance leading to the Fire

Our Mission

Our mission is to gather in one place, for the English-speaking public, all relevant information needed to make the Qur'an more understandable and easier to study. This book tries to do this by providing the following:

1. The Arabic Text for those who are able to read Arabic
2. Transliteration of the Arabic text for those who are unable to read the Arabic script. This will give them a sample of the sound of the Qur'an, which they could not otherwise comprehend from reading the English meaning.
3. The meaning of the qur'an (translated by Dr. Muhammad Taqi-ud-Din Al-Hilali, Ph.D. and Dr. Muhammad Muhsin Khan)
4. Explanation (abridged Tafsir) by Ibn Kathir (translated by Safi-ur-Rahman al-Mubarakpuri)

We hope that by doing this an ordinary English-speaker will be able to pick up a copy of this book and study and comprehend The Glorious Qur'an in a way that is acceptable to the understanding of the Rightly-guided Muslim Ummah (Community).

Biography of Hafiz Ibn Kathir
(701 H - 774 H)

By the Honored Shaykh `Abdul-Qadir Al-Arna'ut, may Allah protect him.

He is the respected Imam, Abu Al-Fida', `Imad Ad-Din Isma il bin 'Umar bin Kathir Al-Qurashi Al-Busrawi - Busraian in origin; Dimashqi in training, learning and residence.

Ibn Kathir was born in the city of Busra in 701 H. His father was the Friday speaker of the village, but he died while Ibn Kathir was only four years old. Ibn Kathir's brother, Shaykh Abdul-Wahhab, reared him and taught him until he moved to Damascus in 706 H., when he was five years old.

Ibn Kathir's Teachers

Ibn Kathir studied Fiqh - Islamic jurisprudence - with Burhan Ad-Din, Ibrahim bin `Abdur-Rahman Al-Fizari, known as Ibn Al-Firkah (who died in 729 H). Ibn Kathir heard Hadiths from `Isa bin Al-Mutim, Ahmad bin Abi Talib, (Ibn Ash-Shahnah) (who died in 730 H), Ibn Al-Hajjar, (who died in 730 H), and the Hadith narrator of Ash-Sham (modern day Syria and surrounding areas); Baha Ad-Din Al-Qasim bin Muzaffar bin `Asakir (who died in 723 H), and Ibn Ash-Shirdzi, Ishaq bin Yahya Al-Ammuddi, also known as `Afif Ad-Din, the Zahiriyyah Shaykh who died in 725 H, and Muhammad bin Zarrad. He remained with Jamal Ad-Din, Yusuf bin Az-Zaki AlMizzi who died in 724 H, he benefited from his knowledge and also married his daughter. He also read with Shaykh Al-Islam, Taqi Ad-Din Ahmad bin `Abdul-Halim bin `Abdus-Salam bin Taymiyyah who died in 728 H. He also read with the Imam Hafiz and historian Shams Ad-Din, Muhammad bin Ahmad bin Uthman bin Qaymaz Adh-Dhahabi, who died in 748 H. Also, Abu Musa Al-Qarafai, Abu Al-Fath Ad-Dabbusi and

'Ali bin `Umar As-Suwani and others who gave him permission to transmit the knowledge he learned with them in Egypt.

In his book, Al-Mu jam Al-Mukhtas, Al-Hafiz Adh-Dhaliabi wrote that Ibn Kathir was, "The Imam, scholar of jurisprudence, skillful scholar of Hadith, renowned Faqih and scholar of Tafsir who wrote several beneficial books."

Further, in Ad-Durar Al-Kdminah, Al-Hafiz Ibn Hajar AlAsqalani said, "Ibn Kathir worked on the subject of the Hadith in the areas of texts and chains of narrators. He had a good memory, his books became popular during his lifetime, and people benefited from them after his death."

Also, the renowned historian Abu Al-Mahasin, Jamal Ad-Din Yusuf bin Sayf Ad-Din (Ibn Taghri Bardi), said in his book, AlManhal As-Safi, "He is the Shaykh, the Imam, the great scholar `Imad Ad-Din Abu Al-Fida'. He learned extensively and was very active in collecting knowledge and writing. He was excellent in the areas of Fiqh, Tafsfr and Hadith. He collected knowledge, authored (books), taught, narrated Hadith and wrote. He had immense knowledge in the fields of Hadith, Tafsir, Fiqh, the Arabic language, and so forth. He gave Fatawa (religious verdicts) and taught until he died, may Allah grant him mercy. He was known for his precision and vast knowledge, and as a scholar of history, Hadith and Tafsir."

Ibn Kathir's Students

Ibn Hajji was one of Ibn Kathir's students, and he described Ibn Kathir: "He had the best memory of the Hadith texts. He also had the most knowledge concerning the narrators and authenticity, his contemporaries and teachers admitted to these qualities. Every time I met him I gained some benefit from him."

Also, Ibn Al-`Imad Al-Hanbali said in his book, Shadhardt Adh-Dhahab, "He is the renowned Hafiz `Imad Ad-Din, whose memory was excellent, whose forgetfulness was miniscule, whose understanding was adequate, and who had good knowledge in the Arabic language." Also, Ibn Habib said about Ibn Kathir, "He heard knowledge and collected it and wrote various books. He brought comfort to the ears with his Fatwas and narrated Hadith and brought benefit to other people. The papers that contained his Fatwas were transmitted to the various (Islamic) provinces. Further, he was known for his precision and encompassing knowledge."

Ibn Kathir's Books

1 - One of the greatest books that Ibn Kathir wrote was his Tafsir of the Noble Qur'an, which is one of the best Tafsir that rely on narrations [of Ahadith, the Tafsir of the Companions, etc.]. The Tafsir by Ibn Kathir was printed many times and several scholars have summarized it.

2- The History Collection known as Al-Biddyah, which was printed in 14 volumes under the name Al-Bidayah wanNihdyah, and contained the stories of the Prophets and previous nations, the Prophet's Seerah (life story) and Islamic history until his time. He also added a book Al-Fitan, about the Signs of the Last Hour.

3- At-Takmil ft Ma`rifat Ath-Thiqat wa Ad-Du'afa wal Majdhil which Ibn Kathir collected from the books of his two Shaykhs Al-Mizzi and Adh-Dhahabi; Al-Kdmal and Mizan Al-Ftiddl. He added several benefits regarding the subject of Al-Jarh and AtT'adil.

4- Al-Hadi was-Sunan ft Ahadith Al-Masdnfd was-Sunan which is also known by, Jami` Al-Masdnfd. In this book, Ibn Kathir collected the narrations of Imams Ahmad bin Hanbal, Al-Bazzar, Abu Ya`la Al-Mawsili, Ibn Abi Shaybah and from the six collections of Hadith: the Two Sahihs [Al-Bukhari and Muslim] and the Four Sunan [Abu Dawud, At-Tirmidhi, AnNasa and Ibn Majah]. Ibn Kathir divided this book according to areas of Fiqh.

5-Tabaqat Ash-Shaf iyah which also contains the virtues of Imam Ash-Shafi.

6- Ibn Kathir wrote references for the Ahadith of Adillat AtTanbfh, from the Shafi school of Fiqh.

7- Ibn Kathir began an explanation of Sahih Al-Bukhari, but he did not finish it.

8- He started writing a large volume on the Ahkam (Laws), but finished only up to the Hajj rituals.

9- He summarized Al-Bayhaqi's 'Al-Madkhal. Many of these books were not printed.

10- He summarized `Ulum Al-Hadith, by Abu `Amr bin AsSalah and called it Mukhtasar `Ulum Al-Hadith. Shaykh Ahmad Shakir, the Egyptian Muhaddith, printed this book along with his commentary on it and called it Al-Ba'th Al-Hathfth fi Sharh Mukhtasar `Ulum Al-Hadith.

11- As-Sfrah An-Nabawiyyah, which is contained in his book Al-Biddyah, and both of these books are in print.

12- A research on Jihad called Al-Ijtihad ft Talabi Al-Jihad, which was printed several times.

Ibn Kathir's Death

Al-Hafiz Ibn Hajar Al-Asgalani said, "Ibn Kathir lost his sight just before his life ended. He died in Damascus in 774 H." May Allah grant mercy upon Ibn Kathir and make him among the residents of His Paradise.

PREFACE

In the name of Allah, Most Gracious, Most Merciful.

About this book

The previous publication of this book included some background information to the chapters of the Qur'an by an Islamic scholar known as Abul Ala Maududi. This information was used to shed more light on the chapters by giving a summery of why each chapter was given its name, It's period of revelation and the circumstances surrounding its revelatiom. However, some Muslims objected to the inclusion of the contributions of Maududi.

In this new publication of Tafsir Ibn Kathir, we have removed all traces of the contribution of Abul Ala Maududi. Personally, I do not know the reasons for the objections to Maududi, but this work concerns only the tafsir of Ibn Kathir, so we have not included anything from Maududi in it. We have also corrected all the typing and formatting errors found in the previous publication. We have not alter the structure of the book. The reader is still able to read the full Arabic Text of the thirty Parts of the Qur'an and follow its meanings in the English language. The transliteration of the Arabic text should also give the reader a taste of the sound of the original Arabic.

May Almighty Allah accept this effort from us, and make it a source of blessings for us in this world and in the next. I bear witness that there is none worthy of worship but Allah and I bear witness that Muhammad (may the peace and blessings of Allah be upon him) is the slave and messenger of Allah.

Performing Prostration While Reading the Qur'an

Question:

Could you please give a list of the Qur'anic verses when a prostration is recommended? What happens if we read these verses and not perform a prostration?

A. Jalil

Answer:

There are 15 verses in the Qur'an that mention prostration before God Almighty as a good action by God-fearing believers. Therefore, it is strongly recommended to perform such a prostration when we read or listen to any of these verses, whether during prayer or in any situation.

Some scholars are of the view that even if one has not performed ablution, one should prostrate oneself. These verses are given here, starting with the Arabic title of the surah which is followed by two numbers, the first indicating the surah, and the second indicating the verse,: Al-Araf 7: 206; Al-Raad 13: 15; Al-Nahl 16: 50; Al-Isra 17: 109; Maryam 19: 58; Al-Hajj 22: 18 & 22: 77; Al-Furqan 25: 60; Al-Naml 27: 26;

Al-Sajdah 32: 15; Saad 38: 25; Fussilat 41: 38; Al-Najm 53: 62; Al-Inshiqaq 84: 21 and Al-Alaq 96: 19.

If you do not perform a prostration when you read or listen to any of these verses, you have done badly because you miss out on the reward of performing a prostration for God. You incur no sin and violate no divine order.

Reference:
http://archive.arabnews.com/?page=5&section=0&article=97811&d=1&m=7&y=2007

The Glorious Qur'an Juz' 13 (Part 13): Chapter (Surah) 12: Yusuf (Joseph) 053 To Chapter (Surah) 14: Ibrahim (Abraham) 052

PART 13 FULL ARABIC TEXT

Chapter (Surah) 12: Yusuf 053-111

﴿ ۞ وَمَآ أُبَرِّئُ نَفْسِىٓ ۚ إِنَّ ٱلنَّفْسَ لَأَمَّارَةٌۢ بِٱلسُّوٓءِ إِلَّا مَا رَحِمَ رَبِّىٓ ۚ إِنَّ رَبِّى غَفُورٌ رَّحِيمٌ ۝ وَقَالَ ٱلْمَلِكُ ٱئْتُونِى بِهِۦٓ أَسْتَخْلِصْهُ لِنَفْسِى ۖ فَلَمَّا كَلَّمَهُۥ قَالَ إِنَّكَ ٱلْيَوْمَ لَدَيْنَا مَكِينٌ أَمِينٌ ۝ قَالَ ٱجْعَلْنِى عَلَىٰ خَزَآئِنِ ٱلْأَرْضِ ۖ إِنِّى حَفِيظٌ عَلِيمٌ ۝ وَكَذَٰلِكَ مَكَّنَّا لِيُوسُفَ فِى ٱلْأَرْضِ يَتَبَوَّأُ مِنْهَا حَيْثُ يَشَآءُ ۚ نُصِيبُ بِرَحْمَتِنَا مَن نَّشَآءُ ۖ وَلَا نُضِيعُ أَجْرَ ٱلْمُحْسِنِينَ ۝ وَلَأَجْرُ ٱلْءَاخِرَةِ خَيْرٌ لِّلَّذِينَ ءَامَنُوا۟ وَكَانُوا۟ يَتَّقُونَ ۝ وَجَآءَ إِخْوَةُ يُوسُفَ فَدَخَلُوا۟ عَلَيْهِ فَعَرَفَهُمْ وَهُمْ لَهُۥ مُنكِرُونَ ۝ وَلَمَّا جَهَّزَهُم بِجَهَازِهِمْ قَالَ ٱئْتُونِى بِأَخٍ لَّكُم مِّنْ أَبِيكُمْ ۚ أَلَا تَرَوْنَ أَنِّىٓ أُوفِى ٱلْكَيْلَ وَأَنَا۠ خَيْرُ ٱلْمُنزِلِينَ ۝ فَإِن لَّمْ تَأْتُونِى بِهِۦ فَلَا كَيْلَ لَكُمْ عِندِى وَلَا تَقْرَبُونِ ۝ قَالُوا۟ سَنُرَٰوِدُ عَنْهُ أَبَاهُ وَإِنَّا لَفَٰعِلُونَ ۝ وَقَالَ لِفِتْيَٰنِهِ ٱجْعَلُوا۟ بِضَٰعَتَهُمْ فِى رِحَالِهِمْ لَعَلَّهُمْ يَعْرِفُونَهَآ إِذَا ٱنقَلَبُوٓا۟ إِلَىٰٓ أَهْلِهِمْ لَعَلَّهُمْ يَرْجِعُونَ ۝ فَلَمَّا رَجَعُوٓا۟ إِلَىٰٓ أَبِيهِمْ قَالُوا۟ يَٰٓأَبَانَا مُنِعَ مِنَّا ٱلْكَيْلُ فَأَرْسِلْ مَعَنَآ أَخَانَا نَكْتَلْ وَإِنَّا لَهُۥ لَحَٰفِظُونَ ۝ قَالَ هَلْ ءَامَنُكُمْ عَلَيْهِ إِلَّا كَمَآ أَمِنتُكُمْ عَلَىٰٓ أَخِيهِ مِن قَبْلُ ۖ فَٱللَّهُ خَيْرٌ حَٰفِظًا ۖ وَهُوَ أَرْحَمُ ٱلرَّٰحِمِينَ ۝ وَلَمَّا فَتَحُوا۟ مَتَٰعَهُمْ وَجَدُوا۟ بِضَٰعَتَهُمْ رُدَّتْ إِلَيْهِمْ ۖ قَالُوا۟ يَٰٓأَبَانَا مَا نَبْغِى ۖ هَٰذِهِۦ بِضَٰعَتُنَا رُدَّتْ إِلَيْنَا ۖ وَنَمِيرُ أَهْلَنَا وَنَحْفَظُ أَخَانَا وَنَزْدَادُ كَيْلَ بَعِيرٍ ۖ ذَٰلِكَ كَيْلٌ يَسِيرٌ ۝ قَالَ لَنْ أُرْسِلَهُۥ

مَعَكُمْ حَتَّىٰ تُؤْتُونِ مَوْثِقًا مِّنَ ٱللَّهِ لَتَأْتُنَّنِى بِهِۦٓ إِلَّآ أَن يُحَاطَ بِكُمْ ۖ فَلَمَّآ ءَاتَوْهُ مَوْثِقَهُمْ قَالَ ٱللَّهُ عَلَىٰ مَا نَقُولُ وَكِيلٌ ۝ وَقَالَ يَـٰبَنِىَّ لَا تَدْخُلُوا۟ مِنۢ بَابٍ وَٰحِدٍ وَٱدْخُلُوا۟ مِنْ أَبْوَٰبٍ مُّتَفَرِّقَةٍ ۖ وَمَآ أُغْنِى عَنكُم مِّنَ ٱللَّهِ مِن شَىْءٍ ۖ إِنِ ٱلْحُكْمُ إِلَّا لِلَّهِ ۖ عَلَيْهِ تَوَكَّلْتُ ۖ وَعَلَيْهِ فَلْيَتَوَكَّلِ ٱلْمُتَوَكِّلُونَ ۝ وَلَمَّا دَخَلُوا۟ مِنْ حَيْثُ أَمَرَهُمْ أَبُوهُم مَّا كَانَ يُغْنِى عَنْهُم مِّنَ ٱللَّهِ مِن شَىْءٍ إِلَّا حَاجَةً فِى نَفْسِ يَعْقُوبَ قَضَىٰهَا ۚ وَإِنَّهُۥ لَذُو عِلْمٍ لِّمَا عَلَّمْنَـٰهُ وَلَـٰكِنَّ أَكْثَرَ ٱلنَّاسِ لَا يَعْلَمُونَ ۝ وَلَمَّا دَخَلُوا۟ عَلَىٰ يُوسُفَ ءَاوَىٰٓ إِلَيْهِ أَخَاهُ ۖ قَالَ إِنِّىٓ أَنَا۠ أَخُوكَ فَلَا تَبْتَئِسْ بِمَا كَانُوا۟ يَعْمَلُونَ ۝ فَلَمَّا جَهَّزَهُم بِجَهَازِهِمْ جَعَلَ ٱلسِّقَايَةَ فِى رَحْلِ أَخِيهِ ثُمَّ أَذَّنَ مُؤَذِّنٌ أَيَّتُهَا ٱلْعِيرُ إِنَّكُمْ لَسَـٰرِقُونَ ۝ قَالُوا۟ وَأَقْبَلُوا۟ عَلَيْهِم مَّاذَا تَفْقِدُونَ ۝ قَالُوا۟ نَفْقِدُ صُوَاعَ ٱلْمَلِكِ وَلِمَن جَآءَ بِهِۦ حِمْلُ بَعِيرٍ وَأَنَا۠ بِهِۦ زَعِيمٌ ۝ قَالُوا۟ تَٱللَّهِ لَقَدْ عَلِمْتُم مَّا جِئْنَا لِنُفْسِدَ فِى ٱلْأَرْضِ وَمَا كُنَّا سَـٰرِقِينَ ۝ قَالُوا۟ فَمَا جَزَٰٓؤُهُۥٓ إِن كُنتُمْ كَـٰذِبِينَ ۝ قَالُوا۟ جَزَٰٓؤُهُۥ مَن وُجِدَ فِى رَحْلِهِۦ فَهُوَ جَزَٰٓؤُهُۥ ۚ كَذَٰلِكَ نَجْزِى ٱلظَّـٰلِمِينَ ۝ فَبَدَأَ بِأَوْعِيَتِهِمْ قَبْلَ وِعَآءِ أَخِيهِ ثُمَّ ٱسْتَخْرَجَهَا مِن وِعَآءِ أَخِيهِ ۚ كَذَٰلِكَ كِدْنَا لِيُوسُفَ ۖ مَا كَانَ لِيَأْخُذَ أَخَاهُ فِى دِينِ ٱلْمَلِكِ إِلَّآ أَن يَشَآءَ ٱللَّهُ ۚ نَرْفَعُ دَرَجَـٰتٍ مَّن نَّشَآءُ ۗ وَفَوْقَ كُلِّ ذِى عِلْمٍ عَلِيمٌ ۝ قَالُوٓا۟ إِن يَسْرِقْ فَقَدْ سَرَقَ أَخٌ لَّهُۥ مِن قَبْلُ ۚ فَأَسَرَّهَا يُوسُفُ فِى نَفْسِهِۦ وَلَمْ يُبْدِهَا لَهُمْ ۚ قَالَ أَنتُمْ شَرٌّ مَّكَانًا ۖ وَٱللَّهُ أَعْلَمُ بِمَا تَصِفُونَ ۝ قَالُوا۟ يَـٰٓأَيُّهَا ٱلْعَزِيزُ إِنَّ لَهُۥٓ أَبًا شَيْخًا كَبِيرًا فَخُذْ أَحَدَنَا مَكَانَهُۥٓ ۖ إِنَّا نَرَىٰكَ مِنَ ٱلْمُحْسِنِينَ ۝ قَالَ مَعَاذَ ٱللَّهِ أَن نَّأْخُذَ إِلَّا مَن وَجَدْنَا مَتَـٰعَنَا عِندَهُۥٓ إِنَّآ إِذًا لَّظَـٰلِمُونَ ۝ فَلَمَّا ٱسْتَيْـَٔسُوا۟ مِنْهُ خَلَصُوا۟ نَجِيًّا ۖ قَالَ كَبِيرُهُمْ أَلَمْ

تَعْلَمُوٓاْ أَنَّ أَبَاكُمْ قَدْ أَخَذَ عَلَيْكُم مَّوْثِقًا مِّنَ ٱللَّهِ وَمِن قَبْلُ مَا فَرَّطتُمْ فِى يُوسُفَ ۖ فَلَنْ أَبْرَحَ ٱلْأَرْضَ حَتَّىٰ يَأْذَنَ لِىٓ أَبِىٓ أَوْ يَحْكُمَ ٱللَّهُ لِى ۖ وَهُوَ خَيْرُ ٱلْحَٰكِمِينَ ۞ ٱرْجِعُوٓاْ إِلَىٰٓ أَبِيكُمْ فَقُولُواْ يَٰٓأَبَانَآ إِنَّ ٱبْنَكَ سَرَقَ وَمَا شَهِدْنَآ إِلَّا بِمَا عَلِمْنَا وَمَا كُنَّا لِلْغَيْبِ حَٰفِظِينَ ۞ وَسْـَٔلِ ٱلْقَرْيَةَ ٱلَّتِى كُنَّا فِيهَا وَٱلْعِيرَ ٱلَّتِىٓ أَقْبَلْنَا فِيهَا ۖ وَإِنَّا لَصَٰدِقُونَ ۞ قَالَ بَلْ سَوَّلَتْ لَكُمْ أَنفُسُكُمْ أَمْرًا ۖ فَصَبْرٌ جَمِيلٌ ۖ عَسَى ٱللَّهُ أَن يَأْتِيَنِى بِهِمْ جَمِيعًا ۚ إِنَّهُۥ هُوَ ٱلْعَلِيمُ ٱلْحَكِيمُ ۞ وَتَوَلَّىٰ عَنْهُمْ وَقَالَ يَٰٓأَسَفَىٰ عَلَىٰ يُوسُفَ وَٱبْيَضَّتْ عَيْنَاهُ مِنَ ٱلْحُزْنِ فَهُوَ كَظِيمٌ ۞ قَالُواْ تَٱللَّهِ تَفْتَؤُاْ تَذْكُرُ يُوسُفَ حَتَّىٰ تَكُونَ حَرَضًا أَوْ تَكُونَ مِنَ ٱلْهَٰلِكِينَ ۞ قَالَ إِنَّمَآ أَشْكُواْ بَثِّى وَحُزْنِىٓ إِلَى ٱللَّهِ وَأَعْلَمُ مِنَ ٱللَّهِ مَا لَا تَعْلَمُونَ ۞ يَٰبَنِىَّ ٱذْهَبُواْ فَتَحَسَّسُواْ مِن يُوسُفَ وَأَخِيهِ وَلَا تَا۟يْـَٔسُواْ مِن رَّوْحِ ٱللَّهِ ۖ إِنَّهُۥ لَا يَا۟يْـَٔسُ مِن رَّوْحِ ٱللَّهِ إِلَّا ٱلْقَوْمُ ٱلْكَٰفِرُونَ ۞ فَلَمَّا دَخَلُواْ عَلَيْهِ قَالُواْ يَٰٓأَيُّهَا ٱلْعَزِيزُ مَسَّنَا وَأَهْلَنَا ٱلضُّرُّ وَجِئْنَا بِبِضَٰعَةٍ مُّزْجَىٰةٍ فَأَوْفِ لَنَا ٱلْكَيْلَ وَتَصَدَّقْ عَلَيْنَآ ۖ إِنَّ ٱللَّهَ يَجْزِى ٱلْمُتَصَدِّقِينَ ۞ قَالَ هَلْ عَلِمْتُم مَّا فَعَلْتُم بِيُوسُفَ وَأَخِيهِ إِذْ أَنتُمْ جَٰهِلُونَ ۞ قَالُوٓاْ أَءِنَّكَ لَأَنتَ يُوسُفُ ۖ قَالَ أَنَا۠ يُوسُفُ وَهَٰذَآ أَخِى ۖ قَدْ مَنَّ ٱللَّهُ عَلَيْنَآ ۖ إِنَّهُۥ مَن يَتَّقِ وَيَصْبِرْ فَإِنَّ ٱللَّهَ لَا يُضِيعُ أَجْرَ ٱلْمُحْسِنِينَ ۞ قَالُواْ تَٱللَّهِ لَقَدْ ءَاثَرَكَ ٱللَّهُ عَلَيْنَا وَإِن كُنَّا لَخَٰطِـِٔينَ ۞ قَالَ لَا تَثْرِيبَ عَلَيْكُمُ ٱلْيَوْمَ ۖ يَغْفِرُ ٱللَّهُ لَكُمْ ۖ وَهُوَ أَرْحَمُ ٱلرَّٰحِمِينَ ۞ ٱذْهَبُواْ بِقَمِيصِى هَٰذَا فَأَلْقُوهُ عَلَىٰ وَجْهِ أَبِى يَأْتِ بَصِيرًا وَأْتُونِى بِأَهْلِكُمْ أَجْمَعِينَ ۞ وَلَمَّا فَصَلَتِ ٱلْعِيرُ قَالَ أَبُوهُمْ إِنِّى لَأَجِدُ رِيحَ يُوسُفَ ۖ لَوْلَآ أَن تُفَنِّدُونِ ۞ قَالُواْ تَٱللَّهِ إِنَّكَ لَفِى ضَلَٰلِكَ ٱلْقَدِيمِ ۞

فَلَمَّآ أَن جَآءَ ٱلْبَشِيرُ أَلْقَىٰهُ عَلَىٰ وَجْهِهِۦ فَٱرْتَدَّ بَصِيرًا ۖ قَالَ أَلَمْ أَقُل لَّكُمْ إِنِّىٓ أَعْلَمُ مِنَ ٱللَّهِ مَا لَا تَعْلَمُونَ ۝ قَالُوا۟ يَـٰٓأَبَانَا ٱسْتَغْفِرْ لَنَا ذُنُوبَنَآ إِنَّا كُنَّا خَـٰطِـِٔينَ ۝ قَالَ سَوْفَ أَسْتَغْفِرُ لَكُمْ رَبِّىٓ ۖ إِنَّهُۥ هُوَ ٱلْغَفُورُ ٱلرَّحِيمُ ۝ فَلَمَّا دَخَلُوا۟ عَلَىٰ يُوسُفَ ءَاوَىٰٓ إِلَيْهِ أَبَوَيْهِ وَقَالَ ٱدْخُلُوا۟ مِصْرَ إِن شَآءَ ٱللَّهُ ءَامِنِينَ ۝ وَرَفَعَ أَبَوَيْهِ عَلَى ٱلْعَرْشِ وَخَرُّوا۟ لَهُۥ سُجَّدًا ۖ وَقَالَ يَـٰٓأَبَتِ هَـٰذَا تَأْوِيلُ رُءْيَـٰىَ مِن قَبْلُ قَدْ جَعَلَهَا رَبِّى حَقًّا ۖ وَقَدْ أَحْسَنَ بِىٓ إِذْ أَخْرَجَنِى مِنَ ٱلسِّجْنِ وَجَآءَ بِكُم مِّنَ ٱلْبَدْوِ مِنۢ بَعْدِ أَن نَّزَغَ ٱلشَّيْطَـٰنُ بَيْنِى وَبَيْنَ إِخْوَتِىٓ ۚ إِنَّ رَبِّى لَطِيفٌ لِّمَا يَشَآءُ ۚ إِنَّهُۥ هُوَ ٱلْعَلِيمُ ٱلْحَكِيمُ ۝ ۞ رَبِّ قَدْ ءَاتَيْتَنِى مِنَ ٱلْمُلْكِ وَعَلَّمْتَنِى مِن تَأْوِيلِ ٱلْأَحَادِيثِ ۚ فَاطِرَ ٱلسَّمَـٰوَٰتِ وَٱلْأَرْضِ أَنتَ وَلِىِّۦ فِى ٱلدُّنْيَا وَٱلْـَٔاخِرَةِ ۖ تَوَفَّنِى مُسْلِمًا وَأَلْحِقْنِى بِٱلصَّـٰلِحِينَ ۝ ذَٰلِكَ مِنْ أَنۢبَآءِ ٱلْغَيْبِ نُوحِيهِ إِلَيْكَ ۖ وَمَا كُنتَ لَدَيْهِمْ إِذْ أَجْمَعُوٓا۟ أَمْرَهُمْ وَهُمْ يَمْكُرُونَ ۝ وَمَآ أَكْثَرُ ٱلنَّاسِ وَلَوْ حَرَصْتَ بِمُؤْمِنِينَ ۝ وَمَا تَسْـَٔلُهُمْ عَلَيْهِ مِنْ أَجْرٍ ۚ إِنْ هُوَ إِلَّا ذِكْرٌ لِّلْعَـٰلَمِينَ ۝ وَكَأَيِّن مِّنْ ءَايَةٍ فِى ٱلسَّمَـٰوَٰتِ وَٱلْأَرْضِ يَمُرُّونَ عَلَيْهَا وَهُمْ عَنْهَا مُعْرِضُونَ ۝ وَمَا يُؤْمِنُ أَكْثَرُهُم بِٱللَّهِ إِلَّا وَهُم مُّشْرِكُونَ ۝ أَفَأَمِنُوٓا۟ أَن تَأْتِيَهُمْ غَـٰشِيَةٌ مِّنْ عَذَابِ ٱللَّهِ أَوْ تَأْتِيَهُمُ ٱلسَّاعَةُ بَغْتَةً وَهُمْ لَا يَشْعُرُونَ ۝ قُلْ هَـٰذِهِۦ سَبِيلِىٓ أَدْعُوٓا۟ إِلَى ٱللَّهِ ۚ عَلَىٰ بَصِيرَةٍ أَنَا۠ وَمَنِ ٱتَّبَعَنِى ۖ وَسُبْحَـٰنَ ٱللَّهِ وَمَآ أَنَا۠ مِنَ ٱلْمُشْرِكِينَ ۝ وَمَآ أَرْسَلْنَا مِن قَبْلِكَ إِلَّا رِجَالًا نُّوحِىٓ إِلَيْهِم مِّنْ أَهْلِ ٱلْقُرَىٰٓ ۗ أَفَلَمْ يَسِيرُوا۟ فِى ٱلْأَرْضِ فَيَنظُرُوا۟ كَيْفَ كَانَ عَـٰقِبَةُ ٱلَّذِينَ مِن قَبْلِهِمْ ۗ وَلَدَارُ ٱلْـَٔاخِرَةِ خَيْرٌ لِّلَّذِينَ ٱتَّقَوْا۟ ۗ أَفَلَا تَعْقِلُونَ ۝ حَتَّىٰٓ إِذَا ٱسْتَيْـَٔسَ ٱلرُّسُلُ وَظَنُّوٓا۟ أَنَّهُمْ قَدْ كُذِبُوا۟ جَآءَهُمْ نَصْرُنَا فَنُجِّىَ مَن نَّشَآءُ ۖ وَلَا يُرَدُّ بَأْسُنَا عَنِ ٱلْقَوْمِ

ٱلۡمُجۡرِمِينَ ۝ لَقَدۡ كَانَ فِى قَصَصِهِمۡ عِبۡرَةٌ لِّأُوْلِى ٱلۡأَلۡبَٰبِۗ مَا كَانَ حَدِيثًا يُفۡتَرَىٰ وَلَٰكِن تَصۡدِيقَ ٱلَّذِى بَيۡنَ يَدَيۡهِ وَتَفۡصِيلَ كُلِّ شَىۡءٍ وَهُدًى وَرَحۡمَةً لِّقَوۡمٍ يُؤۡمِنُونَ ۝

(Yusuf 053-111)

Chapter (Surah) 13: Ar-Ra'd 001-043

بِسۡمِ ٱللَّهِ ٱلرَّحۡمَٰنِ ٱلرَّحِيمِ

الٓمٓرۚ تِلۡكَ ءَايَٰتُ ٱلۡكِتَٰبِۗ وَٱلَّذِىٓ أُنزِلَ إِلَيۡكَ مِن رَّبِّكَ ٱلۡحَقُّ وَلَٰكِنَّ أَكۡثَرَ ٱلنَّاسِ لَا يُؤۡمِنُونَ ۝ ٱللَّهُ ٱلَّذِى رَفَعَ ٱلسَّمَٰوَٰتِ بِغَيۡرِ عَمَدٍ تَرَوۡنَهَاۖ ثُمَّ ٱسۡتَوَىٰ عَلَى ٱلۡعَرۡشِۖ وَسَخَّرَ ٱلشَّمۡسَ وَٱلۡقَمَرَۖ كُلٌّ يَجۡرِى لِأَجَلٍ مُّسَمًّىۚ يُدَبِّرُ ٱلۡأَمۡرَ يُفَصِّلُ ٱلۡأَيَٰتِ لَعَلَّكُم بِلِقَآءِ رَبِّكُمۡ تُوقِنُونَ ۝ وَهُوَ ٱلَّذِى مَدَّ ٱلۡأَرۡضَ وَجَعَلَ فِيهَا رَوَٰسِىَ وَأَنۡهَٰرًاۖ وَمِن كُلِّ ٱلثَّمَرَٰتِ جَعَلَ فِيهَا زَوۡجَيۡنِ ٱثۡنَيۡنِۖ يُغۡشِى ٱلَّيۡلَ ٱلنَّهَارَۚ إِنَّ فِى ذَٰلِكَ لَأَيَٰتٍ لِّقَوۡمٍ يَتَفَكَّرُونَ ۝ وَفِى ٱلۡأَرۡضِ قِطَعٌ مُّتَجَٰوِرَٰتٌ وَجَنَّٰتٌ مِّنۡ أَعۡنَٰبٍ وَزَرۡعٌ وَنَخِيلٌ صِنۡوَانٌ وَغَيۡرُ صِنۡوَانٍ يُسۡقَىٰ بِمَآءٍ وَٰحِدٍ وَنُفَضِّلُ بَعۡضَهَا عَلَىٰ بَعۡضٍ فِى ٱلۡأُكُلِۚ إِنَّ فِى ذَٰلِكَ لَأَيَٰتٍ لِّقَوۡمٍ يَعۡقِلُونَ ۝ ۞ وَإِن تَعۡجَبۡ فَعَجَبٌ قَوۡلُهُمۡ أَءِذَا كُنَّا تُرَٰبًا أَءِنَّا لَفِى خَلۡقٍ جَدِيدٍۗ أُوْلَٰٓئِكَ ٱلَّذِينَ كَفَرُوا۟ بِرَبِّهِمۡۖ وَأُوْلَٰٓئِكَ ٱلۡأَغۡلَٰلُ فِىٓ أَعۡنَاقِهِمۡۖ وَأُوْلَٰٓئِكَ أَصۡحَٰبُ ٱلنَّارِۖ هُمۡ فِيهَا خَٰلِدُونَ ۝ وَيَسۡتَعۡجِلُونَكَ بِٱلسَّيِّئَةِ قَبۡلَ ٱلۡحَسَنَةِ وَقَدۡ خَلَتۡ مِن قَبۡلِهِمُ ٱلۡمَثُلَٰتُۗ وَإِنَّ رَبَّكَ لَذُو مَغۡفِرَةٍ لِّلنَّاسِ عَلَىٰ ظُلۡمِهِمۡۖ وَإِنَّ رَبَّكَ لَشَدِيدُ ٱلۡعِقَابِ ۝ وَيَقُولُ ٱلَّذِينَ كَفَرُوا۟ لَوۡلَآ أُنزِلَ عَلَيۡهِ ءَايَةٌ مِّن رَّبِّهِۦٓۗ إِنَّمَآ أَنتَ مُنذِرٌۖ وَلِكُلِّ قَوۡمٍ هَادٍ ۝ ٱللَّهُ يَعۡلَمُ مَا تَحۡمِلُ كُلُّ أُنثَىٰ وَمَا تَغِيضُ ٱلۡأَرۡحَامُ وَمَا تَزۡدَادُۖ وَكُلُّ شَىۡءٍ عِندَهُۥ بِمِقۡدَارٍ ۝ عَٰلِمُ ٱلۡغَيۡبِ وَٱلشَّهَٰدَةِ ٱلۡكَبِيرُ ٱلۡمُتَعَالِ ۝ سَوَآءٌ مِّنكُم مَّنۡ أَسَرَّ ٱلۡقَوۡلَ وَمَن جَهَرَ بِهِۦ وَمَنۡ هُوَ

مُسْتَخْفٍ بِٱلَّيْلِ وَسَارِبٌ بِٱلنَّهَارِ ۞ لَهُۥ مُعَقِّبَٰتٌ مِّنۢ بَيْنِ يَدَيْهِ وَمِنْ خَلْفِهِۦ يَحْفَظُونَهُۥ مِنْ أَمْرِ ٱللَّهِ ۗ إِنَّ ٱللَّهَ لَا يُغَيِّرُ مَا بِقَوْمٍ حَتَّىٰ يُغَيِّرُوا۟ مَا بِأَنفُسِهِمْ ۗ وَإِذَآ أَرَادَ ٱللَّهُ بِقَوْمٍ سُوٓءًا فَلَا مَرَدَّ لَهُۥ ۚ وَمَا لَهُم مِّن دُونِهِۦ مِن وَالٍ ۞ هُوَ ٱلَّذِى يُرِيكُمُ ٱلْبَرْقَ خَوْفًا وَطَمَعًا وَيُنشِئُ ٱلسَّحَابَ ٱلثِّقَالَ ۞ وَيُسَبِّحُ ٱلرَّعْدُ بِحَمْدِهِۦ وَٱلْمَلَٰٓئِكَةُ مِنْ خِيفَتِهِۦ وَيُرْسِلُ ٱلصَّوَٰعِقَ فَيُصِيبُ بِهَا مَن يَشَآءُ وَهُمْ يُجَٰدِلُونَ فِى ٱللَّهِ وَهُوَ شَدِيدُ ٱلْمِحَالِ ۞ لَهُۥ دَعْوَةُ ٱلْحَقِّ ۖ وَٱلَّذِينَ يَدْعُونَ مِن دُونِهِۦ لَا يَسْتَجِيبُونَ لَهُم بِشَىْءٍ إِلَّا كَبَٰسِطِ كَفَّيْهِ إِلَى ٱلْمَآءِ لِيَبْلُغَ فَاهُ وَمَا هُوَ بِبَٰلِغِهِۦ ۚ وَمَا دُعَآءُ ٱلْكَٰفِرِينَ إِلَّا فِى ضَلَٰلٍ ۞ وَلِلَّهِ يَسْجُدُ مَن فِى ٱلسَّمَٰوَٰتِ وَٱلْأَرْضِ طَوْعًا وَكَرْهًا وَظِلَٰلُهُم بِٱلْغُدُوِّ وَٱلْءَاصَالِ ۩ ۞ قُلْ مَن رَّبُّ ٱلسَّمَٰوَٰتِ وَٱلْأَرْضِ قُلِ ٱللَّهُ ۚ قُلْ أَفَٱتَّخَذْتُم مِّن دُونِهِۦٓ أَوْلِيَآءَ لَا يَمْلِكُونَ لِأَنفُسِهِمْ نَفْعًا وَلَا ضَرًّا ۚ قُلْ هَلْ يَسْتَوِى ٱلْأَعْمَىٰ وَٱلْبَصِيرُ أَمْ هَلْ تَسْتَوِى ٱلظُّلُمَٰتُ وَٱلنُّورُ ۗ أَمْ جَعَلُوا۟ لِلَّهِ شُرَكَآءَ خَلَقُوا۟ كَخَلْقِهِۦ فَتَشَٰبَهَ ٱلْخَلْقُ عَلَيْهِمْ ۚ قُلِ ٱللَّهُ خَٰلِقُ كُلِّ شَىْءٍ وَهُوَ ٱلْوَٰحِدُ ٱلْقَهَّٰرُ ۞ أَنزَلَ مِنَ ٱلسَّمَآءِ مَآءً فَسَالَتْ أَوْدِيَةٌۢ بِقَدَرِهَا فَٱحْتَمَلَ ٱلسَّيْلُ زَبَدًا رَّابِيًا ۚ وَمِمَّا يُوقِدُونَ عَلَيْهِ فِى ٱلنَّارِ ٱبْتِغَآءَ حِلْيَةٍ أَوْ مَتَٰعٍ زَبَدٌ مِّثْلُهُۥ ۚ كَذَٰلِكَ يَضْرِبُ ٱللَّهُ ٱلْحَقَّ وَٱلْبَٰطِلَ ۚ فَأَمَّا ٱلزَّبَدُ فَيَذْهَبُ جُفَآءً ۖ وَأَمَّا مَا يَنفَعُ ٱلنَّاسَ فَيَمْكُثُ فِى ٱلْأَرْضِ ۚ كَذَٰلِكَ يَضْرِبُ ٱللَّهُ ٱلْأَمْثَالَ ۞ لِلَّذِينَ ٱسْتَجَابُوا۟ لِرَبِّهِمُ ٱلْحُسْنَىٰ ۚ وَٱلَّذِينَ لَمْ يَسْتَجِيبُوا۟ لَهُۥ لَوْ أَنَّ لَهُم مَّا فِى ٱلْأَرْضِ جَمِيعًا وَمِثْلَهُۥ مَعَهُۥ لَٱفْتَدَوْا۟ بِهِۦٓ ۚ أُو۟لَٰٓئِكَ لَهُمْ سُوٓءُ ٱلْحِسَابِ وَمَأْوَىٰهُمْ جَهَنَّمُ ۖ وَبِئْسَ ٱلْمِهَادُ ۞ ۞ أَفَمَن يَعْلَمُ أَنَّمَآ أُنزِلَ إِلَيْكَ مِن رَّبِّكَ ٱلْحَقُّ كَمَنْ هُوَ أَعْمَىٰٓ ۚ إِنَّمَا يَتَذَكَّرُ أُو۟لُوا۟ ٱلْأَلْبَٰبِ ۞ ٱلَّذِينَ يُوفُونَ بِعَهْدِ ٱللَّهِ وَلَا يَنقُضُونَ ٱلْمِيثَٰقَ ۞ وَٱلَّذِينَ يَصِلُونَ مَآ أَمَرَ ٱللَّهُ بِهِۦٓ أَن يُوصَلَ

وَيَخْشَوْنَ رَبَّهُمْ وَيَخَافُونَ سُوٓءَ ٱلْحِسَابِ ۝ وَٱلَّذِينَ صَبَرُوا۟ ٱبْتِغَآءَ وَجْهِ رَبِّهِمْ وَأَقَامُوا۟ ٱلصَّلَوٰةَ وَأَنفَقُوا۟ مِمَّا رَزَقْنَـٰهُمْ سِرًّا وَعَلَانِيَةً وَيَدْرَءُونَ بِٱلْحَسَنَةِ ٱلسَّيِّئَةَ أُو۟لَـٰٓئِكَ لَهُمْ عُقْبَى ٱلدَّارِ ۝ جَنَّـٰتُ عَدْنٍ يَدْخُلُونَهَا وَمَن صَلَحَ مِنْ ءَابَآئِهِمْ وَأَزْوَٰجِهِمْ وَذُرِّيَّـٰتِهِمْ ۖ وَٱلْمَلَـٰٓئِكَةُ يَدْخُلُونَ عَلَيْهِم مِّن كُلِّ بَابٍ ۝ سَلَـٰمٌ عَلَيْكُم بِمَا صَبَرْتُمْ ۚ فَنِعْمَ عُقْبَى ٱلدَّارِ ۝ وَٱلَّذِينَ يَنقُضُونَ عَهْدَ ٱللَّهِ مِنۢ بَعْدِ مِيثَـٰقِهِۦ وَيَقْطَعُونَ مَآ أَمَرَ ٱللَّهُ بِهِۦٓ أَن يُوصَلَ وَيُفْسِدُونَ فِى ٱلْأَرْضِ ۙ أُو۟لَـٰٓئِكَ لَهُمُ ٱللَّعْنَةُ وَلَهُمْ سُوٓءُ ٱلدَّارِ ۝ ٱللَّهُ يَبْسُطُ ٱلرِّزْقَ لِمَن يَشَآءُ وَيَقْدِرُ ۚ وَفَرِحُوا۟ بِٱلْحَيَوٰةِ ٱلدُّنْيَا وَمَا ٱلْحَيَوٰةُ ٱلدُّنْيَا فِى ٱلْـَٔاخِرَةِ إِلَّا مَتَـٰعٌ ۝ وَيَقُولُ ٱلَّذِينَ كَفَرُوا۟ لَوْلَآ أُنزِلَ عَلَيْهِ ءَايَةٌ مِّن رَّبِّهِۦ ۗ قُلْ إِنَّ ٱللَّهَ يُضِلُّ مَن يَشَآءُ وَيَهْدِىٓ إِلَيْهِ مَنْ أَنَابَ ۝ ٱلَّذِينَ ءَامَنُوا۟ وَتَطْمَئِنُّ قُلُوبُهُم بِذِكْرِ ٱللَّهِ ۗ أَلَا بِذِكْرِ ٱللَّهِ تَطْمَئِنُّ ٱلْقُلُوبُ ۝ ٱلَّذِينَ ءَامَنُوا۟ وَعَمِلُوا۟ ٱلصَّـٰلِحَـٰتِ طُوبَىٰ لَهُمْ وَحُسْنُ مَـَٔابٍ ۝ كَذَٰلِكَ أَرْسَلْنَـٰكَ فِىٓ أُمَّةٍ قَدْ خَلَتْ مِن قَبْلِهَآ أُمَمٌ لِّتَتْلُوَا۟ عَلَيْهِمُ ٱلَّذِىٓ أَوْحَيْنَآ إِلَيْكَ وَهُمْ يَكْفُرُونَ بِٱلرَّحْمَـٰنِ ۚ قُلْ هُوَ رَبِّى لَآ إِلَـٰهَ إِلَّا هُوَ عَلَيْهِ تَوَكَّلْتُ وَإِلَيْهِ مَتَابِ ۝ وَلَوْ أَنَّ قُرْءَانًا سُيِّرَتْ بِهِ ٱلْجِبَالُ أَوْ قُطِّعَتْ بِهِ ٱلْأَرْضُ أَوْ كُلِّمَ بِهِ ٱلْمَوْتَىٰ ۗ بَل لِّلَّهِ ٱلْأَمْرُ جَمِيعًا ۗ أَفَلَمْ يَا۟يْـَٔسِ ٱلَّذِينَ ءَامَنُوٓا۟ أَن لَّوْ يَشَآءُ ٱللَّهُ لَهَدَى ٱلنَّاسَ جَمِيعًا ۗ وَلَا يَزَالُ ٱلَّذِينَ كَفَرُوا۟ تُصِيبُهُم بِمَا صَنَعُوا۟ قَارِعَةٌ أَوْ تَحُلُّ قَرِيبًا مِّن دَارِهِمْ حَتَّىٰ يَأْتِىَ وَعْدُ ٱللَّهِ ۚ إِنَّ ٱللَّهَ لَا يُخْلِفُ ٱلْمِيعَادَ ۝ وَلَقَدِ ٱسْتُهْزِئَ بِرُسُلٍ مِّن قَبْلِكَ فَأَمْلَيْتُ لِلَّذِينَ كَفَرُوا۟ ثُمَّ أَخَذْتُهُمْ ۖ فَكَيْفَ كَانَ عِقَابِ ۝ أَفَمَنْ هُوَ قَآئِمٌ عَلَىٰ كُلِّ نَفْسٍۭ بِمَا كَسَبَتْ ۗ وَجَعَلُوا۟ لِلَّهِ شُرَكَآءَ قُلْ سَمُّوهُمْ ۚ أَمْ تُنَبِّـُٔونَهُۥ بِمَا لَا يَعْلَمُ فِى ٱلْأَرْضِ أَم بِظَـٰهِرٍ مِّنَ ٱلْقَوْلِ ۗ بَلْ زُيِّنَ لِلَّذِينَ كَفَرُوا۟ مَكْرُهُمْ وَصُدُّوا۟ عَنِ ٱلسَّبِيلِ ۗ وَمَن يُضْلِلِ ٱللَّهُ فَمَا لَهُۥ مِنْ

هَادٍ ۞ لَهُمْ عَذَابٌ فِى ٱلْحَيَوٰةِ ٱلدُّنْيَا ۖ وَلَعَذَابُ ٱلْءَاخِرَةِ أَشَقُّ ۖ وَمَا لَهُم مِّنَ ٱللَّهِ مِن وَاقٍ ۞ مَّثَلُ ٱلْجَنَّةِ ٱلَّتِى وُعِدَ ٱلْمُتَّقُونَ ۖ تَجْرِى مِن تَحْتِهَا ٱلْأَنْهَٰرُ ۖ أُكُلُهَا دَآئِمٌ وَظِلُّهَا ۚ تِلْكَ عُقْبَى ٱلَّذِينَ ٱتَّقَوا۟ ۖ وَّعُقْبَى ٱلْكَٰفِرِينَ ٱلنَّارُ ۞ وَٱلَّذِينَ ءَاتَيْنَٰهُمُ ٱلْكِتَٰبَ يَفْرَحُونَ بِمَآ أُنزِلَ إِلَيْكَ ۖ وَمِنَ ٱلْأَحْزَابِ مَن يُنكِرُ بَعْضَهُۥ ۚ قُلْ إِنَّمَآ أُمِرْتُ أَنْ أَعْبُدَ ٱللَّهَ وَلَآ أُشْرِكَ بِهِۦٓ ۚ إِلَيْهِ أَدْعُوا۟ وَإِلَيْهِ مَـَٔابِ ۞ وَكَذَٰلِكَ أَنزَلْنَٰهُ حُكْمًا عَرَبِيًّا ۚ وَلَئِنِ ٱتَّبَعْتَ أَهْوَآءَهُم بَعْدَمَا جَآءَكَ مِنَ ٱلْعِلْمِ مَا لَكَ مِنَ ٱللَّهِ مِن وَلِىٍّ وَلَا وَاقٍ ۞ وَلَقَدْ أَرْسَلْنَا رُسُلًا مِّن قَبْلِكَ وَجَعَلْنَا لَهُمْ أَزْوَٰجًا وَذُرِّيَّةً ۚ وَمَا كَانَ لِرَسُولٍ أَن يَأْتِىَ بِـَٔايَةٍ إِلَّا بِإِذْنِ ٱللَّهِ ۗ لِكُلِّ أَجَلٍ كِتَابٌ ۞ يَمْحُوا۟ ٱللَّهُ مَا يَشَآءُ وَيُثْبِتُ ۖ وَعِندَهُۥٓ أُمُّ ٱلْكِتَٰبِ ۞ وَإِن مَّا نُرِيَنَّكَ بَعْضَ ٱلَّذِى نَعِدُهُمْ أَوْ نَتَوَفَّيَنَّكَ فَإِنَّمَا عَلَيْكَ ٱلْبَلَٰغُ وَعَلَيْنَا ٱلْحِسَابُ ۞ أَوَلَمْ يَرَوْا۟ أَنَّا نَأْتِى ٱلْأَرْضَ نَنقُصُهَا مِنْ أَطْرَافِهَا ۚ وَٱللَّهُ يَحْكُمُ لَا مُعَقِّبَ لِحُكْمِهِۦ ۚ وَهُوَ سَرِيعُ ٱلْحِسَابِ ۞ وَقَدْ مَكَرَ ٱلَّذِينَ مِن قَبْلِهِمْ فَلِلَّهِ ٱلْمَكْرُ جَمِيعًا ۖ يَعْلَمُ مَا تَكْسِبُ كُلُّ نَفْسٍ ۗ وَسَيَعْلَمُ ٱلْكُفَّٰرُ لِمَنْ عُقْبَى ٱلدَّارِ ۞ وَيَقُولُ ٱلَّذِينَ كَفَرُوا۟ لَسْتَ مُرْسَلًا ۚ قُلْ كَفَىٰ بِٱللَّهِ شَهِيدًۢا بَيْنِى وَبَيْنَكُمْ وَمَنْ عِندَهُۥ عِلْمُ ٱلْكِتَٰبِ ۞

(Ar-Ra'd 001-043)

Chapter (Surah) 14: Ibrahim 001-052

بِسْمِ ٱللَّهِ ٱلرَّحْمَٰنِ ٱلرَّحِيمِ

۞ الٓر ۚ كِتَٰبٌ أَنزَلْنَٰهُ إِلَيْكَ لِتُخْرِجَ ٱلنَّاسَ مِنَ ٱلظُّلُمَٰتِ إِلَى ٱلنُّورِ بِإِذْنِ رَبِّهِمْ إِلَىٰ صِرَٰطِ ٱلْعَزِيزِ ٱلْحَمِيدِ ۞ ٱللَّهِ ٱلَّذِى لَهُۥ مَا فِى ٱلسَّمَٰوَٰتِ وَمَا فِى ٱلْأَرْضِ ۗ وَوَيْلٌ لِّلْكَٰفِرِينَ مِنْ عَذَابٍ شَدِيدٍ ۞ ٱلَّذِينَ يَسْتَحِبُّونَ ٱلْحَيَوٰةَ ٱلدُّنْيَا عَلَى ٱلْءَاخِرَةِ وَيَصُدُّونَ عَن سَبِيلِ ٱللَّهِ وَيَبْغُونَهَا عِوَجًا ۚ أُو۟لَٰٓئِكَ فِى

ضَلَلٍۭ بَعِيدٍ ۝ وَمَآ أَرْسَلْنَا مِن رَّسُولٍ إِلَّا بِلِسَانِ قَوْمِهِۦ لِيُبَيِّنَ لَهُمْ ۖ فَيُضِلُّ ٱللَّهُ مَن يَشَآءُ وَيَهْدِى مَن يَشَآءُ ۚ وَهُوَ ٱلْعَزِيزُ ٱلْحَكِيمُ ۝ وَلَقَدْ أَرْسَلْنَا مُوسَىٰ بِـَٔايَـٰتِنَآ أَنْ أَخْرِجْ قَوْمَكَ مِنَ ٱلظُّلُمَـٰتِ إِلَى ٱلنُّورِ وَذَكِّرْهُم بِأَيَّىٰمِ ٱللَّهِ ۚ إِنَّ فِى ذَٰلِكَ لَـَٔايَـٰتٍ لِّكُلِّ صَبَّارٍ شَكُورٍ ۝ وَإِذْ قَالَ مُوسَىٰ لِقَوْمِهِ ٱذْكُرُوا۟ نِعْمَةَ ٱللَّهِ عَلَيْكُمْ إِذْ أَنجَىٰكُم مِّنْ ءَالِ فِرْعَوْنَ يَسُومُونَكُمْ سُوٓءَ ٱلْعَذَابِ وَيُذَبِّحُونَ أَبْنَآءَكُمْ وَيَسْتَحْيُونَ نِسَآءَكُمْ ۚ وَفِى ذَٰلِكُم بَلَآءٌ مِّن رَّبِّكُمْ عَظِيمٌ ۝ وَإِذْ تَأَذَّنَ رَبُّكُمْ لَئِن شَكَرْتُمْ لَأَزِيدَنَّكُمْ ۖ وَلَئِن كَفَرْتُمْ إِنَّ عَذَابِى لَشَدِيدٌ ۝ وَقَالَ مُوسَىٰٓ إِن تَكْفُرُوٓا۟ أَنتُمْ وَمَن فِى ٱلْأَرْضِ جَمِيعًا فَإِنَّ ٱللَّهَ لَغَنِىٌّ حَمِيدٌ ۝ أَلَمْ يَأْتِكُمْ نَبَؤُا۟ ٱلَّذِينَ مِن قَبْلِكُمْ قَوْمِ نُوحٍ وَعَادٍ وَثَمُودَ ۛ وَٱلَّذِينَ مِنۢ بَعْدِهِمْ ۛ لَا يَعْلَمُهُمْ إِلَّا ٱللَّهُ ۚ جَآءَتْهُمْ رُسُلُهُم بِٱلْبَيِّنَـٰتِ فَرَدُّوٓا۟ أَيْدِيَهُمْ فِىٓ أَفْوَٰهِهِمْ وَقَالُوٓا۟ إِنَّا كَفَرْنَا بِمَآ أُرْسِلْتُم بِهِۦ وَإِنَّا لَفِى شَكٍّ مِّمَّا تَدْعُونَنَآ إِلَيْهِ مُرِيبٍ ۝ ۞ قَالَتْ رُسُلُهُمْ أَفِى ٱللَّهِ شَكٌّ فَاطِرِ ٱلسَّمَـٰوَٰتِ وَٱلْأَرْضِ ۖ يَدْعُوكُمْ لِيَغْفِرَ لَكُم مِّن ذُنُوبِكُمْ وَيُؤَخِّرَكُمْ إِلَىٰٓ أَجَلٍ مُّسَمًّى ۚ قَالُوٓا۟ إِنْ أَنتُمْ إِلَّا بَشَرٌ مِّثْلُنَا تُرِيدُونَ أَن تَصُدُّونَا عَمَّا كَانَ يَعْبُدُ ءَابَآؤُنَا فَأْتُونَا بِسُلْطَـٰنٍ مُّبِينٍ ۝ قَالَتْ لَهُمْ رُسُلُهُمْ إِن نَّحْنُ إِلَّا بَشَرٌ مِّثْلُكُمْ وَلَـٰكِنَّ ٱللَّهَ يَمُنُّ عَلَىٰ مَن يَشَآءُ مِنْ عِبَادِهِۦ ۖ وَمَا كَانَ لَنَآ أَن نَّأْتِيَكُم بِسُلْطَـٰنٍ إِلَّا بِإِذْنِ ٱللَّهِ ۚ وَعَلَى ٱللَّهِ فَلْيَتَوَكَّلِ ٱلْمُؤْمِنُونَ ۝ وَمَا لَنَآ أَلَّا نَتَوَكَّلَ عَلَى ٱللَّهِ وَقَدْ هَدَىٰنَا سُبُلَنَا ۚ وَلَنَصْبِرَنَّ عَلَىٰ مَآ ءَاذَيْتُمُونَا ۚ وَعَلَى ٱللَّهِ فَلْيَتَوَكَّلِ ٱلْمُتَوَكِّلُونَ ۝ وَقَالَ ٱلَّذِينَ كَفَرُوا۟ لِرُسُلِهِمْ لَنُخْرِجَنَّكُم مِّنْ أَرْضِنَآ أَوْ لَتَعُودُنَّ فِى مِلَّتِنَا ۖ فَأَوْحَىٰٓ إِلَيْهِمْ رَبُّهُمْ لَنُهْلِكَنَّ ٱلظَّـٰلِمِينَ ۝ وَلَنُسْكِنَنَّكُمُ ٱلْأَرْضَ مِنۢ بَعْدِهِمْ ۚ

ذَٰلِكَ لِمَنْ خَافَ مَقَامِى وَخَافَ وَعِيدِ ۝ وَٱسْتَفْتَحُوا۟ وَخَابَ كُلُّ جَبَّارٍ عَنِيدٍ ۝ مِّن وَرَآئِهِۦ جَهَنَّمُ وَيُسْقَىٰ مِن مَّآءٍ صَدِيدٍ ۝ يَتَجَرَّعُهُۥ وَلَا يَكَادُ يُسِيغُهُۥ وَيَأْتِيهِ ٱلْمَوْتُ مِن كُلِّ مَكَانٍ وَمَا هُوَ بِمَيِّتٍ ۖ وَمِن وَرَآئِهِۦ عَذَابٌ غَلِيظٌ ۝ مَّثَلُ ٱلَّذِينَ كَفَرُوا۟ بِرَبِّهِمْ ۖ أَعْمَٰلُهُمْ كَرَمَادٍ ٱشْتَدَّتْ بِهِ ٱلرِّيحُ فِى يَوْمٍ عَاصِفٍ ۖ لَّا يَقْدِرُونَ مِمَّا كَسَبُوا۟ عَلَىٰ شَىْءٍ ۚ ذَٰلِكَ هُوَ ٱلضَّلَٰلُ ٱلْبَعِيدُ ۝ أَلَمْ تَرَ أَنَّ ٱللَّهَ خَلَقَ ٱلسَّمَٰوَٰتِ وَٱلْأَرْضَ بِٱلْحَقِّ ۚ إِن يَشَأْ يُذْهِبْكُمْ وَيَأْتِ بِخَلْقٍ جَدِيدٍ ۝ وَمَا ذَٰلِكَ عَلَى ٱللَّهِ بِعَزِيزٍ ۝ وَبَرَزُوا۟ لِلَّهِ جَمِيعًا فَقَالَ ٱلضُّعَفَٰٓؤُا۟ لِلَّذِينَ ٱسْتَكْبَرُوٓا۟ إِنَّا كُنَّا لَكُمْ تَبَعًا فَهَلْ أَنتُم مُّغْنُونَ عَنَّا مِنْ عَذَابِ ٱللَّهِ مِن شَىْءٍ ۚ قَالُوا۟ لَوْ هَدَىٰنَا ٱللَّهُ لَهَدَيْنَٰكُمْ ۖ سَوَآءٌ عَلَيْنَآ أَجَزِعْنَآ أَمْ صَبَرْنَا مَا لَنَا مِن مَّحِيصٍ ۝ وَقَالَ ٱلشَّيْطَٰنُ لَمَّا قُضِىَ ٱلْأَمْرُ إِنَّ ٱللَّهَ وَعَدَكُمْ وَعْدَ ٱلْحَقِّ وَوَعَدتُّكُمْ فَأَخْلَفْتُكُمْ ۖ وَمَا كَانَ لِىَ عَلَيْكُم مِّن سُلْطَٰنٍ إِلَّآ أَن دَعَوْتُكُمْ فَٱسْتَجَبْتُمْ لِى ۖ فَلَا تَلُومُونِى وَلُومُوٓا۟ أَنفُسَكُم ۖ مَّآ أَنَا۠ بِمُصْرِخِكُمْ وَمَآ أَنتُم بِمُصْرِخِىَّ ۖ إِنِّى كَفَرْتُ بِمَآ أَشْرَكْتُمُونِ مِن قَبْلُ ۗ إِنَّ ٱلظَّٰلِمِينَ لَهُمْ عَذَابٌ أَلِيمٌ ۝ وَأُدْخِلَ ٱلَّذِينَ ءَامَنُوا۟ وَعَمِلُوا۟ ٱلصَّٰلِحَٰتِ جَنَّٰتٍ تَجْرِى مِن تَحْتِهَا ٱلْأَنْهَٰرُ خَٰلِدِينَ فِيهَا بِإِذْنِ رَبِّهِمْ ۖ تَحِيَّتُهُمْ فِيهَا سَلَٰمٌ ۝ أَلَمْ تَرَ كَيْفَ ضَرَبَ ٱللَّهُ مَثَلًا كَلِمَةً طَيِّبَةً كَشَجَرَةٍ طَيِّبَةٍ أَصْلُهَا ثَابِتٌ وَفَرْعُهَا فِى ٱلسَّمَآءِ ۝ تُؤْتِىٓ أُكُلَهَا كُلَّ حِينٍۭ بِإِذْنِ رَبِّهَا ۗ وَيَضْرِبُ ٱللَّهُ ٱلْأَمْثَالَ لِلنَّاسِ لَعَلَّهُمْ يَتَذَكَّرُونَ ۝ وَمَثَلُ كَلِمَةٍ خَبِيثَةٍ كَشَجَرَةٍ خَبِيثَةٍ ٱجْتُثَّتْ مِن فَوْقِ ٱلْأَرْضِ مَا لَهَا مِن قَرَارٍ ۝ يُثَبِّتُ ٱللَّهُ ٱلَّذِينَ ءَامَنُوا۟ بِٱلْقَوْلِ ٱلثَّابِتِ فِى ٱلْحَيَوٰةِ ٱلدُّنْيَا وَفِى ٱلْأَخِرَةِ ۖ وَيُضِلُّ ٱللَّهُ ٱلظَّٰلِمِينَ ۚ وَيَفْعَلُ ٱللَّهُ مَا يَشَآءُ ۝ ۞ أَلَمْ تَرَ إِلَى ٱلَّذِينَ بَدَّلُوا۟ نِعْمَتَ ٱللَّهِ كُفْرًا وَأَحَلُّوا۟

قَوْمَهُمْ دَارَ ٱلْبَوَارِ ۝ جَهَنَّمَ يَصْلَوْنَهَا ۖ وَبِئْسَ ٱلْقَرَارُ ۝ وَجَعَلُوا۟ لِلَّهِ أَندَادًا لِّيُضِلُّوا۟ عَن سَبِيلِهِ ۗ قُلْ تَمَتَّعُوا۟ فَإِنَّ مَصِيرَكُمْ إِلَى ٱلنَّارِ ۝ قُل لِّعِبَادِيَ ٱلَّذِينَ ءَامَنُوا۟ يُقِيمُوا۟ ٱلصَّلَوٰةَ وَيُنفِقُوا۟ مِمَّا رَزَقْنَٰهُمْ سِرًّا وَعَلَانِيَةً مِّن قَبْلِ أَن يَأْتِيَ يَوْمٌ لَّا بَيْعٌ فِيهِ وَلَا خِلَٰلٌ ۝ ٱللَّهُ ٱلَّذِي خَلَقَ ٱلسَّمَٰوَٰتِ وَٱلْأَرْضَ وَأَنزَلَ مِنَ ٱلسَّمَاءِ مَاءً فَأَخْرَجَ بِهِۦ مِنَ ٱلثَّمَرَٰتِ رِزْقًا لَّكُمْ ۖ وَسَخَّرَ لَكُمُ ٱلْفُلْكَ لِتَجْرِيَ فِي ٱلْبَحْرِ بِأَمْرِهِۦ ۖ وَسَخَّرَ لَكُمُ ٱلْأَنْهَٰرَ ۝ وَسَخَّرَ لَكُمُ ٱلشَّمْسَ وَٱلْقَمَرَ دَائِبَيْنِ ۖ وَسَخَّرَ لَكُمُ ٱللَّيْلَ وَٱلنَّهَارَ ۝ وَءَاتَىٰكُم مِّن كُلِّ مَا سَأَلْتُمُوهُ ۚ وَإِن تَعُدُّوا۟ نِعْمَتَ ٱللَّهِ لَا تُحْصُوهَا ۗ إِنَّ ٱلْإِنسَٰنَ لَظَلُومٌ كَفَّارٌ ۝ وَإِذْ قَالَ إِبْرَٰهِيمُ رَبِّ ٱجْعَلْ هَٰذَا ٱلْبَلَدَ ءَامِنًا وَٱجْنُبْنِي وَبَنِيَّ أَن نَّعْبُدَ ٱلْأَصْنَامَ ۝ رَبِّ إِنَّهُنَّ أَضْلَلْنَ كَثِيرًا مِّنَ ٱلنَّاسِ ۖ فَمَن تَبِعَنِي فَإِنَّهُۥ مِنِّي ۖ وَمَنْ عَصَانِي فَإِنَّكَ غَفُورٌ رَّحِيمٌ ۝ رَّبَّنَا إِنِّي أَسْكَنتُ مِن ذُرِّيَّتِي بِوَادٍ غَيْرِ ذِي زَرْعٍ عِندَ بَيْتِكَ ٱلْمُحَرَّمِ رَبَّنَا لِيُقِيمُوا۟ ٱلصَّلَوٰةَ فَٱجْعَلْ أَفْئِدَةً مِّنَ ٱلنَّاسِ تَهْوِي إِلَيْهِمْ وَٱرْزُقْهُم مِّنَ ٱلثَّمَرَٰتِ لَعَلَّهُمْ يَشْكُرُونَ ۝ رَبَّنَا إِنَّكَ تَعْلَمُ مَا نُخْفِي وَمَا نُعْلِنُ ۗ وَمَا يَخْفَىٰ عَلَى ٱللَّهِ مِن شَيْءٍ فِي ٱلْأَرْضِ وَلَا فِي ٱلسَّمَاءِ ۝ ٱلْحَمْدُ لِلَّهِ ٱلَّذِي وَهَبَ لِي عَلَى ٱلْكِبَرِ إِسْمَٰعِيلَ وَإِسْحَٰقَ ۚ إِنَّ رَبِّي لَسَمِيعُ ٱلدُّعَاءِ ۝ رَبِّ ٱجْعَلْنِي مُقِيمَ ٱلصَّلَوٰةِ وَمِن ذُرِّيَّتِي ۚ رَبَّنَا وَتَقَبَّلْ دُعَاءِ ۝ رَبَّنَا ٱغْفِرْ لِي وَلِوَٰلِدَيَّ وَلِلْمُؤْمِنِينَ يَوْمَ يَقُومُ ٱلْحِسَابُ ۝ وَلَا تَحْسَبَنَّ ٱللَّهَ غَٰفِلًا عَمَّا يَعْمَلُ ٱلظَّٰلِمُونَ ۚ إِنَّمَا يُؤَخِّرُهُمْ لِيَوْمٍ تَشْخَصُ فِيهِ ٱلْأَبْصَٰرُ ۝ مُهْطِعِينَ مُقْنِعِي رُءُوسِهِمْ لَا يَرْتَدُّ إِلَيْهِمْ طَرْفُهُمْ ۖ وَأَفْئِدَتُهُمْ هَوَاءٌ ۝ وَأَنذِرِ ٱلنَّاسَ يَوْمَ يَأْتِيهِمُ ٱلْعَذَابُ فَيَقُولُ ٱلَّذِينَ ظَلَمُوا۟ رَبَّنَا أَخِّرْنَا إِلَىٰ أَجَلٍ قَرِيبٍ نُّجِبْ دَعْوَتَكَ وَنَتَّبِعِ ٱلرُّسُلَ ۗ أَوَلَمْ تَكُونُوا۟ أَقْسَمْتُم مِّن قَبْلُ مَا لَكُم مِّن زَوَالٍ ۝ وَسَكَنتُمْ فِي

$$\begin{array}{c}
\text{مَسَـٰكِنِ ٱلَّذِينَ ظَلَمُوٓاْ أَنفُسَهُمْ وَتَبَيَّنَ لَكُمْ كَيْفَ فَعَلْنَا بِهِمْ وَضَرَبْنَا لَكُمُ ٱلْأَمْثَالَ ۝ وَقَدْ مَكَرُواْ مَكْرَهُمْ وَعِندَ ٱللَّهِ مَكْرُهُمْ وَإِن كَانَ مَكْرُهُمْ لِتَزُولَ مِنْهُ ٱلْجِبَالُ ۝ فَلَا تَحْسَبَنَّ ٱللَّهَ مُخْلِفَ وَعْدِهِۦ رُسُلَهُۥٓ إِنَّ ٱللَّهَ عَزِيزٌ ذُو ٱنتِقَامٍ ۝ يَوْمَ تُبَدَّلُ ٱلْأَرْضُ غَيْرَ ٱلْأَرْضِ وَٱلسَّمَـٰوَٰتُ وَبَرَزُواْ لِلَّهِ ٱلْوَٰحِدِ ٱلْقَهَّارِ ۝ وَتَرَى ٱلْمُجْرِمِينَ يَوْمَئِذٍ مُّقَرَّنِينَ فِى ٱلْأَصْفَادِ ۝ سَرَابِيلُهُم مِّن قَطِرَانٍ وَتَغْشَىٰ وُجُوهَهُمُ ٱلنَّارُ ۝ لِيَجْزِىَ ٱللَّهُ كُلَّ نَفْسٍ مَّا كَسَبَتْ إِنَّ ٱللَّهَ سَرِيعُ ٱلْحِسَابِ ۝ هَـٰذَا بَلَـٰغٌ لِّلنَّاسِ وَلِيُنذَرُواْ بِهِۦ وَلِيَعْلَمُوٓاْ أَنَّمَا هُوَ إِلَـٰهٌ وَٰحِدٌ وَلِيَذَّكَّرَ أُوْلُواْ ٱلْأَلْبَـٰبِ ۝}
\end{array}$$

(Ibrahim 001-052)

CHAPTER (SURAH) 12: YUSUF (JOSEPH), VERSES 053-111

Surah: 12 Ayah: 53

$$\text{﴿ وَمَآ أُبَرِّئُ نَفْسِىٓ إِنَّ ٱلنَّفْسَ لَأَمَّارَةٌۢ بِٱلسُّوٓءِ إِلَّا مَا رَحِمَ رَبِّىٓ إِنَّ رَبِّى غَفُورٌ رَّحِيمٌ ۝ ﴾}$$

53. "And I free not myself (from the blame). Verily, the (human) self is inclined to evil, except when my Lord bestows His Mercy (upon whom He wills). Verily, my Lord is Oft-Forgiving, Most Merciful."

Transliteration

53. Wama obarri-o nafsee inna alnnafsa laammaratun bialssoo-i illa ma rahima rabbee inna rabbee ghafoorun raheemun

Tafsir Ibn Kathir

It was said Yusuf peace be upon him is the one who said, (in order that he (the `Aziz) may know that I betrayed him not) with his wife, [see Ayah 52, Volume 4]

(in (his) absence).) until the end of Ayah (53) He said, `I sent back the emissary, so that the king would investigate my innocence and the `Aziz be certain that,

(I betrayed him not), with his wife,

(in (his) absence. And, verily, Allah guides not the plot of the betrayers.)' This is the only explanation presented by Ibn Jarir At-Tabari and Ibn Abi Hatim, but the first view is stronger and more obvious because it is a continuation of what the wife of the `Aziz

Chapter 12: Yusuf (Joseph), Verses 053-111

said in the presence of the king. Yusuf was not present at all during this time, for he was released later on and brought to the king by his order.

Surah: 12 Ayah: 54 & Ayah: 55

﴿ وَقَالَ ٱلْمَلِكُ ٱئْتُونِى بِهِۦٓ أَسْتَخْلِصْهُ لِنَفْسِى فَلَمَّا كَلَّمَهُۥ قَالَ إِنَّكَ ٱلْيَوْمَ لَدَيْنَا مَكِينٌ أَمِينٌ ۝ ﴾

54. And the king said: "Bring him to me that I may attach him to my person." Then, when he spoke to him, he said: "Verily, this day, you are with us high in rank and fully trusted."

﴿ قَالَ ٱجْعَلْنِى عَلَىٰ خَزَآئِنِ ٱلْأَرْضِ إِنِّى حَفِيظٌ عَلِيمٌ ۝ ﴾

55. (Yûsuf (Joseph)) said: "Set me over the storehouses of the land; I will indeed guard them with full knowledge" (as a minister of finance in Egypt).

Transliteration

54. Waqala almaliku i/toonee bihi astakhlishu linafsee falamma kallamahu qala innaka alyawma ladayna makeenun ameenun   55. Qala ijAAalnee AAala khaza-ini al-ardi innee hafeethun AAaleemun

Tafsir Ibn Kathir

Yusuf's Rank with the King of Egypt

Allah states that when he became aware of Yusuf's innocence and his innocense of what he was accused of, the king said,

(Bring him to me that I may attach him to my person.), `that I may make him among my close aids and associates,'

(Then, when he spoke to him), when the king spoke to Yusuf and further recognized his virtues, great ability, brilliance, good conduct and perfect mannerism, he said to him,

(Verily, this day, you are with us high in rank and fully trusted.) The king said to Yusuf, `You have assumed an exalted status with us and are indeed fully trusted.' Yusuf, peace be upon him said,

(Set me over the storehouses of the land; I will indeed guard them with full knowledge.) Yusuf praised himself, for this is allowed when one's abilities are unknown and there is a need to do so. He said that he is,

(Hafiz), an honest guard,

(`Alim), having knowledge and wisdom about the job he is to be entrusted with. Prophet Yusuf asked the king to appoint him as minister of finance for the land, responsible for the harvest storehouses, in which they would collect produce for the years of drought which he told them will come. He wanted to be the guard, so that he could dispense the harvest in the wisest, best and most beneficial way. The king accepted Yusuf's offer, for he was eager to draw Yusuf close to him and to honor him. So Allah said next,

Surah: 12 Ayah: 56 & Ayah: 57

﴿ وَكَذَٰلِكَ مَكَّنَّا لِيُوسُفَ فِى ٱلْأَرْضِ يَتَبَوَّأُ مِنْهَا حَيْثُ يَشَآءُ ۚ نُصِيبُ بِرَحْمَتِنَا مَن نَّشَآءُ ۖ وَلَا نُضِيعُ أَجْرَ ٱلْمُحْسِنِينَ ۝ ﴾

56. Thus did We give full authority to Yûsuf (Joseph) in the land, to take possession therein, when or where he likes. We bestow of Our Mercy on whom We will, and We make not to be lost the reward of Al-Muhsinûn (the good doers).

﴿ وَلَأَجْرُ ٱلْأَخِرَةِ خَيْرٌ لِّلَّذِينَ ءَامَنُوا۟ وَكَانُوا۟ يَتَّقُونَ ۝ ﴾

57. And verily, the reward of the Hereafter is better for those who believe and used to fear Allâh and keep their duty to Him (by abstaining from all kinds of sins and evil deeds and by performing all kinds of righteous good deeds).

Transliteration

56. Wakathalika makanna liyoosufa fee al-ardi yatabawwao minha haythu yashao nuseebu birahmatina man nashao wala nudeeAAu ajra almuhsineena 57. Walaajru al-akhirati khayrun lillatheena amanoo wakanoo yattaqoona

Tafsir Ibn Kathir

Yusuf's Reign in Egypt

(Thus did We give full authority to Yusuf in the land), in Egypt,

(to take possession therein, when or where he likes.) As-Suddi and `Abdur-Rahman bin Zayd bin Aslam said that this part of the Ayah means, "To do whatever he wants therein." Ibn Jarir at Tabari said that it means, "He used to move about freely in the land after being imprisoned, suffering from hardship and the disgrace of slavery." Allah said next,

(We bestow of Our mercy on whom We will, and We make not to be lost the reward of the good doers.) Allah says here, We did not let the patience of Yusuf, from the harm his brothers exerted on him and being imprisoned because of the wife of the `Aziz, to be lost. Instead, Allah the Exalted and Most Honored rewarded him with His aid and victory,

(And We make not to be lost the reward of the good doers. And verily, the reward of the Hereafter is better for those who believed and had Taqwa.) Allah states that what He has prepared for His Prophet Yusuf, peace be upon him, in the Hereafter is much greater, substantial and honored than the authority He gave him in this life. Allah said about His Prophet Sulayman (Solomon), peace be upon him,

Chapter 12: Yusuf (Joseph), Verses 053-111 *15*

("This is Our gift, so spend or withhold, no account will be asked of you." And verily, for him is a near access to Us, and a good (final) return (Paradise).) (38:39-40) Yusuf, peace be upon him, was appointed minister of finance by Ar-Rayyan bin Al-Walid, king of Egypt at the time, instead of the `Aziz who bought him and the husband of she who tried to seduce him. The king of Egypt embraced Islam at the hands of Yusuf, peace be upon him, according to Mujahid.

Surah: 12 Ayah: 58, Ayah: 59, Ayah: 60, Ayah: 61 & Ayah: 62

﴿ وَجَاۤءَ إِخْوَةُ يُوسُفَ فَدَخَلُواْ عَلَيْهِ فَعَرَفَهُمْ وَهُمْ لَهُۥ مُنكِرُونَ ۝ ﴾

58. And Yûsuf's (Joseph) brethren came and they entered unto him, and he recognized them, but they recognized him not.

﴿ وَلَمَّا جَهَّزَهُم بِجَهَازِهِمْ قَالَ ٱئْتُونِى بِأَخٍ لَّكُم مِّنْ أَبِيكُمْ ۚ أَلَا تَرَوْنَ أَنِّىٓ أُوفِى ٱلْكَيْلَ وَأَنَاْ خَيْرُ ٱلْمُنزِلِينَ ۝ ﴾

59. And when he had furnished them forth with provisions (according to their need), he said: "Bring me a brother of yours from your father(he meant Benjamin). See you not that I give full measure, and that I am the best of the hosts?

﴿ فَإِن لَّمْ تَأْتُونِى بِهِۦ فَلَا كَيْلَ لَكُمْ عِندِى وَلَا تَقْرَبُونِ ۝ ﴾

60. "But if you bring him not to me, there shall be no measure (of corn) for you with me, nor shall you come near me."

﴿ قَالُواْ سَنُرَٰوِدُ عَنْهُ أَبَاهُ وَإِنَّا لَفَـٰعِلُونَ ۝ ﴾

61. They said: "We shall try to get permission (for him) from his father, and verily, we shall do it."

﴿ وَقَالَ لِفِتْيَـٰنِهِ ٱجْعَلُواْ بِضَـٰعَتَهُمْ فِى رِحَالِهِمْ لَعَلَّهُمْ يَعْرِفُونَهَآ إِذَا ٱنقَلَبُوٓاْ إِلَىٰٓ أَهْلِهِمْ لَعَلَّهُمْ يَرْجِعُونَ ۝ ﴾

62. And (Yûsuf (Joseph)) told his servants to put their money (with which they had bought the corn) into their bags, so that they might know it when they go back to their people; in order that they might come again.

Transliteration

58. Wajaa ikhwatu yoosufa fadakhaloo AAalayhi faAAarafahum wahum lahu munkiroona 59. Walamma jahhazahum bijahazihim qala i/toonee bi-akhin lakum min abeekum ala tarawna annee oofee alkayla waana khayru almunzileena 60. Fa-in lam ta/toonee bihi fala kayla lakum AAindee wala taqrabooni 61. Qaloo sanurawidu AAanhu abahu wa-inna lafaAAiloona 62. Waqala lifityanihi ijAAaloo bidaAAatahum

fee rihalihim laAAallahum yaAArifoonaha itha inqalaboo ila ahlihim laAAallahum yarjiAAoona

Tafsir Ibn Kathir

Yusuf's Brothers travel to Egypt

As-Suddi, Muhammad bin Ishaq and several others said that the reason why Yusuf's brothers went to Egypt, is that after Yusuf became minister of Egypt and the seven years of abundance passed, then came the seven years of drought that struck all areas of Egypt. The drought also reached the area of Kana`an (Canaan), where Prophet Ya`qub, peace be upon him, and his children resided. Prophet Yusuf efficiently guarded the people's harvest and collected it, and what he collected became a great fortune for the people. This also permitted Yusuf to give gifts to the people who sought his aid from various areas who came to buy food and provisions for their families. Yusuf would not give a family man more than whatever a camel could carry, as annual provisions for them. Yusuf himself did not fill his stomach from this food, nor did the king and his aids eat except one meal a day. By doing so, the people could sustain themselves with what they had for the remainder of the seven years. Indeed, Yusuf was a mercy from Allah sent to the people of Egypt. Yusuf's brothers were among those who came to Egypt to buy food supplies, by the order of their father. They knew that the `Aziz of Egypt was selling food to people who need it for a low price, so they took some merchandise from their land with them to exchange it for food. They were ten, because Ya`qub peace be upon him kept his son and Yusuf's brother Binyamin with him. Binyamin was the dearest of his sons to him after Yusuf. When Prophet Yusuf's brothers entered on him in his court and the center of his authority, he knew them the minute he saw them. However, they did not recognize him because they got rid of him when he was still young, and sold him to a caravan of travelers while unaware of their destination. They could not have imagined that Yusuf would end up being a minister, and this is why they did not recognize him, while he did recognize them. As-Suddi said that Yusuf started talking to his brothers and asked them, "What brought you to my land" They said, "O, `Aziz, we came to buy provisions." He asked them, "You might be spies." They said, "Allah forbids." He asked them, "Where are you from" They said, "From the area of Kana`an, and our father is Allah's Prophet Ya`qub." He asked them, "Does he have other children besides you" They said, "Yes, we were twelve brothers. Our youngest died in the desert, and he used to be the dearest to his father. His full brother is alive and his father kept him, so that his closeness compensates him for losing our youngest brother (who died)." Yusuf ordered that his brothers be honored and allowed to remain,

(And when he furnished them with their provisions,) according to their needs and gave them what they wanted to buy, he said to them, "Bring me your brother from your father's side whom you mentioned, so that I know that you have told me the truth." He continued,

(See you not that I give full measure, and that I am the best of the hosts) encouraging them to return to him. He then threatened them,

Chapter 12: Yusuf (Joseph), Verses 053-111

(But if you bring him not to me, there shall be no measure (of corn) for you with me.) He threatened them that if the next time they come without Binyamin with them, they will not be allowed to buy the food that they need,

("...nor shall you come near me." They said: "We shall try to get permission (for him) from his father, and verily, we shall do it.") They said, `We will try our best to bring him with us, so that we spare no effort to prove to you that we are truthful in what we told you about ourselves.' Allah said,

(And (Yusuf) told his servants), or his slaves,

(to put their money), or the merchandise they brought with them to exchange for food,

(into their bags,), while they were unaware,

(in order that they might come again.) It was said that Yusuf did this because he feared that his brothers might not have any more merchandise they could bring with them to exchange for food.

Surah: 12 Ayah: 63 & Ayah: 64

﴿ فَلَمَّا رَجَعُوٓاْ إِلَىٰٓ أَبِيهِمْ قَالُوا۟ يَـٰٓأَبَانَا مُنِعَ مِنَّا ٱلْكَيْلُ فَأَرْسِلْ مَعَنَآ أَخَانَا نَكْتَلْ وَإِنَّا لَهُۥ لَحَـٰفِظُونَ ﴿٦٣﴾

63. So, when they returned to their father, they said: "O our father! No more measure of grain shall we get (unless we take our brother). So send our brother with us, and we shall get our measure and truly we will guard him."

﴿ قَالَ هَلْ ءَامَنُكُمْ عَلَيْهِ إِلَّا كَمَآ أَمِنتُكُمْ عَلَىٰٓ أَخِيهِ مِن قَبْلُ فَٱللَّهُ خَيْرٌ حَـٰفِظًا وَهُوَ أَرْحَمُ ٱلرَّٰحِمِينَ ﴿٦٤﴾

64. He said: "Can I entrust him to you except as I entrusted his brother (Yûsuf (Joseph)) to you aforetime? But Allâh is the Best to guard, and He is the Most Merciful of those who show mercy."

Transliteration

63. Falamma rajaAAoo ila abeehim qaloo ya abana muniAAa minna alkaylu faarsil maAAana akhana naktal wa-inna lahu lahafithoona 64. Qala hal amanukum AAalayhi illa kama amintukum AAala akheehi min qablu faAllahu khayrun hafithan wahuwa arhamu alrrahimeena

Tafsir Ibn Kathir

Yusuf's Brothers ask Ya`qub's Permission to send Their Brother Binyamin with Them to Egypt

Allah says that when they went back to their father,

(they said: "O our father! No more measure of grain shall we get...") `after this time, unless you send our brother Binyamin with us. So send him with us, and we shall get our measure and we shall certainly guard him.' Some scholars read this Ayah in a way that means, `and he shall get his ration.' They said,

(and truly, we will guard him.), `do not fear for his safety, for he will be returned back to you.' This is what they said to Ya`qub about their brother Yusuf,

("Send him with us tomorrow to enjoy himself and play, and verily, we will take care of him.") (12:12) This is why Prophet Ya`qub said to them,

(Can I entrust him to you except as I entrusted his brother (Yusuf) to you aforetime) He asked them, `Will you do to him except what you did to his brother Yusuf before, when you took him away from me and separated me from him'

(But Allah is the Best to guard, and He is the Most Merciful of those who show mercy.) Ya`qub said, `Allah has the most mercy with me among all those who show mercy, He is compassionate with me for my old age, feebleness and eagerness for my son. I invoke Allah to return him to me, and to allow him and I to be together; for surely, He is the Most Merciful of those who show mercy.'

Surah: 12 Ayah: 65 & Ayah: 66

﴿ وَلَمَّا فَتَحُواْ مَتَـٰعَهُمْ وَجَدُواْ بِضَـٰعَتَهُمْ رُدَّتْ إِلَيْهِمْ ۖ قَالُواْ يَـٰأَبَانَا مَا نَبْغِى ۖ هَـٰذِهِۦ بِضَـٰعَتُنَا رُدَّتْ إِلَيْنَا ۖ وَنَمِيرُ أَهْلَنَا وَنَحْفَظُ أَخَانَا وَنَزْدَادُ كَيْلَ بَعِيرٍ ۖ ذَٰلِكَ كَيْلٌ يَسِيرٌ ﴿٦٥﴾

65. And when they opened their bags, they found their money had been returned to them. They said: "O our father! What (more) can we desire? This, our money has been returned to us, so we shall get (more) food for our family, and we shall guard our brother and add one more measure of a camel's load. This quantity is easy (for the king to give)."

﴿ قَالَ لَنْ أُرْسِلَهُۥ مَعَكُمْ حَتَّىٰ تُؤْتُونِ مَوْثِقًا مِّنَ ٱللَّهِ لَتَأْتُنَّنِى بِهِۦٓ إِلَّآ أَن يُحَاطَ بِكُمْ ۖ فَلَمَّآ ءَاتَوْهُ مَوْثِقَهُمْ قَالَ ٱللَّهُ عَلَىٰ مَا نَقُولُ وَكِيلٌ ﴿٦٦﴾

66. He (Ya'qûb (Jacob)) said: "I will not send him with you until you swear a solemn oath to me in Allâh's Name, that you will bring him back to me unless you are

yourselves surrounded (by enemies)," And when they had sworn their solemn oath, he said: "Allâh is the Witness over what we have said."

Transliteration

65. Walamma fatahoo mataAAahum wajadoo bidaAAatahum ruddat ilayhim qaloo ya abana ma nabghee hathihi bidaAAatuna ruddat ilayna wanameeru ahlana wanahfathu akhana wanazdadu kayla baAAeerin thalika kaylun yaseerun   66. Qala lan orsilahu maAAakum hatta tu/tooni mawthiqan mina Allahi lata/tunnanee bihi illa an yuhata bikum falamma atawhu mawthiqahum qala Allahu AAala ma naqoolu wakeelun

Tafsir Ibn Kathir

They find Their Money returned to Their Bags

Allah says, when Yusuf's brothers opened their bags, they found their merchandise inside them, for Yusuf had ordered his servants to return it to their bags. When they found their merchandise in their bags,

(They said: "O our father! What (more) can we desire..."), what more can we ask for,

(This, our money has been returned to us;) Qatadah commented (that they said), "What more can we ask for, our merchandise was returned to us and the `Aziz has given us the sufficient load we wanted" They said next,

(so we shall get (more) food for our family,), `if you send our brother with us the next time we go to buy food for our family,'

(and we shall guard our brother and add one more measure of a camel's load.) since Yusuf, peace be upon him, gave each man a camel's load of corn.

(This quantity is easy (for the king to give).) They said these words to make their case more appealing, saying that taking their brother with them is worth this gain,

(He (Ya`qub (Jacob)) said: "I will not send him with you until you swear a solemn oath to me in Allah's Name..."), until you swear by Allah with the strongest oath,

(that you will bring him back to me unless you are yourselves surrounded (by enemies)), unless you were all overwhelmed and were unable to rescue him,

(And when they had sworn their solemn oath), he affirmed it further, saying,

(Allah is the Witness to what we have said.) Ibn Ishaq commented, "Ya`qub did that because he had no choice but to send them to bring necessary food supplies for their survival. So he sent Binyamin with them."

Surah: 12 Ayah: 67 & Ayah: 68

﴿ وَقَالَ يَـٰبَنِىَّ لَا تَدْخُلُوا۟ مِنۢ بَابٍ وَٰحِدٍ وَٱدْخُلُوا۟ مِنْ أَبْوَٰبٍ مُّتَفَرِّقَةٍ ۖ وَمَآ أُغْنِى عَنكُم مِّنَ ٱللَّهِ مِن شَىْءٍ ۖ إِنِ ٱلْحُكْمُ إِلَّا لِلَّهِ ۖ عَلَيْهِ تَوَكَّلْتُ ۖ وَعَلَيْهِ فَلْيَتَوَكَّلِ ٱلْمُتَوَكِّلُونَ ﴾ ۶۷

67. And he said: "O my sons! Do not enter by one gate, but enter by different gates, and I cannot avail you against Allâh at all. Verily! The decision rests only with Allâh. In him, I put my trust and let all those that trust, put their trust in Him."

﴿ وَلَمَّا دَخَلُوا۟ مِنْ حَيْثُ أَمَرَهُمْ أَبُوهُم مَّا كَانَ يُغْنِى عَنْهُم مِّنَ ٱللَّهِ مِن شَىْءٍ إِلَّا حَاجَةً فِى نَفْسِ يَعْقُوبَ قَضَىٰهَا ۚ وَإِنَّهُۥ لَذُو عِلْمٍ لِّمَا عَلَّمْنَـٰهُ وَلَـٰكِنَّ أَكْثَرَ ٱلنَّاسِ لَا يَعْلَمُونَ ﴾ ۶۸

68. And when they entered according to their father's advice, it did not avail them in the least against (the Will of) Allâh; it was but a need of Ya'qûb's (Jacob) inner-self which he discharged. And verily, he was endowed with knowledge because We had taught him, but most men know not.

Transliteration

67. Waqala ya baniyya la tadkhuloo min babin wahidin waodkhuloo min abwabin mutafarriqatin wama oghnee AAankum mina Allahi min shay-in ini alhukmu illa lillahi AAalayhi tawakkaltu waAAalayhi falyatawakkali almutawakkiloona 68. Walamma dakhaloo min haythu amarahum aboohum ma kana yughnee AAanhum mina Allahi min shay-in illa hajatan fee nafsi yaAAqooba qadaha wa-innahu lathoo AAilmin lima AAallamnahu walakinna akthara alnnasi la yaAAlamoona

Tafsir Ibn Kathir

Ya`qub orders His Children to enter Egypt from Different Gates

Allah says that Ya`qub, peace be upon him, ordered his children, when he sent Binyamin with them to Egypt, to enter from different gates rather than all of them entering from one gate. Ibn `Abbas, Muhammad bin Ka`b, Mujahid, Ad-Dahhak Qatadah, As-Suddi and several others said that he feared the evil eye for them, because they were handsome and looked beautiful and graceful. He feared that people might direct the evil eye at them, because the evil eye truly harms, by Allah's decree, and brings down the mighty warrior-rider from his horse. He next said, (and I cannot avail you against Allah at all.) this precaution will not resist Allah's decision and appointed decree. Verily, whatever Allah wills, cannot be resisted or stopped,

("Verily, the decision rests only with Allah. In Him, I put my trust and let all those that trust, put their trust in Him." And when they entered according to their father's

Chapter 12: Yusuf (Joseph), Verses 053-111

advice, it did not avail them in the least against (the will of) Allah; it was but a need of Ya`qub's inner self which he discharged.), as a precaution against the evil eye,

(And verily, he was endowed with knowledge because We had taught him,) he had knowledge that he implemented, according to Qatadah and Ath-Thawri. Ibn Jarir said that this part of the Ayah means, he has knowledge that We taught him,

(but most men know not.)

Surah: 12 Ayah: 69

﴿ وَلَمَّا دَخَلُواْ عَلَىٰ يُوسُفَ ءَاوَىٰٓ إِلَيْهِ أَخَاهُ ۖ قَالَ إِنِّىٓ أَنَا۠ أَخُوكَ فَلَا تَبْتَئِسْ بِمَا كَانُواْ يَعْمَلُونَ ۝ ﴾

69. And when they went in before Yûsuf (Joseph), he took his brother (Benjamin) to himself and said: "Verily! I am your brother, so grieve not for what they used to do."

Transliteration

69. Walamma dakhaloo AAala yoosufa awa ilayhi akhahu qala innee ana akhooka fala tabta-is bima kanoo yaAAmaloona

Tafsir Ibn Kathir

Yusuf comforts Binyamin

Allah states that when Yusuf's brothers went in before him along with his full brother Binyamin, he invited them to a place of honor as privileged guests. He granted them gifts and generous hospitality and kindness. He met his brother in confidence and told him the story of what happened to him and that he was in fact his brother. He said to him, (grieve not) nor feel sad for what they did to me.' He ordered Binyamin to hide the news from them and to refrain from telling them that the `Aziz is his brother Yusuf. He plotted with him to keep him in Egypt enjoying honor and great hospitality.

Surah: 12 Ayah: 70, Ayah: 71 & Ayah: 72

﴿ فَلَمَّا جَهَّزَهُم بِجَهَازِهِمْ جَعَلَ ٱلسِّقَايَةَ فِى رَحْلِ أَخِيهِ ثُمَّ أَذَّنَ مُؤَذِّنٌ أَيَّتُهَا ٱلْعِيرُ إِنَّكُمْ لَسَٰرِقُونَ ۝ ﴾

70. So when he had furnished them forth with their provisions, he put the (golden) bowl into his brother's bag. Then a crier cried: "O you (in) the caravan! Surely, you are thieves!"

﴿ قَالُواْ وَأَقْبَلُواْ عَلَيْهِم مَّاذَا تَفْقِدُونَ ۝ ﴾

71. They, turning towards them, said: "What is it that you have lost?"

$$﴿ قَالُوا۟ نَفْقِدُ صُوَاعَ ٱلْمَلِكِ وَلِمَن جَآءَ بِهِۦ حِمْلُ بَعِيرٍ وَأَنَا۠ بِهِۦ زَعِيمٌ ﴾$$

72. They said: "We have lost the (golden) bowl of the king and for him who produces it is (the reward of) a camel load; and I will be bound by it."

Transliteration

70. Falamma jahhazahum bijahazihim jaAAala alssiqayata fee rahli akheehi thumma aththana muaththinun ayyatuha alAAeeru innakum lasariqoona 71. Qaloo waaqbaloo AAalayhim matha tafqidoona 72. Qaloo nafqidu suwaAAa almaliki waliman jaa bihi himlu baAAeerin waana bihi zaAAeemun

Tafsir Ibn Kathir

Yusuf had His Golden Bowl placed in Binyamin's Bag; a Plot to keep Him in Egypt

After Yusuf supplied them with their provisions, he ordered some of his servants to place his silver bowl (in Binyamin's bag), according to the majority of scholars. Some scholars said that the king's bowl was made from gold. Ibn Zayd added that the king used it to drink from, and later, measured food grains with it since food became scarce in that time, according to Ibn `Abbas, Mujahid, Qatadah, Ad-Dahhak and `Abdur-Rahman bin Zayd. Shu`bah said that Abu Bishr narrated that Sa`id bin Jubayr said that Ibn `Abbas said that the king's bowl was made from silver and he used it to drink with. Yusuf had the bowl placed in Binyamin's bag while they were unaware, and then had someone herald,

(O you (in) the caravan! Surely, you are thieves!) They looked at the man who was heralding this statement and asked him,

("What is it that you have lost" They said: "We have lost the bowl of the king..."), which he used to measure food grains,

(and for him who produces it is a camel load;), as a reward,

(and I will be bound by it.), as assurance of delivery of the reward.

Surah: 12 Ayah: 73, Ayah: 74, Ayah: 75 & Ayah: 76

$$﴿ قَالُوا۟ تَٱللَّهِ لَقَدْ عَلِمْتُم مَّا جِئْنَا لِنُفْسِدَ فِى ٱلْأَرْضِ وَمَا كُنَّا سَٰرِقِينَ ﴾$$

73. They said: "By Allâh! Indeed you know that we came not to make mischief in the land, and we are no thieves!"

$$﴿ قَالُوا۟ فَمَا جَزَٰٓؤُهُۥٓ إِن كُنتُمْ كَٰذِبِينَ ﴾$$

74. They (Yûsuf's (Joseph) men) said: "What then shall be the penalty of him, if you are (proved to be) liars."

Chapter 12: Yusuf (Joseph), Verses 053-111   *23*

﴿ قَالُوا۟ جَزَآؤُهُۥ مَن وُجِدَ فِى رَحْلِهِۦ فَهُوَ جَزَآؤُهُۥ ۚ كَذَٰلِكَ نَجْزِى ٱلظَّٰلِمِينَ ۝ ﴾

75. They (Yûsuf's (Joseph) brothers) said: "His penalty should be that he, in whose bag it is found, should be held for the punishment (of the crime). Thus we punish the Zâlimûn (wrong-doers)!"

﴿ فَبَدَأَ بِأَوْعِيَتِهِمْ قَبْلَ وِعَآءِ أَخِيهِ ثُمَّ ٱسْتَخْرَجَهَا مِن وِعَآءِ أَخِيهِ ۚ كَذَٰلِكَ كِدْنَا لِيُوسُفَ ۖ مَا كَانَ لِيَأْخُذَ أَخَاهُ فِى دِينِ ٱلْمَلِكِ إِلَّآ أَن يَشَآءَ ٱللَّهُ ۚ نَرْفَعُ دَرَجَٰتٍ مَّن نَّشَآءُ ۗ وَفَوْقَ كُلِّ ذِى عِلْمٍ عَلِيمٌ ۝ ﴾

76. So he (Yûsuf (Joseph)) began (the search) in their bags before the bag of his brother. Then he brought it out of his brother's bag. Thus did We plan for Yûsuf (Joseph). He could not take his brother by the law of the king (as a slave), except that Allâh willed it. (So Allâh made the brothers to bind themselves with their way of "punishment, i.e. enslaving of a thief.") We raise to degrees whom We will, but over all those endowed with knowledge is the All-Knowing (Allâh).

Transliteration

73. Qaloo taAllahi laqad AAalimtum ma ji/na linufsida fee al-ardi wama kunna sariqeena 74. Qaloo fama jazaohu in kuntum kathibeena 75. Qaloo jazaohu man wujida fee rahlihi fahuwa jazaohu kathalika najzee aththalimeena 76. Fabadaa bi-awAAiyatihim qabla wiAAa-i akheehi thumma istakhrajaha min wiAAa-i akheehi kathalika kidna liyoosufa ma kana liya/khutha akhahu fee deeni almaliki illa an yashaa Allahu narfaAAu darajatin man nashao wafawqa kulli thee AAilmin AAaleemun

Tafsir Ibn Kathir

After Yusuf's servants accused his brothers of theft, they said,

(By Allah! Indeed you know that we came not to make mischief in the land, and we are no thieves!) `Ever since you knew us, you, due to our good conduct, became certain that,

(we came not to make mischief in the land, and we are no thieves!) They said, `Theft is not in our character, as you came to know.' Yusuf's men said,

`(What then shall be the penalty of him), in reference to the thief, if it came out that he is one of you,'

(if you are (proved to be) liars) They asked them, `What should be the thief's punishment if he is one of you'

(They said: "His penalty should be that he, in whose bag it is found, should be held for the punishment. Thus we punish the wrongdoers!") This was the law of Prophet

Ibrahim, peace be upon him, that the thief be given as a slave to the victim of theft. This is what Yusuf wanted, and this is why he started with their bags first before his brother's bag, to perfect the plot,

(Then he brought it out of his brother's bag.) Therefore, Yusuf took Binyamin as a slave according to their judgement and the law which they believed in. So Allah said;

(Thus did We plan for Yusuf.) and this is a good plot that Allah likes and prefers, because it seeks a certain benefit using wisdom and the benefit of all. Allah said next,

(He could not take his brother by the law of the king,) as a captive, for this was not the law of king of Egypt, according to Ad-Dahhak and several other scholars. Allah only allowed Yusuf to take his brother as a captive after his brothers agreed to this judgement beforehand, and he knew that this was their law. This is why Allah praised him when He said,

(We raise to degrees whom We will,) just as He said in another Ayah,

(Allah will exalt in degree those of you who believe.) (58:11) Allah said next,

(but over all those endowed with knowledge is the All-Knowing.) Al-Hasan commented, "There is no knowledgeable person, but there is another person with more knowledge until it ends at Allah the Exalted and Most Honored. In addition, `Abdur-Razzaq recorded that Sa`id bin Jubayr said, "We were with Ibn `Abbas when he narrated an amazing Hadith. A man in the audience said, `All praise is to Allah! There is an all-knowing above every person endowed with knowledge.' Ibn `Abbas responded, `Worse it is that which you said! Allah is the All-Knowing and His knowledge is above the knowledge of every knowledgeable person.' Simak narrated that `Ikrimah said that Ibn `Abbas said about Allah's statement,

(but over all those endowed with knowledge is the All-Knowing (Allah).) "This person has more knowledge than that person, and Allah is above all knowledgeable persons." Similar was narrated from `Ikrimah. Qatadah said, "Over every person endowed with knowledge is a more knowledgeable person until all knowledge ends with Allah. Verily, knowledge started from Allah, and from Him the scholars learn, and to Him all knowledge returns." `Abdullah bin Mas`ud read the Ayah this way, (عَلِيمٌ عَالِمٍ كُلِّ وَفَوْقَ) "And above every scholar, is the All-Knower (Allah)."

Surah: 12 Ayah: 77

﴿ ۞ قَالُوٓاْ إِن يَسْرِقْ فَقَدْ سَرَقَ أَخٌ لَّهُۥ مِن قَبْلُ ۚ فَأَسَرَّهَا يُوسُفُ فِى نَفْسِهِۦ وَلَمْ يُبْدِهَا لَهُمْ ۚ قَالَ أَنتُمْ شَرٌّ مَّكَانًا ۚ وَٱللَّهُ أَعْلَمُ بِمَا تَصِفُونَ ۝ ﴾

77. They ((Yûsuf's (Joseph) brothers) said: "If he steals, there was a brother of his (Yûsuf (Joseph)) who did steal before (him)." But these things did Yûsuf (Joseph) keep in himself, revealing not the secrets to them. He said (within himself): "You are in worst case, and Allâh is the Best Knower of that which you describe!"

Chapter 12: Yusuf (Joseph), Verses 053-111

Transliteration

77. Qaloo in yasriq faqad saraqa akhun lahu min qablu faasarraha yoosufu fee nafsihi walam yubdiha lahum qala antum sharrun makanan waAllahu aAAlamu bima tasifoona

Tafsir Ibn Kathir

Yusuf's Brothers accuse Him of Theft!

After Yusuf's brothers saw that the king's bowl was taken out of Binyamin's bag, they said,

(If he steals, there was a brother of his who did steal before.) They tried to show themselves as innocent from being like Binyamin, saying that he did just like a brother of his did beforehand, meaning Yusuf, peace be upon him! Allah said,

(But these things did Yusuf keep in himself), meaning the statement that he said afterwards,

(You are in an evil situation, and Allah is the Best Knower of that which you describe!) Yusuf said this to himself and did not utter it aloud, thus intending to hide what he wanted to say to himself even before he said it. Al-`Awfi reported that Ibn `Abbas said about Allah's statement,

(But these things did Yusuf keep in himself), "He kept in himself (his statement next),

(You are in an evil situation, and Allah is the Best Knower of that which you describe!)."

Surah: 12 Ayah: 78 & Ayah: 79

﴿ قَالُوا۟ يَـٰٓأَيُّهَا ٱلْعَزِيزُ إِنَّ لَهُۥٓ أَبًا شَيْخًا كَبِيرًا فَخُذْ أَحَدَنَا مَكَانَهُۥٓ ۖ إِنَّا نَرَىٰكَ مِنَ ٱلْمُحْسِنِينَ ۝ ﴾

78. They said: "O ruler of the land! Verily, he has an old father (who will grieve for him); so take one of us in his place. Indeed we think that you are one of the Muhsinûn (good-doers)."

﴿ قَالَ مَعَاذَ ٱللَّهِ أَن نَّأْخُذَ إِلَّا مَن وَجَدْنَا مَتَـٰعَنَا عِندَهُۥٓ إِنَّآ إِذًا لَّظَـٰلِمُونَ ۝ ﴾

79. He said: "Allâh forbid, that we should take anyone but him with whom we found our property. Indeed (if we did so), we should be Zâlimûn (wrong-doers)."

Transliteration

78. Qaloo ya ayyuha alAAazeezu inna lahu aban shaykhan kabeeran fakhuth ahadana makanahu inna naraka mina almuhsineena 79. Qala maAAatha Allahi an na/khutha illa man wajadna mataAAana AAindahu inna ithan lathalimoona

Tafsir Ibn Kathir

Yusuf's Brothers offer taking One of Them instead of Binyamin as a Slave, Yusuf rejects the Offer

When it was decided that Benyamin was to be taken and kept with Yusuf according to the law they adhered by, Yusuf's brothers started requesting clemency and raising compassion in his heart for them,

(They said, "O `Aziz! Verily, he has an old father...") who loves him very much and is comfor- ted by his presence from the son that he lost,

(so take one of us in his place.), instead of Binyamin to remain with you,

(Indeed we think that you are one of the doers of good.), the good doers, just, and accepting fairness,

(He said: "Allah forbid, that we should take anyone but him with whom we found our property..."), `according to the judgement that you gave for his punishment,

(Indeed, we should be wrongdoers.), if we take an innocent man instead of the guilty man. '

Surah: 12 Ayah: 80, Ayah: 81 & Ayah: 82

﴿ فَلَمَّا ٱسْتَيْـَٔسُوا۟ مِنْهُ خَلَصُوا۟ نَجِيًّا ۖ قَالَ كَبِيرُهُمْ أَلَمْ تَعْلَمُوٓا۟ أَنَّ أَبَاكُمْ قَدْ أَخَذَ عَلَيْكُم مَّوْثِقًا مِّنَ ٱللَّهِ وَمِن قَبْلُ مَا فَرَّطتُمْ فِى يُوسُفَ ۖ فَلَنْ أَبْرَحَ ٱلْأَرْضَ حَتَّىٰ يَأْذَنَ لِىٓ أَبِىٓ أَوْ يَحْكُمَ ٱللَّهُ لِى ۖ وَهُوَ خَيْرُ ٱلْحَٰكِمِينَ ﴾

80. So, when they despaired of him, they held a conference in private. The eldest among them said: "Know you not that your father did take an oath from you in Allâh's Name, and before this you did fail in your duty with Yûsuf (Joseph)? Therefore I will not leave this land until my father permits me, or Allâh decides my case (by releasing Benjamin) and He is the Best of the judges.

﴿ ٱرْجِعُوٓا۟ إِلَىٰٓ أَبِيكُمْ فَقُولُوا۟ يَٰٓأَبَانَآ إِنَّ ٱبْنَكَ سَرَقَ وَمَا شَهِدْنَآ إِلَّا بِمَا عَلِمْنَا وَمَا كُنَّا لِلْغَيْبِ حَٰفِظِينَ ﴾

81. "Return to your father and say, 'O our father! Verily, your son (Benjamin) has stolen, and we testify not except according to what we know, and we could not know the Unseen!

﴿ وَسْـَٔلِ ٱلْقَرْيَةَ ٱلَّتِى كُنَّا فِيهَا وَٱلْعِيرَ ٱلَّتِىٓ أَقْبَلْنَا فِيهَا ۖ وَإِنَّا لَصَٰدِقُونَ ﴾

82. "And ask (the people of) the town where we have been, and the caravan in which we returned; and indeed we are telling the truth."

Chapter 12: Yusuf (Joseph), Verses 053-111

Transliteration

80. Falamma istay-asoo minhu khalasoo najiyyan qala kabeeruhum alam taAAlamoo anna abakum qad akhatha AAalaykum mawthiqan mina Allahi wamin qablu ma farrattum fee yoosufa falan abraha al-arda hatta ya/thana lee abee aw yahkuma Allahu lee wahuwa khayru alhakimeena 81. IrjiAAoo ila abeekum faqooloo ya abana inna ibnaka saraqa wama shahidna illa bima AAalimna wama kunna lilghaybi hafitheena 82. Wais-ali alqaryata allatee kunna feeha waalAAeera allatee aqbalna feeha wa-inna lasadiqoona

Tafsir Ibn Kathir

Yusuf's Brothers consult Each Other in Confidence; the Advice Their Eldest Brother gave Them

Allah narrates to us that Yusuf's brothers were desperate because they could not secure the release of their brother Binyamin, even though they had given a promise and sworn to their father to bring him back. They were unable to fulfill their promise to their father, so,

(in private), away from people's eyes,

(they consulted), among themselves,

(The eldest among them said), and his name, as we mentioned, was Rubil, or Yahudha. He was the one among them who recommended throwing Yusuf into a well, rather than killing him. So Rubil said to them,

a`(Know you not that your father did take an oath from you in Allah's Name,) that you will return Binyamin to him However, you were not able to fulfill this promise and, before you caused Yusuf to be lost from his father,

(Therefore I will not leave this land), I will not leave Egypt,

(until my father permits me,) allows me to go back to him while he is pleased with me,

(or Allah decides my case) by using the sword, or, they says; by allowing me to secure the release of my brother,

(and He is the Best of the judges.), He next ordered them to narrate to their father what happened so that they could present their excuse about that happened to Binyamin and as claim their innocence before him. Rubil said to them (to say to their father),

(and we could not know the Unseen!) or, `we did not know that your son had committed theft,' according to Qatadah and `Ikrimah. `Abdur-Rahman bin Zayd bin Aslam said that it means, `we did not know that Binyamin stole something that belonged to the king, we only stated the punishment of the thief,'

(And ask (the people of) the town where we have been,), in reference to Egypt, according to Qatadah, or another town.

(and the caravan in which we returned), `about our truthfulness, honesty, protection and sincere guardianship,

(and indeed we are telling the truth.) in what we have told you, that Binyamin stole and was taken as a captive as compensation for his theft.'

Surah: 12 Ayah: 83, Ayah: 84, Ayah: 85 & Ayah: 86

﴿ قَالَ بَلْ سَوَّلَتْ لَكُمْ أَنفُسُكُمْ أَمْرًا فَصَبْرٌ جَمِيلٌ عَسَى ٱللَّهُ أَن يَأْتِيَنِى بِهِمْ جَمِيعًا إِنَّهُۥ هُوَ ٱلْعَلِيمُ ٱلْحَكِيمُ ﴾

83. He (Ya'qûb (Jacob)) said: "Nay, but your own selves have beguiled you into something. So patience is most fitting (for me). May be Allâh will bring them (back) all to me. Truly He! only He is All-Knowing, All-Wise."

﴿ وَتَوَلَّىٰ عَنْهُمْ وَقَالَ يَـٰأَسَفَىٰ عَلَىٰ يُوسُفَ وَٱبْيَضَّتْ عَيْنَاهُ مِنَ ٱلْحُزْنِ فَهُوَ كَظِيمٌ ﴾

84. And he turned away from them and said: "Alas, my grief for Yûsuf (Joseph)!" And he lost his sight because of the sorrow that he was suppressing.

﴿ قَالُوا۟ تَٱللَّهِ تَفْتَؤُا۟ تَذْكُرُ يُوسُفَ حَتَّىٰ تَكُونَ حَرَضًا أَوْ تَكُونَ مِنَ ٱلْهَـٰلِكِينَ ﴾

85. They said: "By Allâh! You will never cease remembering Yûsuf (Joseph) until you become weak with old age, or until you be of the dead."

﴿ قَالَ إِنَّمَآ أَشْكُوا۟ بَثِّى وَحُزْنِىٓ إِلَى ٱللَّهِ وَأَعْلَمُ مِنَ ٱللَّهِ مَا لَا تَعْلَمُونَ ﴾

86. He said: "I only complain of my grief and sorrow to Allâh, and I know from Allâh that which you know not.

Transliteration

83. Qala bal sawwalat lakum anfusukum amran fasabrun jameelun AAasa Allahu an ya/tiyanee bihim jameeAAan innahu huwa alAAaleemu alhakeemu 84. Watawalla AAanhum waqala ya asafa AAala yoosufa waibyaddat AAaynahu mina alhuzni fahuwa katheemun 85. Qaloo taAllahi taftao tathkuru yoosufa hatta takoona haradan aw takoona mina alhalikeena 86. Qala innama ashkoo baththee wahuznee ila Allahi waaAAlamu mina Allahi ma la taAAlamoona

Chapter 12: Yusuf (Joseph), Verses 053-111

Tafsir Ibn Kathir

Allah's Prophet Ya`qub receives the Grievous News

Allah's Prophet Ya`qub repeated to his children the same words he said to them when they brought false blood on Yusuf' shirt,

(Nay, but your own selves have beguiled you into something. So patience is most fitting (for me).) Muhammad bin Ishaq said, "When they went back to Ya`qub and told him what happened, he did not believe them and thought that this was a repetition of what they did to Yusuf. So he said,

(Nay, but your own selves have beguiled you into something. So patience is most fitting (for me).) Some said that since this new development came after what they did before (to Yusuf), they were given the same judgement to this later incident that was given to them when they did what they did (to Yusuf). Therefore, Ya`qub's statement here is befitting,

(Nay, but your own selves have beguiled you into something. So patience is most fitting (for me).) He then begged Allah to bring back his three sons: Yusuf, Binyamin and Rubil to him." Rubil had remained in Egypt awaiting Allah's decision about his case, either his father's permission ordering him to go back home, or to secure the release of his brother in confidence. This is why Ya`qub said,

(May be Allah will bring them (back) all to me. Truly, He! Only He is All-Knowing,), in my distress,

(the All-Wise), in His decisions and the decree and preordainment He appoints. Allah said next,

(And he turned away from them and said: "Alas, my grief for Yusuf!") He turned away from his children and remembered his old grief for Yusuf,

(Alas, my grief for Yusuf!) The new grief, losing Binyamin and Rubil, renewed his old sadness that he kept to himself. `Abdur-Razzaq narrated that Ath-Thawri said that Sufyan Al-`Usfuri said that Sa`id bin Jubayr said, "Only this nation (the following of Prophet Muhammad ) were given Al-Istirja'. Have you not heard the statement of Ya`qub, peace be upon him,

("Alas, my grief for Yusuf !" And he lost his sight because of the sorrow that he was suppressing.)" Ya`qub suppressed his sorrow and did not complain to a created being, according to Qatadah and other scholars. Ad-Dahhak also commented, "Ya`qub was aggrieved, sorrowful and sad." Ya`qub's children felt pity for him and said, while feeling sorrow and compassion,

(By Allah! You will never cease remembering Yusuf), `you will keep remembering Yusuf,

(until you become weak with old age,), until your strength leaves you,' (or until you be of the dead.) They said, `if you continue like this, we fear for you that you might die of grief,'

(He said: "I only complain of my grief and sorrow to Allah.") When they said these words to him, Ya`qub said, (I only complain of my grief and sorrow) for the afflictions that struck me,

(to Allah,) alone,

(and I know from Allah that which you know not.) I anticipate from Allah each and every type of goodness.' Ibn `Abbas commented on the meaning of,

(and I know from Allah that which you know not.) "The vision that Yusuf saw is truthful and Allah will certainly make it come true."

Surah: 12 Ayah: 87 & Ayah: 88

﴿ يَـٰبَنِىَّ ٱذْهَبُواْ فَتَحَسَّسُواْ مِن يُوسُفَ وَأَخِيهِ وَلَا تَاْيْـَٔسُواْ مِن رَّوْحِ ٱللَّهِ إِنَّهُۥ لَا يَاْيْـَٔسُ مِن رَّوْحِ ٱللَّهِ إِلَّا ٱلْقَوْمُ ٱلْكَـٰفِرُونَ ﴾

87. "O my sons! Go you and inquire about Yûsuf (Joseph) and his brother, and never give up hope of Allâh's Mercy. Certainly no one despairs of Allâh's Mercy, except the people who disbelieve."

﴿ فَلَمَّا دَخَلُواْ عَلَيْهِ قَالُواْ يَـٰٓأَيُّهَا ٱلْعَزِيزُ مَسَّنَا وَأَهْلَنَا ٱلضُّرُّ وَجِئْنَا بِبِضَـٰعَةٍ مُّزْجَىٰةٍ فَأَوْفِ لَنَا ٱلْكَيْلَ وَتَصَدَّقْ عَلَيْنَآ إِنَّ ٱللَّهَ يَجْزِى ٱلْمُتَصَدِّقِينَ ﴾

88. Then, when they entered unto him (Yûsuf (Joseph)) they said: "O ruler of the land! A hard time has hit us and our family, and we have brought but poor capital, so pay us full measure and be charitable to us. Truly, Allâh does reward the charitable."

Transliteration

87. Ya baniyya ithhaboo fatahassasoo min yoosufa waakheehi wala tay-asoo min rawhi Allahi innahu la yay-asu min rawhi Allahi illa alqawmu alkafiroona 88. Falamma dakhaloo AAalayhi qaloo ya ayyuha alAAazeezu massana waahlana alddurru waji/na bibidaAAatin muzjatin faawfi lana alkayla watasaddaq AAalayna inna Allaha yajzee almutasaddiqeena

Tafsir Ibn Kathir

Ya`qub orders His Children to inquire about Yusuf and His Brother

Allah states that Ya`qub, peace be upon him, ordered his children to go back and inquire about the news of Yusuf and his brother Binyamin, in a good manner, not as spies. He encouraged them, delivered to them the good news and ordered them not to despair of Allah's mercy. He ordered them to never give up hope in Allah, nor to ever discontinue trusting in Him for what they seek to accomplish. He said to them that only the disbelieving people despair of Allah's mercy.

Yusuf's Brothers stand before Him

Allah said next,

(Then, when they entered unto him), when they went back to Egypt and entered upon Yusuf,

(they said: "O Aziz! A hard time has hit us and our family..."), because of severe droughts and the scarcity of food,

(and we have brought but poor capital,) means, `we brought money for the food we want to buy, but it is not substantial,' according to Mujahid, Al-Hasan and several others. Allah said that they said next,

(so pay us full measure) meaning, `in return for the little money we brought, give us the full measure that you gave us before.' Ibn Mas`ud read this Ayah in a way that means, "So give the full load on our animals and be charitable with us." Ibn Jurayj commented, "So be charitable to us by returning our brother to us." And when Sufyan bin `Uyaynah was asked if the Sadaqah (charity) was prohibited for any Prophet before our Prophet , he said, "Have you not heard the Ayah,

(so pay us full measure and be charitable to us. Truly, Allah does reward the charitable.)" Ibn Jarir At-Tabari collected this statement.

Surah: 12 Ayah: 89, Ayah: 90, Ayah: 91 & Ayah: 92

﴿ قَالَ هَلْ عَلِمْتُم مَّا فَعَلْتُم بِيُوسُفَ وَأَخِيهِ إِذْ أَنتُمْ جَـٰهِلُونَ ﴾

89. He said: "Do you know what you did with Yûsuf (Joseph) and his brother, when you were ignorant?"

﴿ قَالُوٓا۟ أَءِنَّكَ لَأَنتَ يُوسُفُ قَالَ أَنَا۟ يُوسُفُ وَهَـٰذَآ أَخِى قَدْ مَنَّ ٱللَّهُ عَلَيْنَآ إِنَّهُۥ مَن يَتَّقِ وَيَصْبِرْ فَإِنَّ ٱللَّهَ لَا يُضِيعُ أَجْرَ ٱلْمُحْسِنِينَ ﴾

90. They said: "Are you indeed Yûsuf (Joseph)?" He said: "I am Yûsuf (Joseph), and this is my brother (Benjamin). Allâh has indeed been gracious to us. Verily, he who fears Allâh with obedience to Him (by abstaining from sins and evil deeds, and by performing righteous good deeds), and is patient, then surely, Allâh makes not the reward of the Muhsinûn (good-doers - see V.2:112) to be lost."

﴿ قَالُوا۟ تَٱللَّهِ لَقَدْ ءَاثَرَكَ ٱللَّهُ عَلَيْنَا وَإِن كُنَّا لَخَـٰطِـِٔينَ ﴾

91. They said: "By Allâh! Indeed Allâh has preferred you above us, and we certainly have been sinners."

﴿ قَالَ لَا تَثْرِيبَ عَلَيْكُمُ ٱلْيَوْمَ يَغْفِرُ ٱللَّهُ لَكُمْ وَهُوَ أَرْحَمُ ٱلرَّاحِمِينَ ۞ ﴾

92. He said: "No reproach on you this day; may Allâh forgive you, and He is the Most Merciful of those who show mercy!

Transliteration

89. Qala hal AAalimtum ma faAAaltum biyoosufa waakheehi ith antum jahiloona 90. Qaloo a-innaka laanta yoosufa qala ana yoosufu wahatha akhee qad manna Allahu AAalayna innahu man yattaqi wayasbir fa-inna Allaha la yudeeAAu ajra almuhsineena 91. Qaloo taAllahi laqad atharaka Allahu AAalayna wa-in kunna lakhati-eena 92. Qala la tathreeba AAalaykumu alyawma yaghfiru Allahu lakum wahuwa arhamu alrrahimeena

Tafsir Ibn Kathir

Yusuf reveals His True Identity to His Brothers and forgives Them

Allah says, when Yusuf's brothers told him about the afflictions and hardship, and shortages in food they suffered from in the aftermath of the drought that struck them, and he remembered his father's grief for losing his two children, he felt compassion, pity and mercy for his father and brothers. He felt this way, especially since he was enjoying kingship, authority and power, so he cried and revealed his true identity to them when he asked them,

(Do you know what you did with Yusuf and his brother, when you were ignorant) meaning, `when you separated between Yusuf and his brother,'

(when you were ignorant) He said, `What made you do this is your ignorance of the tremendous sin you were about to commit.' It appears, and Allah knows best, that Yusuf revealed his identity to his brothers only then by Allah's command, just as he hid his identity from them in the first two meetings, by Allah's command. When the affliction became harder, Allah sent His relief from that affliction, just as He said He does,

(Verily, along with every hardship is relief. Verily, along with every hardship is relief.)(94:5-6) This is when they said to Yusuf,

(Are you indeed Yusuf), in amazement, because they had been meeting him for more than two years while unaware of who he really was. Yet, he knew who they were and hid this news from them. Therefore, they asked in astonishment,

(Are you indeed Yusuf He said: "I am Yusuf, and this is my brother...") Yusuf said next,

`(Allah has indeed been gracious to us.) by gathering us together after being separated all this time,'

("Verily, he who has Taqwa, and is patient, then surely, Allah makes not the reward of the gooddoers to be lost." They said: "By Allah! Indeed Allah has preferred you above us.") They affirmed Yusuf's virtue above them, being blessed with beauty, conduct, richness, kingship, authority and, above all, prophethood. They admitted their error and acknowledged that they made a mistake against him,

(He said: "No reproach on you this day.") He said to them, `There will be no blame for you today or admonishment, and I will not remind you after today of your error against me.' He then multiplied his generosity by invoking Allah for them for mercy,

(may Allah forgive you, and He is the Most Merciful of those who show mercy!)

Surah: 12 Ayah: 93, Ayah: 94 & Ayah: 95

﴿ اذْهَبُواْ بِقَمِيصِى هَـٰذَا فَأَلْقُوهُ عَلَىٰ وَجْهِ أَبِى يَأْتِ بَصِيرًا وَأْتُونِى بِأَهْلِكُمْ أَجْمَعِينَ ﴾

93. "Go with this shirt of mine, and cast it over the face of my father, he will become clear-sighted, and bring me all your family."

﴿ وَلَمَّا فَصَلَتِ ٱلْعِيرُ قَالَ أَبُوهُمْ إِنِّى لَأَجِدُ رِيحَ يُوسُفَ لَوْلَآ أَن تُفَنِّدُونِ ﴾

94. And when the caravan departed, their father said: "I do indeed feel the smell of Yûsuf (Joseph), if only you think me not a dotard (a person who has weakness of mind because of old age)."

﴿ قَالُواْ تَٱللَّهِ إِنَّكَ لَفِى ضَلَـٰلِكَ ٱلْقَدِيمِ ﴾

95. They said: "By Allâh! Certainly, you are in your old error."

Transliteration

93. Ithhaboo biqameesee hatha faalqoohu AAala wajhi abee ya/ti baseeran wa/toonee bi-ahlikum ajmaAAeena 94. Walamma fasalati alAAeeru qala aboohum innee laajidu reeha yoosufa lawla an tufannidooni 95. Qaloo taAllahi innaka lafee dalalika alqadeemi

Tafsir Ibn Kathir

Ya`qub finds the Scent of Yusuf in his Shirt!

Yusuf said, `Take this shirt of mine,

(and cast it over the face of my father, his vision will return),' because Ya`qub had lost his sight from excessive crying,

(and bring to me all your family.) all the children of Ya`qub.

(And when the caravan departed) from Egypt,

(their father said...), Ya`qub, peace be upon him, said to the children who remained with him,

`(I do indeed feel the smell of Yusuf, if only you think me not senile.), except that you might think me senile because of old age.' `Abdur-Razzaq narrated that Ibn `Abbas said, "When the caravan departed (from Egypt), a wind started blowing and brought the scent of Yusuf's shirt to Ya`qub. He said,

(I do indeed feel the smell of Yusuf, if only you think me not senile.) He found his scent from a distance of eight days away!" Similar was also reported through Sufyan Ath-Thawri and Shu`bah and others reported it from Abu Sinan. Ya`qub said to them,

(if only you think me not senile.) Ibn `Abbas, Mujahid, `Ata, Qatadah and Sa'id bin Jubayr commented, "If only you think me not a fool!" Mujahid and Al-Hasan said that it means, "If only you think me not old." Their answer to him was,

(Certainly, you are in your old Dalal.) meaning, `in your old error,' according to Ibn `Abbas. Qatadah commented, "They meant that, `because of your love for Yusuf you will never forget him.' So they uttered a harsh word to their father that they should never have uttered to him, nor to a Prophet of Allah." Similar was said by As-Suddi and others.

Surah: 12 Ayah: 96, Ayah: 97 & Ayah: 98

﴿ فَلَمَّآ أَن جَآءَ ٱلْبَشِيرُ أَلْقَىٰهُ عَلَىٰ وَجْهِهِۦ فَٱرْتَدَّ بَصِيرًا ۖ قَالَ أَلَمْ أَقُل لَّكُمْ إِنِّىٓ أَعْلَمُ مِنَ ٱللَّهِ مَا لَا تَعْلَمُونَ ﴾

96. Then, when the bearer of the glad tidings arrived, he cast it (the shirt) over his face, and he became clear-sighted. He said: "Did I not say to you, 'I know from Allâh that which you know not.' "

﴿ قَالُوا۟ يَـٰٓأَبَانَا ٱسْتَغْفِرْ لَنَا ذُنُوبَنَآ إِنَّا كُنَّا خَـٰطِـِٔينَ ﴾

97. They said: "O our father! Ask forgiveness (from Allâh) for our sins, indeed we have been sinners."

﴿ قَالَ سَوْفَ أَسْتَغْفِرُ لَكُمْ رَبِّىٓ ۖ إِنَّهُۥ هُوَ ٱلْغَفُورُ ٱلرَّحِيمُ ﴾

98. He said: "I will ask my Lord for forgiveness for you, verily He! Only He is the Oft-Forgiving, the Most Merciful."

Transliteration

96. Falamma an jaa albasheeru alqahu AAala wajhihi fairtadda baseeran qala alam aqul lakum innee aAAlamu mina Allahi ma la taAAlamoona   97. Qaloo ya abana istaghfir lana thunoobana inna kunna khati-eena   98. Qala sawfa astaghfiru lakum rabbee innahu huwa alghafooru alrraheemu

Tafsir Ibn Kathir

Yahudha brings Yusuf's Shirt and Good News

Ibn `Abbas and Ad-Dahhak said;

(good news) means information. Mujahid and As-Suddi said that the bearer of good news was Yahudha, son of Ya`qub. As-Suddi added, "He brought it (Yusuf's shirt) because it was he who brought Yusuf's shirt stained with the false blood. So he liked to erase that error with this good act, by bringing Yusuf's shirt and placing it on his father's face. His father's sight was restored to him." Ya`qub said to his children,

(Did I not say to you, `I know from Allah that which you know not'), that I know that Allah will return Yusuf to me and that,

(I do indeed feel the smell of Yusuf, if only you think me not senile.)

Yusuf's Brothers feel Sorry and Regretful

This is when Yusuf's brothers said to their father, with humble- ness,

("O our father! Ask forgiveness (from Allah) for our sins, indeed we have been sinners." He said: "I will ask my Lord for forgiveness for you, verily, He! Only He is the Oft-Forgiving, the Most Merciful.") and He forgives those who repent to Him. `Abdullah bin Mas`ud, Ibrahim At-Taymi, `Amr bin Qays, Ibn Jurayj and several others said that Prophet Ya`qub delayed fulfilling their request until the latter part of the night.

Surah: 12 Ayah: 99 & Ayah: 100

﴿ فَلَمَّا دَخَلُواْ عَلَىٰ يُوسُفَ ءَاوَىٰٓ إِلَيْهِ أَبَوَيْهِ وَقَالَ ٱدْخُلُواْ مِصْرَ إِن شَآءَ ٱللَّهُ ءَامِنِينَ ۝ ﴾

99. Then, when they came in before Yûsuf (Joseph), he took his parents to himself and said: "Enter Egypt, if Allâh wills, in security."

﴿ وَرَفَعَ أَبَوَيْهِ عَلَى ٱلْعَرْشِ وَخَرُّواْ لَهُۥ سُجَّدًا ۖ وَقَالَ يَـٰٓأَبَتِ هَـٰذَا تَأْوِيلُ رُءْيَـٰىَ مِن قَبْلُ قَدْ جَعَلَهَا رَبِّى حَقًّا ۖ وَقَدْ أَحْسَنَ بِىٓ إِذْ أَخْرَجَنِى مِنَ ٱلسِّجْنِ وَجَآءَ بِكُم مِّنَ ٱلْبَدْوِ مِنۢ بَعْدِ أَن نَّزَغَ ٱلشَّيْطَـٰنُ بَيْنِى وَبَيْنَ إِخْوَتِىٓ ۚ إِنَّ رَبِّى لَطِيفٌ لِّمَا يَشَآءُ ۚ إِنَّهُۥ هُوَ ٱلْعَلِيمُ ٱلْحَكِيمُ ۝ ﴾

100. And he raised his parents to the throne and they fell down before him prostrate. And he said: "O my father! This is the interpretation of my dream aforetime! My Lord has made it come true! He was indeed good to me, when He took me out of the prison, and brought you (all here) out of the bedouin-life, after Shaitân

(Satan) had sown enmity between me and my brothers. Certainly, my Lord is the Most Courteous and Kind unto whom He wills. Truly He! Only He is the All-Knowing, the All-Wise.

Transliteration

99. Falamma dakhaloo AAala yoosufa awa ilayhi abawayhi waqala odkhuloo misra in shaa Allahu amineena 100. WarafaAAa abawayhi AAala alAAarshi wakharroo lahu sujjadan waqala ya abati hatha ta/weelu ru/yaya min qablu qad jaAAalaha rabbee haqqan waqad ahsana bee ith akhrajanee mina alssijni wajaa bikum mina albadwi min baAAdi an nazagha alshshaytanu baynee wabayna ikhwatee inna rabbee lateefun lima yashao innahu huwa alAAaleemu alhakeemu

Tafsir Ibn Kathir

Yusuf welcomes His Parents; His Dream comes True

Allah states that Ya`qub went to Yusuf in Egypt. Yusuf had asked his brothers to bring all of their family, and they all departed their area and left Kana`an to Egypt. When Yusuf received news of their approach to Egypt, he went out to receive them. The king ordered the princes and notable people to go out in the receiving party with Yusuf to meet Allah's Prophet Ya`qub, peace be upon him. It is said that the king also went out with them to meet Ya`qub. Yusuf said to his family, after they entered unto him and he took them to himself,

(and said: "Enter Egypt, if Allah wills, in security.") He said to them, `enter Egypt', meaning, `reside in Egypt', and added, `if Allah wills, in security', in reference to the hardship and famine that they suffered. Allah said next,

(and he took his parents to himself) As-Suddi and `Abdur-Rahman bin Zayd bin Aslam said that his parents were his father and maternal aunt, as his mother had died long ago. Muhammad bin Ishaq and Ibn Jarir At-Tabari said, "His father and mother were both alive." Ibn Jarir added, "There is no evidence that his mother had died before then. Rather, the apparent words of the Qur'an testify that she was alive." This opinion has the apparent and suitable meaning that this story testifies to. Allah said next,

(And he raised his parents to Al-'Arsh) he raised them to his bedstead where he sat, according to Ibn `Abbas, Mujahid and several others. Allah said,

(and they fell down before him prostrate.) Yusuf's parents and brothers prostrated before him, and they were eleven men,

(And he said: "O my father! This is the Ta'wil (interpretation) of my dream aforetime..."), in reference to the dream that he narrated to his father before,

(إِنِّى رَأَيْتُ أَحَدَ عَشَرَ كَوْكَبًا)

Chapter 12: Yusuf (Joseph), Verses 053-111

(I saw (in a dream) eleven stars...) In the laws of these and previous Prophets, it was allowed for the people to prostrate before the men of authority, when they met them. This practice was allowed in the law of Adam until the law of `Isa, peace be upon them, but was later prohibited in our law. Islam made prostration exclusively for Allah Alone, the Exalted and Most Honored. The implication of this statement was collected from Qatadah and other scholars. When Mu`adh bin Jabal visited the Sham area, he found them prostrating before their priests. When he returned (to Al-Madinah), he prostrated before the Messenger of Allah, who asked him,

$$\text{«مَا هَذَا يَا مُعَاذُ؟»}$$

(What is this, O, Mu`adh) Mu`adh said, "I saw that they prostrate before their priests. However, you, O Messenger of Allah, deserve more to be prostrated before." The Messenger said,

$$\text{«لَوْ كُنْتُ آمِرًا أَحَدًا أَنْ يَسْجُدَ لِأَحَدٍ، لَأَمَرْتُ الْمَرْأَةَ أَنْ تَسْجُدَ لِزَوْجِهَا لِعِظَمِ حَقِّهِ عَلَيْهَا»}$$

(If I were to order anyone to prostrate before anyone else (among the creation), I would have ordered the wife to prostrate before her husband because of the enormity of his right on her.) Therefore, this practice was allowed in previous laws, as we stated. This is why they (Ya`qub and his wife and eleven sons) prostrated before Yusuf, who said at that time,

(O my father! This is the Ta'wil of my dream aforetime! My Lord has made it come true!) using the word, `Ta'wil', to describe what became of the matter, later on. Allah said in another Ayah,

(Await they just for its Ta'wil On the Day the event is finally fulfilled...), meaning, on the Day of Judgement what they were promised of good or evil will surely come to them. Yusuf said,

(My Lord has made it come true!) mentioning that Allah blessed him by making his dream come true,

(He was indeed good to me, when He took me out of the prison, and brought you (all here) out of the bedouin life,) out of the desert, for they lived a bedouin life and raised cattle, according to Ibn Jurayj and others. He also said that they used to live in the Arava, Ghur area of Palestine, in Greater Syria. Yusuf said next,

(after Shaytan had sown enmity between me and my brothers. Certainly, my Lord is the Most Courteous and Kind unto whom He wills.) for when Allah wills something, He brings forth its reasons and elements of existence, then wills it into existence and makes it easy to attain,

(Truly, He! Only He is the All-Knowing.) what benefits His servants,

(the All-Wise.) in His statements, actions, decrees, preordain- ment and what He chooses and wills.

Surah: 12 Ayah: 101

$$﴿ ۞ رَبِّ قَدْ ءَاتَيْتَنِى مِنَ ٱلْمُلْكِ وَعَلَّمْتَنِى مِن تَأْوِيلِ ٱلْأَحَادِيثِ ۚ فَاطِرَ ٱلسَّمَـٰوَٰتِ وَٱلْأَرْضِ أَنتَ وَلِىِّۦ فِى ٱلدُّنْيَا وَٱلْـَٔاخِرَةِ ۖ تَوَفَّنِى مُسْلِمًا وَأَلْحِقْنِى بِٱلصَّـٰلِحِينَ ﴾$$

101. "My Lord! You have indeed bestowed on me of the sovereignty, and taught me something of the interpretation of dreams - the (Only) Creator of the heavens and the earth! You are my Walî (Protector, Helper, Supporter, Guardian, God, Lord) in this world and in the Hereafter. Cause me to die as a Muslim (the one submitting to Your Will), and join me with the righteous."

Transliteration

101. Rabbi qad ataytanee mina almulki waAAallamtanee min ta/weeli al-ahadeethi fatira alssamawati waal-ardi anta waliyyee fee alddunya waal-akhirati tawaffanee musliman waalhiqnee bialssaliheena

Tafsir Ibn Kathir

Yusuf begs Allah to die as A Muslim

This is the invocation of Yusuf, the truthful one, to his Lord the Exalted and Most Honored. He invoked Allah after His favor was complete on him by being reunited with his parents and brothers, after He had bestowed on him prophethood and kingship. He begged his Lord the Exalted and Ever High, that as He has perfected His bounty on him in this life, to continue it until the Hereafter. He begged Him that, when he dies, he dies as a Muslim, as Ad-Dahhak said, and to join him with the ranks of the righteous, with his brethren the Prophets and Messengers, may Allah's peace and blessings be on them all. It is possible that Yusuf, peace be upon him, said this supplication while dying. In the Two Sahihs it is recorded that `A'ishah, may Allah be pleased with her, said that while dying, the Messenger of Allah was raising his finger and said - thrice,

$$«اللَّهُمَّ فِي الرَّفِيقِ الْأَعْلَى»$$

(O Allah to Ar-Rafiq Al-A`la (the uppermost, highest company in heaven).) It is also possible that long before he died, Yusuf begged Allah to die as a Muslim and be joined with the ranks of the righteous

Chapter 12: Yusuf (Joseph), Verses 053-111

Surah: 12 Ayah: 102, Ayah: 103 & Ayah: 104

﴿ ذَٰلِكَ مِنْ أَنۢبَآءِ ٱلْغَيْبِ نُوحِيهِ إِلَيْكَ ۖ وَمَا كُنتَ لَدَيْهِمْ إِذْ أَجْمَعُوٓا۟ أَمْرَهُمْ وَهُمْ يَمْكُرُونَ ﴾

102. This is of the news of the Ghaib (Unseen) which We reveal to you (O Muhammad (peace be upon him)). You were not (present) with them when they arranged their plan together, and (while) they were plotting.

﴿ وَمَآ أَكْثَرُ ٱلنَّاسِ وَلَوْ حَرَصْتَ بِمُؤْمِنِينَ ﴾

103. And most of mankind will not believe even if you desire it eagerly.

﴿ وَمَا تَسْـَٔلُهُمْ عَلَيْهِ مِنْ أَجْرٍ ۚ إِنْ هُوَ إِلَّا ذِكْرٌ لِّلْعَٰلَمِينَ ﴾

104. And no reward you (O Muhammad (peace be upon him)) ask of them (those who deny your Prophethood) for it; it(the Qur'ân) is no less than a Reminder and an advice unto the 'Alamîn (men and jinn).

Transliteration

102. Thalika min anba-i alghaybi nooheehi ilayka wama kunta ladayhim ith ajmaAAoo amrahum wahum yamkuroona   103. Wama aktharu alnnasi walaw harasta bimu/mineena   104. Wama tas-aluhum AAalayhi min ajrin in huwa illa thikrun lilAAalameena

Tafsir Ibn Kathir

This Story is a Revelation from Allah

Allah narrated to Muhammad, peace be upon him, the story of Yusuf and his brothers and how Allah raised him over them, giving him the better end, triumph, the sovereignty and wisdom (i.e., prophethood), even though they tried to harm and kill him. Allah said, `This and similar stories are part of the unseen incidents of the past, O Muhammad,

(which We reveal to you.) and inform you of, O Muhammad, because it carries a lesson, for you to draw from and a reminder to those who defy you.' Allah said next,

`(You were not (present) with them), you did not witness their conference nor saw them,

(when they arranged their plan together,) to throw Yusuf into the well,

(and (while) they were plotting) against him. We taught you all this through Our Revelation which We sent down to you.' Allah said in other Ayat,

(You were not with them, when they cast lots with their pens..) and,

(And you were not on the western side, when We made clear to Musa the commandment...) (28:44) until,

(And you were not at the side of the Tur when We did call.)(28:46) Allah also said,

(And you were not a dweller among the people of Madyan, reciting Our verses to them.) (28:45) Allah states that Muhammad is His Messenger and that He has taught him the news of what occurred in the past, which carry lessons for people to draw from, so that they acquire their safety in their religious affairs as well as their worldly affairs. Yet, most people did not and will not believe, so Allah said,

(And most of mankind will not believe even if you desire it eagerly.) Allah said in similar Ayat,

(And if you obey most of those on the earth, they will mislead you far away from Allah's path) (6:116), and,

(Verily, in this is an Ayah, yet most of them are not believers.) (26:8) Allah said next,

(And no reward you ask of them for it;) Allah says, `You, O Muhammad, do not ask them in return for this advice and your call to all that is good and righteous, for any price or compensation for delivering it. Rather, you do so seeking Allah's Face and to deliver good and sincere advice to His creatures,

(it (the Qur'an) is no less than a Reminder unto the `Alamin (men and Jinn)) with which they remember, receive guidance and save themselves in this life and the Hereafter.'

Surah: 12 Ayah: 105, Ayah: 106 & Ayah: 107

﴿ وَكَأَيِّن مِّن ءَايَةٍ فِى ٱلسَّمَـوَٰتِ وَٱلْأَرْضِ يَمُرُّونَ عَلَيْهَا وَهُمْ عَنْهَا مُعْرِضُونَ ﴾

105. And how many a sign in the heavens and the earth they pass by, while they are averse therefrom.

﴿ وَمَا يُؤْمِنُ أَكْثَرُهُم بِٱللَّهِ إِلَّا وَهُم مُّشْرِكُونَ ﴾

106. And most of them believe not in Allâh except that they attribute partners unto Him (i.e. they are Mushrikûn i.e. polytheists. See Verse 6: 121).

﴿ أَفَأَمِنُوٓا۟ أَن تَأْتِيَهُمْ غَـٰشِيَةٌ مِّنْ عَذَابِ ٱللَّهِ أَوْ تَأْتِيَهُمُ ٱلسَّاعَةُ بَغْتَةً وَهُمْ لَا يَشْعُرُونَ ﴾

107. Do they then feel secure from the coming against them of the covering veil of the Torment of Allâh, or of the coming against them of the (Final) Hour, all of a sudden while they perceive not?

Transliteration

105. Wakaayyin min ayatin fee alssamawati waal-ardi yamurroona AAalayha wahum AAanha muAAridoona 106. Wama yu/minu aktharuhum biAllahi illa wahum mushrikoona 107. Afaaminoo an ta/tiyahum ghashiyatun min AAathabi Allahi aw ta/tiyahumu alssaAAatu baghtatan wahum la yashAAuroona

Tafsir Ibn Kathir

People neglect to ponder the Signs before Them

Allah states that most people do not think about His signs and proofs of His Oneness that He created in the heavens and earth. Allah created brilliant stars and rotating heavenly objects and planets, all made subservient. There are many plots of fertile land next to each other on earth, and gardens, solid mountains, lively oceans, with their waves smashing against each other, and spacious deserts. There are many live creatures and others that have died; and animals, plants and fruits that are similar in shape, but different in taste, scent, color and attributes. All praise is due to Allah the One and Only, Who created all types of creations, Who Alone will remain and last forever. It is He Who is unique in His Names and Attributes. Allah said next,

(And most of them believe not in Allah except that they attribute partners unto Him.) Ibn `Abbas commented, "They have a part of faith, for when they are asked, `Who created the heavens Who created the earth Who created the mountains' They say, `Allah did.' Yet, they associate others with Him in worship." Similar is said by Mujahid, `Ata, `Ikrimah, Ash-Sha`bi, Qatadah, Ad-Dahhak and `Abdur-Rahman bin Zayd bin Aslam. In the Sahih, it is recorded that during the Hajj season, the idolators used to say in their Talbiyah: "Here we rush to Your service. You have no partners with You, except a partner with You whom You own but he owns not!" Allah said in another Ayah,

(Verily, joining others in worship with Allah is a great Zulm (wrong) indeed.) (31:13) This indeed is the greatest type of Shirk, associating others with Allah in worship. It is recorded in the Two Sahihs that `Abdullah bin Mas`ud said, "I said, `O Allah's Messenger! What is the greatest sin' He said,

(وَمَا يُؤْمِنُ أَكْثَرُهُمْ بِاللَّهِ إِلاَّ وَهُمْ مُّشْرِكُونَ)

(That you call a rival to Allah while He alone created you.)" Al-Hasan Al-Basri commented on Allah's statement,

(And most of them believe not in Allah except that they attribute partners unto Him.) "This is the hypocrite; if he performs good deeds, he does so to show off with the people, and he is an idolator while doing this." Al-Hasan was referring to Allah's statement,

(Verily, the hypocrites seek to deceive Allah, but it is He Who deceives them. And when they stand up for As-Salah, they stand with laziness and to be seen of men, and they do not remember Allah but little.) (4:142) There is another type of hidden Shirk that most people are unaware of. Hammad bin Salamah narrated that `Asim bin Abi An-Najud said that `Urwah said, "Hudhayfah visited an ill man and saw a rope tied around his arm, so he ripped it off while reciting,

(And most of them believe not in Allah except that they attribute partners unto Him.) In a Hadith, from Ibn `Umar collected by At-Tirmidhi who said it was Hasan, the Prophet said,

«مَنْ حَلَفَ بِغَيْرِ اللهِ فَقَدْ أَشْرَكَ»

(He who swears by other than Allah, commits Shirk.) Imam Ahmad, Abu Dawud and other scholars of Hadith narrated that `Abdullah bin Mas`ud said that the Messenger of Allah said,

«إِنَّ الرُّقَى وَالتَّمَائِمَ وَالتِّوَلَةَ شِرْكٌ»

(Verily, Ar-Ruqa, At-Tama'im and At-Tiwalah are all acts of Shirk.) In another narration collected by Ahmad and Abu Dawud, the Prophet said,

«الطِّيَرَةُ شِرْكٌ وَمَا مِنَّا إِلَّا، وَلَكِنَّ اللهَ يُذْهِبُهُ بِالتَّوَكُّلِ»

(Verily, At-Tiyarah (omen) is Shirk; everyone might feel a glimpse of it, but Allah dissipates it with Tawakkul.)" Allah said next,

(Do they then feel secure from the coming against them of the covering veil of the torment of Allah) Allah asks, `Do these idolators who associate others with Allah in the worship, feel secure from the coming of an encompassing torment from where they perceive not' Allah said in other `Ayat,

(Do then those who devise evil plots feel secure that Allah will not sink them into the earth, or that the torment will not seize them from directions they perceive not Or that He may catch them in the midst of their going to and from, so that there be no escape for them (from Allah's punishment) Or that He may catch them with gradual wasting (of their wealth and health) Truly, Your Lord is indeed full of kindness, Most Merciful.) (16:45-47) and,

(Did the people of the towns then feel secure against the coming of Our punishment by night while they were asleep Or, did the people of the towns then feel secure against the coming of Our punishment in the forenoon while they were playing Did they then feel secure against the plan of Allah None feels secure from the plan of Allah except the people who are the losers.) (7:97-99)

Surah: 12 Ayah: 108

﴿ قُلْ هَـٰذِهِۦ سَبِيلِىٓ أَدْعُوٓا۟ إِلَى ٱللَّهِ ۚ عَلَىٰ بَصِيرَةٍ أَنَا۠ وَمَنِ ٱتَّبَعَنِى ۖ وَسُبْحَـٰنَ ٱللَّهِ وَمَآ أَنَا۠ مِنَ ٱلْمُشْرِكِينَ ﴾

108. Say (O Muhammad (peace be upon him)) "This is my way; I invite unto Allâh (i.e. to the Oneness of Allâh - Islâmic Monotheism) with sure knowledge, I and whosoever follows me (also must invite others to Allâh i.e. to the Oneness of Allâh - Islâmic Monotheism with sure knowledge). And Glorified and Exalted be Allâh (above all that they associate as partners with Him). And I am not of the Mushrikûn (polytheists, pagans, idolaters and disbelievers in the Oneness of Allâh; those who worship others along with Allâh or set up rivals or partners to Allâh)."

Transliteration

108. Qul hathihi sabeelee adAAoo ila Allahi AAala baseeratin ana wamani ittabaAAanee wasubhana Allahi wama ana mina almushrikeena

Tafsir Ibn Kathir

The Messenger's Way

Allah orders His Messenger to say to mankind and the Jinns that this is his way, meaning, his method, path and Sunnah, concentrating on calling to the testimony that there is no deity worthy of worship except Allah alone without partners. The Messenger calls to this testimonial with sure knowledge, certainty and firm evidence. He calls to this way, and those who followed him call to what Allah's Messenger called to with sure knowledge, certainty and evidence, whether logical or religious evidence,

(And Glorified and Exalted be Allah.) This part of the Ayah means, I glorify, honor, revere and praise Allah from having a partner, equal, rival, parent, son, wife, minister or advisor. All praise and honor be to Allah, glorified He is from all that they attribute to Him,

(The seven heavens and the earth and all that is therein, glorify Him, and there is not a thing but glorifies His praise. But you understand not their glorification. Truly, He is Ever Forbearing, Oft-Forgiving.) (17:44)

Surah: 12 Ayah: 109

﴿ وَمَآ أَرْسَلْنَا مِن قَبْلِكَ إِلَّا رِجَالًا نُّوحِىٓ إِلَيْهِم مِّنْ أَهْلِ ٱلْقُرَىٰٓ ۗ أَفَلَمْ يَسِيرُوا۟ فِى ٱلْأَرْضِ فَيَنظُرُوا۟ كَيْفَ كَانَ عَـٰقِبَةُ ٱلَّذِينَ مِن قَبْلِهِمْ ۗ وَلَدَارُ ٱلْـَٔاخِرَةِ خَيْرٌ لِّلَّذِينَ ٱتَّقَوْا۟ ۗ أَفَلَا تَعْقِلُونَ ﴾

109. And We sent not before you (as Messengers) any but men unto whom We revealed, from among the people of townships. Have they not traveled in the

land and seen what was the end of those who were before them? And verily, the home of the Hereafter is the best for those who fear Allâh and obey Him (by abstaining from sins and evil deeds, and by performing righteous good deeds). Do you not then understand?

Transliteration

109. Wama arsalna min qablika illa rijalan noohee ilayhim min ahli alqura afalam yaseeroo fee al-ardi fayanthuroo kayfa kana AAaqibatu allatheena min qablihim waladaru al-akhirati khayrun lillatheena ittaqaw afala taAAqiloona

Tafsir Ibn Kathir

All of the Prophets are Humans and Men

Allah states that He only sent Prophets and Messengers from among men and not from among women, as this Ayah clearly states. Allah did not reveal religious and legislative laws to any woman from among the daughters of Adam. This is the belief of Ahlus-Sunnah wal-Jama`ah. Shaykh Abu Al-Hasan, `Ali bin Isma`il Al-Ash`ari mentioned that it is the view of Ahlus-Sunnah wal-Jama`ah, that there were no female Prophets, but there were truthful believers from among women. Allah mentions the most honorable of the truthful female believers, Maryam, the daughter of `Imran, when He said,

(The Messiah ('Isa), son of Maryam (Mary), was no more than a Messenger; many were the Messengers that passed away before him. His mother was a Siddiqah (truthful believer). They both used to eat food.) (5:75) Therefore, the best description Allah gave her is Siddiqah. Had she been a Prophet, Allah would have mentioned this fact when He was praising her qualities and honor. Therefore, Mary was a truthful believer according to the words of the Qur'an.

All Prophets were Humans not Angels

Ad-Dahhak reported that Ibn `Abbas commented on Allah's statement,

(And We sent not before you (as Messengers) any but men) "They were not from among the residents of the heaven (angels), as you claimed." This statement of Ibn `Abbas is supported by Allah's statements,

(And We never sent before you any of the Messengers, but verily, they ate food and walked in the markets), (25:20)

(And We did not create them with bodies that ate not food, nor were they immortals. Then We fulfilled to them the promise. So We saved them and those whom We willed, but We destroyed extravagants), (21:8-9) and,

(Say: "I am not a new thing among the Messengers.") (46:9) Allah said next,

(from among the people of townships), meaning, from among the people of cities, not that they were sent among the bedouins who are some of the harshest and roughest of all people.

Drawing Lessons from the Incidents of the Past

Allah said next,

(Have they not traveled in the land), meaning, 'Have not these people who rejected you, O Muhammad, traveled in the land,'

(and seen what was the end of those who were before them) that is, the earlier nations that rejected the Messengers, and how Allah destroyed them. A similar end is awaiting all disbelievers. Allah said in another Ayah,

(Have they not traveled through the land, and have they hearts wherewith to understand) (22:46) When they hear this statement, they should realize that Allah destroyed the disbelievers and saved the believers, and this is His way with His creation. This is why Allah said,

(And verily, the home of the Hereafter is the best for those who have Taqwa.) Allah says, 'Just as We saved the faithful in this life, We also wrote safety for them in the Hereafter, which is far better for them than the life of the present world.' Allah said in another Ayah,

(Verily, We will indeed make victorious Our Messengers and those who believe in this world's life and on the Day when the witnesses will stand forth (i.e. Day of Resurrection). The Day when their excuses will be of no profit to the wrongdoers. Theirs will be the curse, and theirs will be the evil abode (in Hellfire).) (40:51-52)

Surah: 12 Ayah: 110

﴿ حَتَّىٰ إِذَا ٱسْتَيْـَٔسَ ٱلرُّسُلُ وَظَنُّوٓا۟ أَنَّهُمْ قَدْ كُذِبُوا۟ جَآءَهُمْ نَصْرُنَا فَنُجِّىَ مَن نَّشَآءُ وَلَا يُرَدُّ بَأْسُنَا عَنِ ٱلْقَوْمِ ٱلْمُجْرِمِينَ ۝ ﴾

110. (They were reprieved) until, when the Messengers gave up hope and thought that they were denied (by their people), then came to them Our Help, and whomsoever We willed were rescued. And Our Punishment cannot be warded off from the people who are Mujrimûn (criminals, sinners, disbelievers, polytheists).

Transliteration

110. Hatta itha istay-asa alrrusulu wathannoo annahum qad kuthiboo jaahum nasruna fanujjiya man nashao wala yuraddu ba/suna AAani alqawmi almujrimeena

Tafsir Ibn Kathir

Allah's Prophets are aided by Victory in Times of Distress and Need

Allah states that He sends His aid and support to His Messengers, peace be upon them, when distress and hardship surround them and they eagerly await Allah's aid. Allah said in another Ayah,

(..and were so shaken that even the Messenger and those who believed along with him said, "When (will come) the help of Allah") (2:214) As for saying of Allah,

(they were denied) There are two recitations for it. One of them is with a Shadda (meaning: they were betrayed by their people). And this is the way `A'ishah, may Allah be pleased with her, recited it. Al-Bukhari said that `Urwah bin Az-Zubayr narrated that he asked `Aishah about the meaning of the following verse,

(`Until when the Messengers give up hope...), Respite will be granted, is it denied or betrayed `A'0ishah replied, "betrayed." `Urwah said, "I said, `They were sure that their people betrayed them, so why use the word `thought" She said, `Yes, they were sure that they betrayed them.' I said,

(and they thought that they were denied (by Allah)) `A'0ishah said, `Allah forbid! The Messengers did not suspect their Lord of such a thing.' I asked, `So what does this Ayah mean' She said, `This Verse is concerned with the Messengers' followers who had faith in their Lord and believed in their Messengers. The period of trials for those followers was long and Allah's help was delayed until the Messengers gave up hope for the conversion of the disbelievers amongst their nation and suspected that even their followers were shaken in their belief, Allah's help then came to them.'" Ibn Jurayj narrated that Ibn Abi Mulaikah said that Ibn `Abbas read this Ayah this way,

(and they thought they were denied.) `Abdullah bin Abi Mulaikah said, "Then Ibn `Abbas said to me that they were humans. He then recited this Ayah,

(..even the Messenger and those who believed along with him said, "When (will come) the help of Allah" Yes! Certainly, the help of Allah is near!)(2:214)" Ibn Jurayj also narrated that Ibn Abi Mulaykah said that `Urwah narrated to him that `Aishah did not agree to this and rejected it. She said, "Nothing that Allah has promised Muhammad, peace be upon him, but Muhammad knew for certainty that it shall come, until he died. However, the Messengers were tried with trials until they thought that those believers, who were with them, did not fully support them." Ibn Abi Mulaykah said that `Urwah narrated that `Aishah recited this Ayah this way, "and they thought that they were betrayed." Therefore, there is another way of reciting this word, and there is a difference of opinion about its meaning. We narrated the meaning that Ibn `Abbas gave. Ibn Mas`ud said, as Sufyan Ath-Thawri narrated from him, that he read the Ayah this way,

(until, when the Messengers gave up hope and thought that they were denied.) `Abdullah commented that this is the recitation that you dislike. Ibn `Abbas also commented on the Ayah,

(until, when the Messengers gave up hope and thought that they were denied) "When the Messengers gave up hope that their people would accept their messages, and their people thought that their Messengers had not said the truth to them, Allah's victory came then,

(and whomsoever We willed were rescued.) Ibn Jarir At-Tabari narrated that Ibrahim bin Abi Hamzah (Hurrah) Al-Jazari said, "A young man from Quraysh asked Sa'id bin

Chapter 12: Yusuf (Joseph), Verses 053-111   *47*

Jubayr `O, Abu `Abdullah! How do you read this word, for when I pass by it, I wish I had not read this Surah,

(until, when the Messengers gave up hope and thought that they were denied...) He said, `Yes, it means, when the Messengers gave up hope that their people will believe in them and those to whom the Messengers were sent thought that the Messengers were not truthful.'" Ad-Dahhak bin Muzahim commented, "I have not seen someone who is called to knowledge and is lazy accepting the invitation, until today! If you traveled to Yemen just to get this explanation, it will still be worth it." Ibn Jarir At-Tabari narrated that Muslim bin Yasar asked Sa`id bin Jubayr about the same Ayah and he gave the same response. Muslim stood up and embraced Sa'id bin Jubayr, saying, "May Allah relieve a distress from you as you relieved a distress from me!" This was reported from Sa'id bin Jubayr through various chains of narration. This is also the Tafsir that Mujahid bin Jabr and several other Salaf scholars gave for this Ayah. However, some scholars said that the Ayah,

(and thought that they were denied), is in reference to the believers who followed the Messengers, while some said it is in reference to the disbelievers among the Messengers' nation. In the latter case, the meaning becomes: `and the disbelievers thought that the Messengers were not given a true promise of victory. ' Ibn Jarir At-Tabari narrated that Tamim bin Hadhlam said, "I heard `Abdullah bin Mas`ud comment on this Ayah,

(until, when the Messengers gave up hope) that their people will believe in them, and their people thought when the respite was long, that the Messengers were not given a true promise."

Surah: 12 Ayah: 111

﴿ لَقَدْ كَانَ فِى قَصَصِهِمْ عِبْرَةٌ لِّأُوْلِى ٱلْأَلْبَٰبِ ۗ مَا كَانَ حَدِيثًا يُفْتَرَىٰ وَلَٰكِن تَصْدِيقَ ٱلَّذِى بَيْنَ يَدَيْهِ وَتَفْصِيلَ كُلِّ شَىْءٍ وَهُدًى وَرَحْمَةً لِّقَوْمٍ يُؤْمِنُونَ ﴾

111. Indeed in their stories, there is a lesson for men of understanding. It (the Qur'an) is not a forged statement but a confirmation of the (Allâh's existing Books) which were before it (i.e. the Taurât (Torah), the Injeel (Gospel) and other Scriptures of Allâh) and a detailed explanation of everything and a guide and a Mercy for the people who believe.

Transliteration

111. Laqad kana fee qasasihim AAibratun li-olee al-albabi ma kana hadeethan yuftara walakin tasdeeqa allathee bayna yadayhi watafseela kulli shay-in wahudan warahmatan liqawmin yu/minoona

Tafsir Ibn Kathir

A Lesson for Men Who have Understanding

Allah states here that the stories of the Messengers and their nations and how we saved the believers and destroyed the disbelievers are,

(a lesson for men of understanding), who have sound minds,

(It is not a forged statement.) Allah says here that this Qur'an could not have been forged; it truly came from Allah,

(but a confirmation of that which was before it) in reference to the previously revealed Divine Books, by which this Qur'an testifies to the true parts that remain in them and denies and refutes the forged parts that were added, changed and falsified by people. The Qur'an accepts or abrogates whatever Allah wills of these Books,

(and a detailed explanation of everything) Meaning the allowed, the prohibited, the preferred and the disliked matters. The Qur'an deals with the acts of worship, the obligatory and recommended matters, forbids the unlawful and discourages from the disliked. The Qur'an contains major facts regarding the existence and about matters of the future in general terms or in detail. The Qur'an tells us about the Lord, the Exalted and Most Honored, and about His Names and Attributes and teaches us that Allah is glorified from being similar in any way to the creation. Hence, the Qur'an is,

(a guide and a mercy for the people who believe.) with which their hearts are directed from misguidance to guidance and from deviation to conformance, and with which they seek the mercy of the Lord of all creation in this life and on the Day of Return. We ask Allah the Most Great to make us among this group in the life of the present world and in the Hereafter, on the Day when those who are successful will have faces that radiate with light, while those whose faces are dark will end up with the losing deal. This is the end of the Tafsir of Surah Yusuf; and all the thanks and praises are due to Allah, and all our trust and reliance are on Him Alone.

CHAPTER (SURAH) 13: AR-RAD (THE THUNDER), VERSES 001-043

(بِسْمِ اللَّهِ الرَّحْمَنِ الرَّحِيمِ)

In the Name of Allah, the Most Gracious, the Most Merciful.

Surah: 13 Ayah: 1

﴿ المر تِلْكَ ءَايَتُ الْكِتَبِ وَالَّذِى أُنزِلَ إِلَيْكَ مِن رَّبِّكَ الْحَقُّ وَلَكِنَّ أَكْثَرَ النَّاسِ لَا يُؤْمِنُونَ ۝ ﴾

1. Alif-Lâm-Mîm-Râ [These letters are one of the miracles of the Qur'ân and none but Allâh (Alone) knows their meanings]. These are the Verses of the Book (the

Qur'ân), and that which has been revealed unto you (Muhammad SAW) from your Lord is the truth, but most men believe not.

Transliteration

1. Alif-lam-meem-ra tilka ayatu alkitabi waallathee onzila ilayka min rabbika alhaqqu walakinna akthara alnnasi la yu/minoona

Tafsir Ibn Kathir

The Qur'an is Allah's Kalam (Speech)

We talked before, in the beginning of Surat Al-Baqarah (chapter 2) about the meaning of the letters that appear in the beginnings of some chapters in the Qur'an. We stated that every Surah that starts with separate letters, affirms that the Qur'an is miraculous and is an evidence that it is a revelation from Allah, and that there is no doubt or denying in this fact. This is why Allah said next,

(These are the verses of the Book), the Qur'an, which Allah described afterwards,

(and that which has been revealed unto you), O Muhammad,

(from your Lord is the truth,) Allah said next,

(but most men believe not.) just as He said in another Ayah,

(And most of mankind will not believe even if you desire it eagerly.) (12:103) Allah declares that even after this clear, plain and unequivocal explanation (the Qur'an), most men will still not believe, due to their rebellion, stubbornness and hypocrisy.

Surah: 13 Ayah: 2

اللَّهُ الَّذِى رَفَعَ السَّمَٰوَٰتِ بِغَيْرِ عَمَدٍ تَرَوْنَهَا ۖ ثُمَّ اسْتَوَىٰ عَلَى الْعَرْشِ ۖ وَسَخَّرَ الشَّمْسَ وَالْقَمَرَ ۖ كُلٌّ يَجْرِى لِأَجَلٍ مُّسَمًّى ۚ يُدَبِّرُ الْأَمْرَ يُفَصِّلُ الْءَايَٰتِ لَعَلَّكُم بِلِقَآءِ رَبِّكُمْ تُوقِنُونَ ۝

Transliteration

2. Allahu allathee rafaAAa alssamawati bighayri AAamadin tarawnaha thumma istawa AAala alAAarshi wasakhkhara alshshamsa waalqamara kullun yajree li-ajalin musamman yudabbiru al-amra yufassilu al-ayati laAAallakum biliqa-i rabbikum tooqinoona

Translation

2. Allâh is He Who raised the heavens without any pillars that you can see. Then, He Istawâ (rose above) the Throne (really in a manner that suits His Majesty). He has subjected the sun and the moon (to continue going round)! Each running (its course) for a term appointed. He regulates all affairs, explaining the Ayât (proofs, evidences,

verses, lessons, signs, revelations, etc.) in detail, that you may believe with certainty in the meeting with your Lord.

Tafsir Ibn Kathir

Clarifying Allah's Perfect Ability

Allah mentions His perfect ability and infinite authority, since it is He Who has raised the heavens without pillars by His permission and order. He, by His leave, order and power, has elevated the heavens high above the earth, distant and far away from reach. The heaven nearest to the present world encompasses the earth from all directions, and is also high above it from every direction. The distance between the first heaven and the earth is five hundred years from every direction, and its thickness is also five hundred years. The second heaven surrounds the first heaven from every direction, encompassing everything that the latter carries, with a thickness also of five hundred years and a distance between them of five hundred years. The same is also true about the third, the fourth, the fifth, the sixth and the seventh heavens. Allah said,

(It is Allah who has created seven heavens and of the earth the like thereof.) (65:12) Allah said next,

(..without any pillars that you can see.) meaning, 'there are pillars, but you cannot see them,' according to Ibn `Abbas, Mujahid, Al-Hasan, Qatadah, and several other scholars. Iyas bin Mu`awiyah said, "The heaven is like a dome over the earth," meaning, without pillars. Similar was reported from Qatadah, and this meaning is better for this part of the Ayah, especially since Allah said in another Ayah,

(He withholds the heaven from falling on the earth except by His permission.)(22:65) Therefore, Allah's statement,

(..that you can see), affirms that there are no pillars. Rather, the heaven is elevated (above the earth) without pillars, as you see. This meaning best affirms Allah's ability and power.

Al-Istawa', Rising above the Throne

Allah said next,

(Then, He rose above (Istawa) the Throne.) We explained the meaning of the Istawa' in Surat Al-A`raf (7:54), and stated that it should be accepted as it is without altering, equating, annulling its meaning, or attempts to explain its true nature. Allah is glorified and praised from all that they attribute to Him.

Allah subjected the Sun and the Moon to rotate continuously

Allah said,

(He has subjected the sun and the moon, each running (its course) for a term appointed.) It was said that the sun and the moon continue their course until they cease doing so upon the commencement of the Final Hour, as Allah stated,

(And the sun runs on its fixed course for a term (appointed).)(36:38) It was also said that the meaning is: until they settle under the Throne of Allah after passing the other side of the earth. So when they, and the rest of the planetary bodies reach there, they are at the furthest distance from the Throne. Because according to the correct view, which the texts prove, it is shaped like a dome, under which is all of the creation. It is not circular like the celestial bodies, because it has pillars by which it is carried. This fact is clear to those who correctly understand the Ayat and authentic Hadiths. All the (praise is due to) Allah and all the favors are from Him. Allah mentioned the sun and the moon here because they are among the brightest seven heavenly objects. Therefore, if Allah subjected these to His power, then it is clear that He has also subjected all other heavenly objects. Allah said in other Ayat,

(Prostrate yourselves not to the sun nor to the moon, but prostrate yourselves to Allah Who created them, if you (really) worship Him.) (41:37) and,

(And (He created) the sun, the moon, the stars subjected to His command. Surely, His is the creation and commandment. Blessed is Allah, the Lord of all that exists!) (7:54) Allah's statement next,

(He explains the Ayat in detail, that you may believe with certainty in the Meeting with your Lord.) means, He explains the signs and clear evidences that testify that there is no deity worthy of worship except Him. These evidences prove that He will resurrect creation if He wills, just as He started it.

Surah: 13 Ayah: 3 & Ayah: 4

﴿ وَهُوَ ٱلَّذِى مَدَّ ٱلْأَرْضَ وَجَعَلَ فِيهَا رَوَٰسِىَ وَأَنْهَٰرًا ۖ وَمِن كُلِّ ٱلثَّمَرَٰتِ جَعَلَ فِيهَا زَوْجَيْنِ ٱثْنَيْنِ ۖ يُغْشِى ٱلَّيْلَ ٱلنَّهَارَ ۚ إِنَّ فِى ذَٰلِكَ لَءَايَٰتٍ لِّقَوْمٍ يَتَفَكَّرُونَ ۝ ﴾

3. And it is He Who spread out the earth, and placed therein firm mountains and rivers and of every kind of fruits He made Zawjain Ithnaîn (two in pairs - may mean two kinds or it may mean: of two sorts, e.g. black and white, sweet and sour, small and big). He brings the night as a cover over the day. Verily, in these things, there are Ayât (proofs, evidences, lessons, signs, etc.) for people who reflect.

﴿ وَفِى ٱلْأَرْضِ قِطَعٌ مُّتَجَٰوِرَٰتٌ وَجَنَّٰتٌ مِّنْ أَعْنَٰبٍ وَزَرْعٌ وَنَخِيلٌ صِنْوَانٌ وَغَيْرُ صِنْوَانٍ يُسْقَىٰ بِمَآءٍ وَٰحِدٍ وَنُفَضِّلُ بَعْضَهَا عَلَىٰ بَعْضٍ فِى ٱلْأُكُلِ ۚ إِنَّ فِى ذَٰلِكَ لَءَايَٰتٍ لِّقَوْمٍ يَعْقِلُونَ ۝ ﴾

4. And in the earth are neighboring tracts, and gardens of vines, and green crops (fields), and date-palms, growing out two or three from a single stem root, or otherwise (one stem root for every palm), watered with the same water; yet some of them We make more excellent than others to eat. Verily, in these things there are Ayât (proofs, evidences, lessons, signs) for the people who understand.

Transliteration

3. Wahuwa allathee madda al-arda wajaAAala feeha rawasiya waanharan wamin kulli alththamarati jaAAala feeha zawjayni ithnayni yughshee allayla alnnahara inna fee thalika laayatin liqawmin yatafakkaroona 4. Wafee al-ardi qitaAAun mutajawiratun wajannatun min aAAnabin wazarAAun wanakheelun sinwanun waghayru sinwanin yusqa bima-in wahidin wanufaddilu baAAdaha AAala baAAdin fee alokuli inna fee thalika laayatin liqawmin yaAAqiloona

Tafsir Ibn Kathir

Allah's Signs on the Earth

After Allah mentioned the higher worlds, He started asserting His power, wisdom and control over the lower parts of the world. Allah said,

(And it is He Who spread out the earth) made it spacious in length and width. Allah has placed on the earth firm mountains and made rivers, springs and water streams run through it, so that the various kinds of fruits and plants of every color, shape, taste and scent are watered with this water,

(and of every kind of fruit He made Zawjayn Ithnayn.), two types from every kind of fruit,

(He brings the night as a cover over the day.) Allah made the day and night pursue each other, when one is about to depart, the other overcomes it, and vice versa. Allah controls time just as He controls space and matter,

(Verily, in these things, there are Ayat for people who reflect.) who reflect on Allah's signs and the evidences of His wisdom. Allah said,

(And in the earth are neighboring tracts,) Meaning, next to each other, some of them are fertile and produce what benefits people, while others are dead, salty and do not produce anything. This meaning was collected from Ibn `Abbas, Mujahid, Sa`id bin Jubayr, Ad-Dahhak and several others. This also covers the various colors and types of diverse areas on the earth; some red, some white, or yellow, or black, some are stony, or flat, or sandy, or thick, or thin, all made to neighbor each other while preserving their own qualities. All this indicates the existence of the Creator Who does what He wills, there is no deity or lord except Him. Allah said next,

(and gardens of vines, and green crops (fields), and date palms...) Allah's statement, next,

(Sinwanun wa (or) Ghayru Sinwan.) `Sinwan' means, growing into two or three from a single stem, such as figs, pomegranate and dates. `Ghayru Sinwan' means, having one stem for every tree, as is the case with most plants. From this meaning, the paternal uncle is called one's `Sinw' of his father. There is an authentic Hadith that states that the Messenger of Allah said to `Umar bin Al-Khattab,

Chapter 13: Ar-Rad (The Thunder), Verses 001-043

»أَمَا شَعَرْتَ أَنَّ عَمَّ الرَّجُلِ صِنْوُ أَبِيهِ«

(Do you not know that man's paternal uncle is the Sinw of his father) Allah said next,

(watered with the same water; yet some of them We make more excellent than others to eat.) Abu Hurayrah narrated that the Prophet commented on Allah's statement,

(yet some of them We make more excellent than others to eat.)

»الدَّقَلُ، وَالْفَارِسِيُّ، وَالْحُلْوُ، وَالْحَامِضُ«

(The Dagal, the Persian, the sweet, the bitter...") At-Tirmidhi collected this Hadith and said, "Hasan Gharib." Therefore, there are differences between plants and fruits with regards to shape, color, taste, scent, blossoms and the shape of their leaves. There are plants that are very sweet or sour, bitter or mild, fresh; some plants have a combination of these attributes, and the taste then changes and becomes another taste, by Allah's will. There is also some that are yellow in color, or red, or white, or black, or blue, and the same can be said about their flowers; and all these variances and complex diversities are watered by the same water. Surely, in this there are signs for those who have sound reasoning, and surely, all this indicates the existence of the Creator Who does what He wills and Whose power made distinctions between various things and created them as He wills. So Allah said,

(Verily, in these things there are Ayat for the people who understand.)

Surah: 13 Ayah: 5

﴿ ۞ وَإِن تَعْجَبْ فَعَجَبٌ قَوْلُهُمْ أَءِذَا كُنَّا تُرَٰبًا أَءِنَّا لَفِى خَلْقٍ جَدِيدٍ ۗ أُو۟لَٰٓئِكَ ٱلَّذِينَ كَفَرُوا۟ بِرَبِّهِمْ ۖ وَأُو۟لَٰٓئِكَ ٱلْأَغْلَٰلُ فِىٓ أَعْنَاقِهِمْ ۖ وَأُو۟لَٰٓئِكَ أَصْحَٰبُ ٱلنَّارِ ۖ هُمْ فِيهَا خَٰلِدُونَ ﴾

5. And if you (O Muhammad (peace be upon him)) wonder (at these polytheists who deny your message of Islâmic Monotheism and have taken besides Allâh others for worship who can neither harm nor benefit), then wondrous is their saying: "When we are dust, shall we indeed then be (raised) in a new creation?" They are those who disbelieve in their Lord! They are those who will have iron chains tying their hands to their necks. They will be dwellers of the Fire to abide therein.

Transliteration

5. Wa-in taAAjab faAAajabun qawluhum a-itha kunna turaban a-inna lafee khalqin jadeedin ola-ika allatheena kafaroo birabbihim waola-ika al-aghlalu fee aAAnaqihim waola-ika as-habu alnnari hum feeha khalidoona

Tafsir Ibn Kathir

Denying Resurrection after Death, is Strange

Allah says to His Messenger Muhammad, peace and blessings be upon him,

(And if you wonder.) at the rejection of the polytheists who deny Resurrection, even though they witness Allah's signs and evidences that He made in His creation which testify that He is able to do everything. Yet, they admit that Allah originated the creation of all things and brought them into existence after they were nothing. However, they deny Allah's claim that He will resurrect the world anew, even though they admit to what is more amazing than what they deny and reject. Therefore, it is amazing that they said,

(When we are dust, shall we indeed then be (raised) in a new creation) It is an obvious fact to every sane and knowledgeable person that creating the heavens and earth is a greater feat than creating men, and that He Who has originated creation is more able to resurrect it anew,

(Do they not see that Allah, Who created the heavens and the earth, and was not wearied by their creation, is able to give life to the dead Yes, He surely is able to do all things)(46:33) Allah described those who deny Resurrection,

(They are those who disbelieved in their Lord! They are those who will have iron chains linking their hands to their necks.) They will be dragged in the Fire by these chains,

(They will be dwellers of the Fire to abide therein forever.), for they will remain in Hell forever and will never escape it or be removed from it.

Surah: 13 Ayah: 6

﴿ وَيَسْتَعْجِلُونَكَ بِٱلسَّيِّئَةِ قَبْلَ ٱلْحَسَنَةِ وَقَدْ خَلَتْ مِن قَبْلِهِمُ ٱلْمَثُلَـٰتُ وَإِنَّ رَبَّكَ لَذُو مَغْفِرَةٍ لِّلنَّاسِ عَلَىٰ ظُلْمِهِمْ وَإِنَّ رَبَّكَ لَشَدِيدُ ٱلْعِقَابِ ۞ ﴾

6. They ask you to hasten the evil before the good, while (many) exemplary punishments have indeed occurred before them. But verily, your Lord is full of Forgiveness for mankind in spite of their wrong-doing. And verily, your Lord is (also) Severe in punishment.

Transliteration

6. WayastaAAjiloonaka bialssayyi-ati qabla alhasanati waqad khalat min qablihimu almathulatu wainna rabbaka lathoo maghfiratin lilnnasi AAala thulmihim wa-inna rabbaka lashadeedu alAAiqabi

Tafsir Ibn Kathir

The Disbelievers ask for the Punishment to be delivered now!

Allah said,

(They ask you to hasten), in reference to the disbelievers,

(the evil before the good,) meaning, the punishment. Allah said in other Ayat that they said,

(And they say: "O you to whom the Dhikr (the Qur'an) has been sent down! Verily, you are a mad man! Why do you not bring angels to us if you are of the truthful" We send not the angels down except with the truth (i.e. for torment), and in that case, they (the disbelieves) would have no respite!)(15:6-8), and two Ayat;

(And they ask you to hasten on the torment!)(29:53-54) Allah also said,

(A questioner asked concerning a torment about to befall.) (70:1),

(Those who believe not therein seek to hasten it, while those who believe are fearful of it, and know that it is the very truth.)(42:18), and,

(They say: "Our Lord! Hasten to us Qittana.)(38:16), meaning, our due torment and reckoning. Allah said that they also supplicated,

(And (remember) when they said: "O Allah! If this (the Qur'an) is indeed the truth from You.)(8:32) They were such rebellious, stubborn disbelievers that they asked the Messenger to bring them Allah's torment. Allah replied,

(while exemplary punishments have indeed occurred before them.) Meaning, `We have exerted Our punishment on the previous disbelieving nations, and made them a lesson and example for those who might take heed from their destruction.' If it was not for His forbearance and forgiveness, Allah would have indeed punished them sooner. Allah said in another Ayah,

(And if Allah were to punish men for that which they earned, He would not leave a moving creature on the surface of the earth.)(35:45) Allah said in this honorable Ayah,

(But verily, your Lord is full of forgiveness for mankind in spite of their wrongdoing.) He is full of forgiveness, pardoning and covering the mistakes of people, in spite of their wrongdoing and the errors committed night and day. Allah next reminds that His punishment is severe, so that fear and hope are both addressed and mentioned. Allah said in other Ayat,

(If they belie you, say: "Your Lord is the Owner of vast mercy, and never will His wrath be turned back from the people who are criminals.")(6:147)

(Verily, your Lord is quick in retribution and certainly He is Oft-Forgiving, Most Merciful.)(7:167), and,

(Declare unto My servants that truly I am the Oft-Forgiving, the Most Merciful. And that My torment is indeed the most painful torment.)(15:49-50) There are many other Ayat that mention both fear and hope.

Surah: 13 Ayah: 7

﴿ وَيَقُولُ ٱلَّذِينَ كَفَرُواْ لَوْلَآ أُنزِلَ عَلَيْهِ ءَايَةٌ مِّن رَّبِّهِۦٓ ۗ إِنَّمَآ أَنتَ مُنذِرٌ وَلِكُلِّ قَوْمٍ هَادٍ ۞ ﴾

7. And the disbelievers say: "Why is not a sign sent down to him from his Lord?" You are only a warner, and to every people there is a guide.

Transliteration

7. Wayaqoolu allatheena kafaroo lawla onzila AAalayhi ayatun min rabbihi innama anta munthirun walikulli qawmin hadin

Tafsir Ibn Kathir

The Idolators ask for a Miracle

Allah states that out of their disbelief and stubbornness, the idolators asked why is not a miracle sent down to the Messenger from his Lord, just like the earlier Messengers For instance, the disbelievers were being stubborn when they asked the Prophet to turn As-Safa into gold, to remove the mountains from around them, and to replace them with green fields and rivers. Allah said,

(And nothing stops Us from sending the Ayat but that the people of old denied them.)(17:59) Allah said here,

(You are only a warner), and your duty is only to convey Allah's Message which He has ordered you,

(Not upon you is their guidance, but Allah guides whom He wills.)(2:272) Allah said;

(And to every people there is a guide.) meaning that for every people there has been a caller, according to Ibn `Abbas and as narrated from him by Ali bin Abi Talhah. Allah said in a similar Ayah, a

(And there never was a nation but a warner had passed among them.)(35:24) Similar has reported from Qatadah and `Abdur-Rahman bin Zayd.

Chapter 13: Ar-Rad (The Thunder), Verses 001-043

Surah: 13 Ayah: 8 & Ayah: 9

﴿ ٱللَّهُ يَعْلَمُ مَا تَحْمِلُ كُلُّ أُنْثَىٰ وَمَا تَغِيضُ ٱلْأَرْحَامُ وَمَا تَزْدَادُ ۖ وَكُلُّ شَيْءٍ عِندَهُۥ بِمِقْدَارٍ ﴾

8. Allâh knows what every female bears, and by how much the wombs fall short (of their time or number) or exceed. Everything with Him is in (due) proportion.

﴿ عَـٰلِمُ ٱلْغَيْبِ وَٱلشَّهَـٰدَةِ ٱلْكَبِيرُ ٱلْمُتَعَالِ ﴾

9. All-Knower of the Unseen and the seen, the Most Great, the Most High.

Transliteration

8. Allahu yaAAlamu ma tahmilu kullu ontha wama tagheedu al-arhamu wama tazdadu wakullu shay-in AAindahu bimiqdarin 9. AAalimu alghaybi waalshshahadati alkabeeru almutaAAali

Tafsir Ibn Kathir

Allah is All-Knower of Al-Ghayb (Unseen)

Allah affirms His perfect knowledge, from which nothing is hidden, and that He has complete knowledge of whatever every female creature is carrying,

(And He knows that which is in the wombs.)(31:34), whether male or female, fair or ugly, miserable or happy, whether it will have a long or a short life. Allah said in other Ayat,

(He knows you well when He created you from the earth, and when you were fetuses.)(53:32), and,

(He creates you in the wombs of your mother: creation after creation in three veils of darkness.)(39:6) meaning stage after stage. Allah also said,

(And indeed We created man out of an extract of clay. Thereafter We made him as a Nutfah in a safe lodging. Then We made the Nutfah into a clot, then We made the clot into a little lump of flesh, then We made out of that little lump of flesh bones, then We clothed the bones with flesh, and then We brought it forth as another creation. So Blessed is Allah, the Best of creators.)(23:12-14) In the two Sahihs it is recorded that `Abdullah bin Mas`ud said that the Messenger of Allah said,

«إِنَّ خَلْقَ أَحَدِكُمْ يُجْمَعُ فِي بَطْنِ أُمِّهِ أَرْبَعِينَ يَوْمًا، ثُمَّ يَكُونُ عَلَقَةً مِثْلَ ذَلِكَ، ثُمَّ يَكُونُ مُضْغَةً مِثْلَ ذَلِكَ، ثُمَّ يَبْعَثُ اللهُ إِلَيْهِ مَلَكًا فَيُؤْمَرُ بِأَرْبَعِ كَلِمَاتٍ، بِكَتْبِ رِزْقِهِ، وَعُمْرِهِ، وَعَمَلِهِ، وَشَقِيٌّ أَوْ سَعِيدٌ»

(The matter of the creation of one of you is put together in the womb of the mother in forty days, and then he becomes a clot of thick blood for a similar period, and then a piece of flesh for a similar period. Then Allah sends an angel who is ordered to write four things. He is ordered to write down his provisions, his life span, his deeds, and whether he will be blessed or wretched.") In another Hadith, the Prophet said,

«فَيَقُولُ الْمَلَكُ: أَيْ رَبِّ أَذَكَرٌ أَمْ أُنْثَى؟ أَيْ رَبِّ أَشَقِيٌّ أَمْ سَعِيدٌ؟ فَمَا الرِّزْقُ؟ فَمَا الْأَجَلُ؟ فَيَقُولُ اللهُ: وَيَكْتُبُ الْمَلَكُ»

(Then the angel asks, "O my Lord! Is it a male or a female, miserable or happy, what is its provisions and life span" Allah then ordains and the angel records it.) Allah said next,

(and by how much the wombs fall short or exceed.) Al-Bukhari recorded that `Abdullah bin `Umar said that the Messenger of Allah said,

«مَفَاتِيحُ الْغَيْبِ خَمْسٌ، لَا يَعْلَمُهُنَّ إِلَّا اللهُ: لَا يَعْلَمُ مَا فِي غَدٍ إِلَّا اللهُ، وَلَا يَعْلَمُ مَا تَغِيضُ الْأَرْحَامُ إِلَّا اللهُ، وَلَا يَعْلَمُ مَتَى يَأْتِي الْمَطَرُ أَحَدٌ إِلَّا اللهُ، وَلَا تَدْرِي نَفْسٌ بِأَيِّ أَرْضٍ تَمُوتُ، وَلَا يَعْلَمُ مَتَى تَقُومُ السَّاعَةُ إِلَّا اللهُ»

(The Keys of the Ghayb (unseen knowledge) are five, nobody knows them but Allah. Nobody knows what will happen tomorrow except Allah; nobody knows what is in the womb except Allah; nobody knows when it will rain except Allah; no soul knows at what place he will die except Allah; and nobody knows when the (Final) Hour will begin except Allah.) Al-`Awfi reported from Ibn `Abbas that he said,

(and by how much the wombs fall short), this refers to miscarriages,

(or exceed), this refers to carrying her fetus in her womb for the full term. Some women carry their fetus for ten months, while others for nine months. Some terms are longer or shorter than others. This is the falling short or exceeding that Allah the Exalted mentioned, and all this occurs by His knowledge." Qatadah commented on Allah's statement,

(Everything with Him is in proportion.) "For a term appointed. Allah has the records of the provisions and terms of His creation and made an appointed term for everything." An authentic Hadith mentioned that one of the Prophet's daughters sent (a messenger) to him requesting him to come as her child was dying, but the Prophet returned the messenger and told him to say to her,

«إِنَّ لِلَّهِ مَا أَخَذَ، وَلَهُ مَا أَعْطَى، وَكُلُّ شَيْءٍ عِنْدَهُ بِأَجَلٍ مُسَمًّى، فَمُرُوهَا فَلْتَصْبِرْ وَلْتَحْتَسِبْ»

(Verily, whatever Allah takes is for Him and whatever He gives is for Him, and everything with Him has a limited fixed term (in this world), and so she should be patient and hope for Allah's reward.) Allah said next,

(All-Knower of the Ghayb (the unseen) and the Shahadah (the witnessable),) Who knows everything that the servants see and all what they cannot see, and none of it ever escapes His knowledge,

(the Most Great), greater than everything,

(the Most High.) above everything,

((Allah) surrounds all things in (His) knowledge.)(65:12), and has full power over all things, the necks are under His control and the servants are subservient to Him, willingly or unwillingly.

Surah: 13 Ayah: 10 & Ayah: 11

﴿ سَوَآءٌ مِّنكُم مَّنْ أَسَرَّ ٱلْقَوْلَ وَمَن جَهَرَ بِهِۦ وَمَنْ هُوَ مُسْتَخْفٍۭ بِٱلَّيْلِ وَسَارِبٌۢ بِٱلنَّهَارِ ﴿١٠﴾ ﴾

10. It is the same (to Him) whether any of you conceal his speech or declares it openly, whether he be hid by night or goes forth freely by day.

﴿ لَهُۥ مُعَقِّبَٰتٌ مِّنۢ بَيْنِ يَدَيْهِ وَمِنْ خَلْفِهِۦ يَحْفَظُونَهُۥ مِنْ أَمْرِ ٱللَّهِ ۗ إِنَّ ٱللَّهَ لَا يُغَيِّرُ مَا بِقَوْمٍ حَتَّىٰ يُغَيِّرُوا۟ مَا بِأَنفُسِهِمْ ۗ وَإِذَآ أَرَادَ ٱللَّهُ بِقَوْمٍ سُوٓءًا فَلَا مَرَدَّ لَهُۥ ۚ وَمَا لَهُم مِّن دُونِهِۦ مِن وَالٍ ﴿١١﴾ ﴾

11. For him (each person), there are angels in succession, before and behind him. They guard him by the Command of Allâh. Verily! Allâh will not change the (good) condition of a people as long as they do not change their state (of goodness) themselves (by committing sins and by being ungrateful and disobedient to Allâh). But when Allâh wills a people's punishment, there can be no turning back of it, and they will find besides Him no protector.

Transliteration

10. Sawaon minkum man asarra alqawla waman jahara bihi waman huwa mustakhfin biallayli wasaribun bialnnahari 11. Lahu muAAaqqibatun min bayni yadayhi wamin khalfihi yahfathoonahu min amri Allahi inna Allaha la yughayyiru ma biqawmin hatta

yughayyiroo ma bi-anfusihim wa-itha arada Allahu biqawmin soo-an fala maradda lahu wama lahum min doonihi min walin

Tafsir Ibn Kathir

Allah's Knowledge encompasses all Things Apparent and Hidden

Allah declares that His knowledge is encompassing all of His creation, those who declare their speech or hide it, He hears it and nothing of it ever escapes His observation. Allah said in other Ayat,

(And if you speak aloud, then verily, He knows the secret and that which is yet more hidden.)(20:7), and,

(And (Allah) knows what you conceal and what you reveal.) `A'ishah said, "All praise is due to Allah Whose hearing has encompassed all voices! By Allah, she who came to complain about her husband to the Messenger of Allah was speaking while I was in another part of the room, yet I did not hear some of what she said. Allah sent down,

(Indeed Allah has heard the statement of her that disputes with you concerning her husband and complains to Allah. And Allah hears the argument between you both. Verily, Allah is All-Hearer, All-Seer.)(58:1) Allah said next,

(whether he be hid by night), in his house in the darkness of the night,

(or goes forth freely by day.) moves about during the daylight; both are encompassed by Allah's knowledge. Allah said in other Ayat,

(Surely, even when they cover themselves with their garments.) (11:5), and,

(Neither you (O Muhammad (peace be upon him)) do any deed nor recite any portion of the Qur'ân, - nor you (mankind) do any deed (good or evil) but We are Witness thereof, when you are doing it. And nothing is hidden from your Lord (so much as) the weight of an atom (or small ant) on the earth or in the heaven. Not what is less than that or what is greater than that but is (written) in a Clear Record. (Tafsir At-Tabarî).)(10:61)

The Guardian Angels

Allah said next,

(For him (each person), there are angels in succession, before and behind him. They guard him by the command of Allah.) Allah states that there are angels who take turns guarding each servant, some by night and some by day. These angels protect each person from harm and accidents. There are also angels who take turns recording the good and evil deeds, some angels do this by day and some by night. There are two angels, one to the right and one to the left of each person, recording the deeds. The angel to the right records the good deeds, while the angel to the left records the evil deeds. There are also two angels that guard and protect each person, one from the back and one from in front. Therefore, there are four angels that surround each person by day and they are replaced by four others at night, two scribes and two guards. An authentic Hadith states,

«يَتَعَاقَبُونَ فِيكُمْ مَلَائِكَةٌ بِاللَّيْلِ وَمَلَائِكَةٌ بِالنَّهَارِ، وَيَجْتَمِعُونَ فِي صَلَاةِ الصُّبْحِ وَصَلَاةِ الْعَصْرِ، فَيَصْعَدُ إِلَيْهِ الَّذِينَ بَاتُوا فِيكُمْ فَيَسْأَلُهُمْ وَهُوَ أَعْلَمُ بِكُمْ: كَيْفَ تَرَكْتُمْ عِبَادِي؟ فَيَقُولُونَ: أَتَيْنَاهُمْ وَهُمْ يُصَلُّونَ، وَتَرَكْنَاهُمْ وَهُمْ يُصَلُّونَ»

(Angels take turns around you, some at night and some by day, and all of them assemble together at the time of the Fajr and `Asr prayers. Then those who have stayed with you throughout the night, ascend to Allah Who asks them, and He knows the answer better than they about you, "How have you left My servants" They reply, "As we have found them praying, we have left them praying.") Imam Ahmad recorded that `Abdullah said that the Messenger of Allah said,

«مَا مِنْكُمْ مِنْ أَحَدٍ إِلَّا وَقَدْ وُكِّلَ بِهِ قَرِينُهُ مِنَ الْجِنِّ وَقَرِينُهُ مِنَ الْمَلَائِكَةِ»

(Verily, every one among you has his companion from the Jinn and his companion from the angels.") They said, "And you too, O Allah's Messenger" He said,

«وَإِيَّايَ، وَلَكِنَّ اللهَ أَعَانَنِي عَلَيْهِ، فَلَا يَأْمُرُنِي إِلَّا بِخَيْرٍ»

(And I too, except that Allah has helped me against him, so he only orders me to do good.) Muslim collected this Hadith. Ibn Abi Hatim narrated that Ibrahim said, "Allah revealed to a Prophet from among the Children of Israel, `Say to your nation: every people of a village or a house who used to obey Allah but changed their behavior to disobeying Him, then He will take away from them what they like and exchange it for what they dislike." Ibrahim next said that this statement has proof in Allah's Book,

(Verily, Allah will not change the (good) condition of a people as long as they do not change their state (of goodness) themselves.)

Surah: 13 Ayah: 12 & Ayah: 13

﴿هُوَ ٱلَّذِى يُرِيكُمُ ٱلْبَرْقَ خَوْفًا وَطَمَعًا وَيُنْشِئُ ٱلسَّحَابَ ٱلثِّقَالَ ۝﴾

12. It is He who shows you the lightning, as a fear (for travelers) and as a hope (for those who wait for rain). And it is He Who brings up (or originates) the clouds, heavy (with water).

$$\left\{ \text{وَيُسَبِّحُ ٱلرَّعْدُ بِحَمْدِهِۦ وَٱلْمَلَٰٓئِكَةُ مِنْ خِيفَتِهِۦ وَيُرْسِلُ ٱلصَّوَٰعِقَ فَيُصِيبُ بِهَا مَن يَشَآءُ وَهُمْ يُجَٰدِلُونَ فِى ٱللَّهِ وَهُوَ شَدِيدُ ٱلْمِحَالِ} \right.$$

13. And Ar-Ra'd (thunder) glorifies and praises Him, and so do the angels because of His Awe, He sends the thunderbolts, and therewith He strikes whom He wills, yet they (disbelievers) dispute about Allâh. And He is Mighty in strength and Severe in punishment.

Transliteration

12. Huwa allathee yureekumu albarqa khawfan watamaAAan wayunshi-o alssahaba aththiqala   13. Wayusabbihu alrraAAdu bihamdihi waalmala-ikatu min kheefatihi wayursilu alssawaAAiqa fayuseebu biha man yashao wahum yujadiloona fee Allahi wahuwa shadeedu almihali

Tafsir Ibn Kathir

Clouds, Thunder and Lightning are Signs of Allah's Power

Allah states that He has full power over Al-Barq (lightning), which is the bright light that originates from within clouds. Ibn Jarir recorded that Ibn `Abbas once wrote to Abu Al-Jald asking about the meaning of Al-Barq, and he said that it is water. Qatadah commented on Allah's statement,

(as a fear and as a hope.) "Fear for travelers, for they feel afraid of its harm and hardship, and hope for residents, awaiting its blessing and benefit and anticipating Allah's provisions." Allah said next,

(And it is He Who brings up the clouds, heavy.) meaning, He originates the clouds that are heavy and close to the ground because of being laden with rain. Mujahid said that this part of the Ayah is about clouds that are heavy with rain. Allah's statement,

(And Ar-Ra'd (thunder) glorifies and praises Him), is similar to His other statement,

(And there is not a thing but glorifies His praise.) (17:44) Imam Ahmad recorded that Ibrahim bin Sa`d said, "My father told me that he was sitting next to Hamid bin `Abdur Rahman in the Masjid. A man from the tribe of Ghifar passed and Hamid sent someone to him to please come to them. When he came, Hamid said to me, `My nephew! Make space for him between me and you, for he had accompanied Allah's Messenger .' When that man came, he sat between me and Hamid and Hamid said to him, `What was the Hadith that you narrated to me from the Messenger of Allah ' He said, `A man from Ghifar said that he heard the Prophet say,

«إِنَّ اللهَ يُنْشِىءُ السَّحَابَ فَيَنْطِقُ أَحْسَنَ النُّطْقِ، وَيَضْحَكُ أَحْسَنَ الضَّحِك»

(Verily, Allah originates the clouds, and they speak in the most beautiful voice and laugh in the most beautiful manner.) It appears, and Allah has the best knowledge, that the cloud's voice is in reference to thunder and its laughter is the lightning. Musa bin `Ubaydah narrated that Sa`d bin Ibrahim said, "Allah sends the rain and indeed, none has a better smile than it, nor more comforting voice. Its smile is lightning and its voice is thunder."

Supplicating to Allah upon hearing Ar-Ra`d (Thunder)

Imam Ahmad recorded that Salim bin `Abdullah narrated that his father said that the Messenger of Allah used to say upon hearing the thunder and thunderbolts,

«اللَّهُمَّ لَا تَقْتُلْنَا بِغَضَبِكَ، وَلَا تُهْلِكْنَا بِعَذَابِكَ، وَعَافِنَا قَبْلَ ذَلِكَ»

(O Allah! Do not kill us with Your anger, nor destroy us with Your torment, and save us before that." This Hadith was recorded by At-Tirmidhi, Al-Bukhari in his book Al-Adab Al-Mufrad, An-Nasa'i in `Amal Al-Yawm wal-Laylah, and Al-Hakim in Al-Mustadrak. When `Abdullah bin Az-Zubayr used to hear thunder, he would stop talking and would supplicate, "All praise is to He Whom Ar-Ra`d (thunder) glorifies and praises, and so do the angels because of His awe." He would then say, "This is a stern warning to the people of earth." Malik collected this Hadith in Al-Muwatta', and Al-Bukhari in Al-Adab Al-Mufrad. Imam Ahmad recorded that Abu Hurayrah said that the Messenger of Allah said,

«قَالَ رَبُّكُمْ عَزَّ وَجَلَّ: لَوْ أَنَّ عَبِيدِي أَطَاعُونِي لَأَسْقَيْتُهُمُ الْمَطَرَ بِاللَّيْلِ، وَأَطْلَعْتُ عَلَيْهِمُ الشَّمْسَ بِالنَّهَارِ، وَلَمَا أَسْمَعْتُهُمْ صَوْتَ الرَّعْدِ»

(Your Lord, the Exalted and Most High, said, `Had My servants obeyed Me, I would have given them rain by night and the sun by day, and would not have made them hear the sound of the Ra`d (thunder).') Allah's statement,

(He sends the thunderbolts, and therewith He strikes whom He wills,) indicates that He sends thunderbolts as punishment upon whom He wills, and this is why thunderbolts increase as time comes to an end. Al-Hafiz Abu Al-Qasim At-Tabarani narrated that Ibn `Abbas said that Arbad bin Qays bin Juzu' bin Julayd bin Ja`far bin Kulab, and `Amir bin At-Tufayl bin Malik came to Al-Madinah to the Messenger of Allah and sat where he was sitting. `Amir bin At-Tufayl said, "O Muhammad! What will you give me if I embrace Islam" The Messenger of Allah said,

«لَكَ مَا لِلْمُسْلِمِينَ وَعَلَيْكَ مَا عَلَيْهِم»

(You will have the rights and duties of all Muslims.) `Amir bin At-Tufayl said, "Will you make me your successor if I embrace Islam" The Messenger of Allah said,

$$\text{«لَيْسَ ذَلِكَ لَكَ وَلَا لِقَوْمِكَ، وَلَكِنْ لَكَ أَعِنَّةَ الْخَيْل»}$$

(That is not your right, nor your people's right. However, I could appoint you a commander of the horsemen (i.e., war).) `Amir said, "I am already the commander of the horsemen of Najd (in the north of Arabia). Give me control over the desert and you keep the cities." The Messenger of Allah refused. When these two men were leaving the Messenger of Allah , `Amir said, "By Allah! I will fill it (Al-Madinah) with horses and men (hostile to Muslims)." The Messenger of Allah replied,

$$\text{«يَمْنَعُكَ الله»}$$

(Rather, Allah will prevent you.) When `Amir and Arbad left, `Amir said, "O Arbad! I will keep Muhammad busy while talking to him, so you can strike him with the sword. Verily, if you kill Muhammad, the people (Muslims) will agree to take blood money and will hate to wage war over his murder. Then we will give them the blood money." Arbad said, "I will do that," and they went back to the Messenger . `Amir said, "O Muhammad! Stand next to me so that I can talk to you." The Messenger stood up, and they both stood next to a wall talking to each other. Arbad wanted to grab his sword, but his hand froze when it touched the sword's handle and he could not take the sword out of its sheath. Arbad did not strike the Messenger as `Amir suggested, and the Messenger of Allah looked at Arbad and realized what he was doing, so he departed. When Arbad and `Amir left the Messenger of Allah and arrived at Al-Harrah of Waqim area, they dismounted from their horses. However, Sa`d bin Mu`adh and Usayd bin Hudayr came out saying, "Come, O enemies of Allah! May Allah curse you." `Amir asked, "Who is this with you, O Sa`d" Sa`d said, "This is Usayd bin Hudayr." They fled until they reached the Riqm area, where Allah struck Arbad with a bolt of lightning and he met his demise. As for `Amir, he went on until he reached the Kharim area, where Allah sent an open ulcer that struck him. During that night, `Amir took refuge in a woman's house, from Banu Salul. `Amir kept touching his open ulcer and saying, "An ulcer as big as a camel's hump, while I am at the house of a woman from Bani Salul, seeking to bring my death in her house!" He rode his horse, but he died while riding it headed to his area. Allah sent down these Ayat (13:8-11) in their case,

(Allah knows what every female bears) until,

(..and they will find besides Him no protector.) Ibn `Abbas commented, "The angels in succession, guard Muhammad, peace be upon him, by the command of Allah." He next mentioned the demise of Arbad by Allah's command, reciting this Ayah,

(He sends the thunderbolts,)" Allah said next,

(yet they (disbelievers) dispute about Allah.) they doubt Allah's greatness and that there is no deity worthy of worship except Him,

(And He is Mighty in strength and Severe in punishment.) Allah's torment is severe against those who rebel against Him, defy Him and persist in disbelief, according to the Tafsir of Ibn Jarir At-Tabari. There is a similar Ayah in the Qur'an,

(So they plotted a plot, and We planned a plan, while they perceived not. Then see how was the end of their plot! Verily, We destroyed them and their nation all together.)(27:50-51) `Ali bin Abi Talib said that,

(And He is Mighty in strength and Severe in punishment (Al-Mihal)), means, His punishment is severe.

Surah: 13 Ayah: 14

﴿ لَهُۥ دَعۡوَةُ ٱلۡحَقِّ ۚ وَٱلَّذِينَ يَدۡعُونَ مِن دُونِهِۦ لَا يَسۡتَجِيبُونَ لَهُم بِشَيۡءٍ إِلَّا كَبَٰسِطِ كَفَّيۡهِ إِلَى ٱلۡمَآءِ لِيَبۡلُغَ فَاهُ وَمَا هُوَ بِبَٰلِغِهِۦ ۚ وَمَا دُعَآءُ ٱلۡكَٰفِرِينَ إِلَّا فِي ضَلَٰلٍ ﴾

14. For Him (Allah, Alone) is the Word of Truth (i.e. none has the right to be worshipped but Allah). And those whom they (polytheists and disbelievers) invoke, answer them no more than one who stretches forth his hand (at the edge of a deep well) for water to reach his mouth, but it reaches him not; and the invocation of the disbelievers is nothing but an error (i.e. of no use).

Transliteration

14. Lahu daAAwatu alhaqqi waallatheena yadAAoona min doonihi la yastajeeboona lahum bishay-in illa kabasiti kaffayhi ila alma-i liyablugha fahu wama huwa bibalighihi wama duAAao alkafireena illa fee dalalin

Tafsir Ibn Kathir

A Parable for the Weakness of the False Gods of the Polytheists

`Ali bin Abi Talib said that Allah's statement,

(For Him is the Word of Truth.) Is in reference to Tawhid, according to Ibn Jarir At-Tabari. Ibn `Abbas, Qatadah, and Malik who narrated it from Muhammad bin Al-Munkadir, said that,

(For Him is the Word of Truth.) means, "La ilaha illallah." Allah said next,

(And those whom they invoke besides Him...), meaning, the example of those who worship others besides Allah,

(like one who stretches forth his hand for water to reach his mouth,) `Ali bin Abi Talib commented, "Like he who stretches his hand on the edge of a deep well to reach the water, even though his hands do not reach it; so how can the water reach his mouth" Mujahid said about, (like one who stretches forth his hand) "Calling the water with his words and pointing at it, but it will never come to him this way." The meaning of this Ayah is that he who stretches his hand to water from far away, to either collect some or draw some from far away, will not benefit from the water which will not reach his mouth, where water should be consumed. Likewise, those idolators who call another deity besides Allah, will never benefit from these deities in this life or the Hereafter, hence Allah's statement,

(and the invocation of the disbelievers is nothing but misguidance.)

Surah: 13 Ayah: 15

﴿ وَلِلَّهِ يَسْجُدُ مَن فِى ٱلسَّمَـٰوَٰتِ وَٱلْأَرْضِ طَوْعًا وَكَرْهًا وَظِلَـٰلُهُم بِٱلْغُدُوِّ وَٱلْأَصَالِ ﴾

15. And unto Allâh (Alone) falls in prostration whoever is in the heavens and the earth, willingly or unwillingly, and so do their shadows in the mornings and in the afternoons.

Transliteration

15. Walillahi yasjudu man fee alssamawati waal-ardi tawAAan wakarhan wathilaluhum bialghuduwwi waal-asali

Tafsir Ibn Kathir

Everything prostrates unto Allah

Allah affirms His might and power, for He has full control over everything, and everything is subservient to Him. Therefore, everything, including the believers, prostrate to Allah willingly, while the disbelievers do so unwillingly,

(and so do their shadows in the mornings), in the beginning of the days,

(and in the afternoons.) towards the end of the days. Allah said in another Ayah,

(Have they not observed things that Allah has created: (how) their shadows incline.) (16:48)

Surah: 13 Ayah: 16

﴿ قُلْ مَن رَّبُّ ٱلسَّمَـٰوَٰتِ وَٱلْأَرْضِ قُلِ ٱللَّهُ قُلْ أَفَٱتَّخَذْتُم مِّن دُونِهِۦ أَوْلِيَآءَ لَا يَمْلِكُونَ لِأَنفُسِهِمْ نَفْعًا وَلَا ضَرًّا قُلْ هَلْ يَسْتَوِى ٱلْأَعْمَىٰ وَٱلْبَصِيرُ أَمْ هَلْ تَسْتَوِى ٱلظُّلُمَـٰتُ وَٱلنُّورُ أَمْ جَعَلُوا۟ لِلَّهِ شُرَكَآءَ خَلَقُوا۟ كَخَلْقِهِۦ فَتَشَـٰبَهَ ٱلْخَلْقُ عَلَيْهِمْ قُلِ ٱللَّهُ خَـٰلِقُ كُلِّ شَىْءٍ وَهُوَ ٱلْوَٰحِدُ ٱلْقَهَّـٰرُ ﴾

16. Say (O Muhammad (peace be upon him)) "Who is the Lord of the heavens and the earth?" Say: "(It is) Allâh." Say: "Have you then taken (for worship) Auliyâ' (protectors) other than Him, such as have no power either for benefit or for harm to themselves?" Say: "Is the blind equal to the one who sees? Or darkness equal to light? Or do they assign to Allâh partners who created the like of His creation, so that the creation (which they made and His creation) seemed alike to them." Say: "Allâh is the Creator of all things; He is the One, the Irresistible."

Transliteration

16. Qul man rabbu alssamawati waal-ardi quli Allahu qul afaittakhathtum min doonihi awliyaa la yamlikoona li-anfusihim nafAAan wala darran qul hal yastawee al-aAAma waalbaseeru am hal tastawee alththulumatu waalnnooru am jaAAaloo lillahi shurakaa khalaqoo kakhalqihi fatashabaha alkhalqu AAalayhim quli Allahu khaliqu kulli shay-in wahuwa alwahidu alqahharu

Tafsir Ibn Kathir

Affirming Tawhid

Allah affirms here that there is no deity worthy of worship except Him, since they admit that He alone created the heavens and the earth and that He is their Lord and the Disposer of all affairs. Yet, they take as lords others besides Allah and worship them, even though these false gods do not have the power to benefit or harm themselves, or those who worship them. Therefore, the polytheists will not benefit or have harm removed from them by these false deities. Are those who worship the false deities instead of Allah equal to those who worship Him alone, without partners, and thus have a light from their Lord This is why Allah said here,

(Say: "Is the blind equal to the one who sees Or darkness equal to light Or do they assign to Allah partners who created the like of His creation, so that the creations seemed alike to them") Allah asks, `Do these polytheists worship gods besides Him that rival Him in what He created Have their false deities created similar creations to those Allah created and, thus, they are confused between the two types of creations, not knowing which was created by others besides Allah' Rather, the Ayah proves that the truth is nothing like this. There is none similar to Allah, nor does He have an equal, a rival, anyone like Him, a minister, a son, or a wife. Allah is glorified in that He is far away from all that is ascribed to Him. These idolators worship gods that they themselves admit were created by Allah and are subservient to Him. They used to say during their Talbiyah: "Here we rush to Your obedience. There is no partner for You, except Your partner, You own him and he owns not." Allah also mentioned their polytheistic statements in other Ayat,

(We worship them only that they may bring us near to Allah.) (39:3) Allah admonished them for this false creed, stating that only those whom He chooses are allowed to intercede with Him,

(Intercession with Him profits not except for him whom He permits.) (34:23)

(And there are many angels in the heavens.....)(53:26), and,

(There is none in the heavens and the earth but comes unto the Most Gracious (Allah) as a servant. Verily, He knows each one of them, and has counted them a full counting. And everyone of them will come to Him alone on the Day of Resurrection.) (19:93-95) If all are Allah's servants, then why do any of them worships each other without proof or evidence that allows them to do so Rather, they rely on sheer opinion and innovation in the religion, even though Allah has sent all of His Prophets and Messengers, from beginning to end, prohibiting this practice (polytheism) and ordering them to refrain from worshipping others besides Allah. They defied their Messengers and rebelled against them, and this is why the word of punishment struck them as a worthy recompense, e

(And your Lord treats no one with injustice) (18:49)

Surah: 13 Ayah: 17

﴿ أَنزَلَ مِنَ ٱلسَّمَآءِ مَآءً فَسَالَتْ أَوْدِيَةٌ بِقَدَرِهَا فَٱحْتَمَلَ ٱلسَّيْلُ زَبَدًا رَّابِيًا وَمِمَّا يُوقِدُونَ عَلَيْهِ فِى ٱلنَّارِ ٱبْتِغَآءَ حِلْيَةٍ أَوْ مَتَـٰعٍ زَبَدٌ مِّثْلُهُۥ ۚ كَذَٰلِكَ يَضْرِبُ ٱللَّهُ ٱلْحَقَّ وَٱلْبَـٰطِلَ ۚ فَأَمَّا ٱلزَّبَدُ فَيَذْهَبُ جُفَآءً ۖ وَأَمَّا مَا يَنفَعُ ٱلنَّاسَ فَيَمْكُثُ فِى ٱلْأَرْضِ ۚ كَذَٰلِكَ يَضْرِبُ ٱللَّهُ ٱلْأَمْثَالَ ﴾

17. He sends down water (rain) from the sky, and the valleys flow according to their measure, but the flood bears away the foam that mounts up to the surface - and (also) from that (ore) which they heat in the fire in order to make ornaments or utensils, rises a foam like unto it, thus does Allâh (by parables) show forth truth and falsehood. Then, as for the foam it passes away as scum upon the banks, while that which is for the good of mankind remains in the earth. Thus Allâh sets forth parables (for the truth and falsehood, i.e. Belief and disbelief).

Transliteration

17. Anzala mina alssama-i maan fasalat awdiyatun biqadariha faihtamala alssaylu zabadan rabiyan wamimma yooqidoona AAalayhi fee alnnari ibtighaa hilyatin aw mataAAin zabadun mithluhu kathalika yadribu Allahu alhaqqa waalbatila faamma alzzabadu fayathhabu jufaan waamma ma yanfaAAu alnnasa fayamkuthu fee al-ardi kathalika yadribu Allahu al-amthala

Tafsir Ibn Kathir

Two Parables proving that Truth remains and Falsehood perishes

This honorable Ayah contains two parables which affirm that truth remains and increases, while falsehood diminishes and perishes. Allah said,

(He sends down water from the sky,) He sends rain,

(and the valleys flow according to their measure,) each valley taking its share according to its capacity, for some valleys are wider and can retain more water than others which are small and thus retain smaller measures of water. This Ayah indicates that hearts differ, for some of them can retain substantial knowledge while others cannot entertain knowledge, but rather are bothered by knowledge,

(but the flood bears away the foam that mounts up to the surface) of the water that ran down the valleys; this is the first parable. Allah said next,

(and (also) from that (ore) which they heat in the fire in order to make ornaments or utensils...) This is the second parable, whereas gold and silver ore is heated with fire to make adornments with it, and iron and copper ore are heated to make pots and the like with it. Foam also rises to the surface of these ores, just as in the case with water,

(thus does Allah (by parables) show forth truth and falsehood.) when they both exist, falsehood does not remain, just as foam does not remain with the water or the gold and silver ores which are heated in fire. Rather, foam dissipates and vanishes,

(Then, as for the foam it passes away as scum upon the banks,) for it carries no benefit and dissipates and scatters on the banks of the valley. The foam also sticks to trees or is dissipated by wind, just as the case with the scum that rises on the surface of gold, silver, iron and copper ores; it all goes away and never returns. However, water, gold and silver remain and are used to man's benefit. This is why Allah said next,

(while that which is for the good of mankind remains in the earth. Thus Allah sets forth parables.) Allah said in a similar Ayah,

(And these similitudes We put forward for mankind; but none will understand them except those who have knowledge.) (29:43) Some of the Salaf (rightly guided ancestors) said, "When I would read a parable in the Qur'an that I could not comprehend, I would cry for myself because Allah the Exalted says,

(But none will understand them except those who have knowledge.)" (29:43) `Ali bin Abi Talhah reported that `Abdullah bin `Abbas commented on Allah's statement,

(He sends down water from the sky, and the valleys flow according to their measure,) "This is a parable that Allah has set; the hearts carry knowledge from Him, and certainty according to the amount of doubt. As for doubt, working good deeds does not benefit while it exists. As for certainty, Allah benefits its people by it, hence Allah's statement,

(Then, as for the foam), which refers to doubt,

(it passes away as scum upon the banks, while that which is for the good of mankind remains in the earth.) in reference to certainty. And just as when jewelry is heated in fire and is rid of its impurity, which remains in the fire, similarly Allah accepts certainty and discards doubt."

The Qur'an and the Sunnah contain Parables that use Water and Fire

Allah has set two examples in the beginning of Surat Al-Baqarah (chapter 2) about the hypocrites, one using fire and another using water. Allah said,

(Their likeness is as the likeness of one who kindled a fire; then, when it illuminated all around him.) (2:17) then He said,

(Or like a rainstorm in the sky, bringing darkness, thunder, and lightning.) (2:19) Allah also has set two parables for the disbelievers in Surat An-Nur (chapter 24), one of them is,

(As for those who disbelieved, their deeds are like a mirage in a desert.)(24:39) The mirage occurs during intense heat. It is recorded in the Two Sahihs that the Messenger of Allah said,

«فَيُقَالُ لِلْيَهُودِ يَوْمَ الْقِيَامَةِ: فَمَا تُرِيدُونَ؟ فَيَقُولُونَ: أَيْ رَبَّنَا عَطِشْنَا فَاسْقِنَا، فَيُقَالُ: أَلَا تَرِدُونَ؟ فَيَرِدُونَ النَّارَ فَإِذَا هِيَ كَسَرَابٍ يَحْطِمُ بَعْضُهَا بَعْضًا»

(It will be said to the Jews on the Day of Resurrection, "What do you desire" They will reply, "We need to drink, for we have become thirsty, O our Lord!" It will be said, "Will you then proceed to drink," and they will head towards the Fire, which will appear as a mirage, its various parts consuming the other parts.") Allah said in the second parable (in Surat An-Nur);

(Or is like the darkness in a vast deep sea.)(24:40) In the Two Sahihs it is recorded that Abu Musa Al-Ash`ari said that the Messenger of Allah said,

«إِنَّ مَثَلَ مَا بَعَثَنِي اللهُ بِهِ مِنَ الْهُدَى وَالْعِلْمِ، كَمَثَلِ غَيْثٍ أَصَابَ أَرْضًا، فَكَانَ مِنْهَا طَائِفَةٌ قَبِلَتِ الْمَاءَ فَأَنْبَتَتِ الْكَلَأَ وَالْعُشْبَ الْكَثِيرَ، وَكَانَتْ مِنْهَا أَجَادِبُ أَمْسَكَتِ الْمَاءَ، فَنَفَعَ اللهُ بِهَا النَّاسَ، فَشَرِبُوا، وَرَعَوْا، وَسَقَوْا، وَزَرَعُوا، وَأَصَابَتْ طَائِفَةً مِنْهَا أُخْرَى، إِنَّمَا هِيَ قِيعَانٌ لَا تُمْسِكُ مَاءً وَلَا تُنْبِتُ كَلَأً، فَذَلِكَ مَثَلُ مَنْ فَقُهَ فِي دِينِ اللهِ وَنَفَعَهُ اللهُ بِمَا بَعَثَنِي وَنَفَعَ بِهِ، فَعَلِمَ وَعَلَّمَ، وَمَثَلُ مَنْ لَمْ يَرْفَعْ بِذَلِكَ رَأْسًا وَلَمْ يَقْبَلْ هُدَى اللهِ الَّذِي أُرْسِلْتُ بِهِ»

(The example of guidance and knowledge with which Allah has sent me is like abundant rain falling on the earth, some of which was fertile soil that absorbed the rain water and brought forth vegetation and grass in abundance. And another portion of it was hard, it held the rain water and Allah benefited the people with it and they utilized it for drinking, grazing, making their animals drink from it and for irrigation purposes. And another portion of it fell on barren land, which could neither hold the water nor bring forth vegetation. The first is the example of the person who comprehends Allah's religion and gets benefit, as well as benefiting others (from the knowledge and guidance) which Allah has revealed through me and learns and then teaches others. The last example is that of a person who does not care for it and does not embrace Allah's guidance revealed through me.) This parable uses water in it. In another Hadith that Imam Ahmad collected, Abu Hurayrah narrated that the Messenger of Allah said,

«مَثَلِي وَمَثَلُكُمْ كَمَثَلِ رَجُلٍ اسْتَوْقَدَ نَارًا فَلَمَّا أَضَاءَتْ مَا حَوْلَهُ، جَعَلَ الْفَرَاشُ وَهَذِهِ الدَّوَابُّ الَّتِي يَقَعْنَ فِي النَّارِ يَقَعْنَ فِيهَا، وَجَعَلَ يَحْجُزُهُنَّ وَيَغْلِبْنَهُ فَيَقْتَحِمْنَ فِيهَا قَالَ : فَذَلِكُمْ مَثَلِي وَمَثَلُكُمْ، أَنَا آخِذٌ بِحُجَزِكُمْ عَنِ النَّارِ، هَلُمَّ عَنِ النَّارِ، فَتَغْلِبُونِي، فَتَقْتَحِمُونَ فِيهَا»

(My example and the example of you is like that of a person who lit a fire. When the fire illuminated his surroundings, butterflies and insects started falling into it, as they usually do, and he started swatting at them to prevent them from falling; but they overwhelmed him and kept falling into the fire. This is the parable of me and you, I am holding you by the waist trying to save you from the Fire, saying, "Go away from the Fire," yet you overwhelm me and fall into it.) The Two Sahihs also collected this Hadith. This is a parable using fire.

Surah: 13 Ayah: 18

﴿ لِلَّذِينَ ٱسْتَجَابُوا لِرَبِّهِمُ ٱلْحُسْنَىٰ وَٱلَّذِينَ لَمْ يَسْتَجِيبُوا لَهُ لَوْ أَنَّ لَهُم مَّا فِي ٱلْأَرْضِ جَمِيعًا وَمِثْلَهُۥ مَعَهُۥ لَٱفْتَدَوْا بِهِۦٓ ۚ أُوْلَٰٓئِكَ لَهُمْ سُوٓءُ ٱلْحِسَابِ وَمَأْوَىٰهُمْ جَهَنَّمُ ۖ وَبِئْسَ ٱلْمِهَادُ ۝ ﴾

18. For those who answered their Lord's Call (believed in the Oneness of Allâh and followed His Messenger Muhammad (peace be upon him) i.e. Islâmic Monotheism) is Al-Husna (i.e. Paradise). But those who answered not His Call (disbelieved in the Oneness of Allâh and followed not His Messenger Muhammad (peace be upon him)) if they had all that is in the earth together with its like, they would offer it in order to save themselves (from the torment, it will be in vain). For them there will be the terrible reckoning. Their dwelling-place will be Hell; and worst indeed is that place for rest.

Transliteration

18. Lillatheena istajaboo lirabbihimu alhusna waallatheena lam yastajeeboo lahu law anna lahum ma fee al-ardi jameeAAan wamithlahu maAAahu laiftadaw bihi ola-ika lahum soo-o alhisabi wama/wahum jahannamu wabi/sa almihadu

Tafsir Ibn Kathir

Blessed and Wretched Ones

Allah mentions the final destination of the blessed ones and the wretched ones,

(For those who answered their Lord's call) obeyed Allah and followed His Messenger (Muhammad, peace be upon him) by obeying his commands and believing in the narrations he brought about the past and the future, theirs will be,

(Al-Husna), which is the good reward. Allah said that Dhul-Qarnayn declared,

(As for him who does wrong, we shall punish him, and then he will be brought back unto his Lord, Who will punish him with a terrible torment (Hell). But as for him who believes and works righteousness, he shall have the best reward (Al-Husna), and we shall speak unto him mild words by our command)(18: 87-88) Allah said in another Ayah,

(For those who have done good is the best (Al-Husna) and even more.) (10: 26) Allah said next,

(But those who answered not His call,) disobeyed Allah,

(if they had all that is in the earth together) meaning, in the Hereafter. This Ayah says: Had the earth's fill of gold and its like with it, they would try to ransom themselves from Allah's torment at that time. However, this will not be accepted from them. Verily, Allah the Exalted will not accept any type of exchange from,

(For them there will be the terrible reckoning.) in the Hereafter, when they will be reckoned for the Naqir and the Qitmir, the big and the small. Verily, he who is reckoned in detail on that Day will receive punishment, hence Allah's statement next,

(Their dwelling place will be Hell; and worst indeed is that place for rest.)

Surah: 13 Ayah: 19

﴿ ۞ أَفَمَن يَعْلَمُ أَنَّمَآ أُنزِلَ إِلَيْكَ مِن رَّبِّكَ ٱلْحَقُّ كَمَنْ هُوَ أَعْمَىٰٓ إِنَّمَا يَتَذَكَّرُ أُوْلُواْ ٱلْأَلْبَـٰبِ ﴾

19. Shall he then who knows that what has been revealed unto you (O Muhammad (peace be upon him)) from your Lord is the truth be like him who is blind? But it is only the men of understanding that pay heed.

Transliteration

19. Afaman yaAAlamu annama onzila ilayka min rabbika alhaqqu kaman huwa aAAma innama yatathakkaru oloo al-albabi

Tafsir Ibn Kathir

The Believer and the Disbeliever are never Equal

Allah says, `They could never be equal; those among people who know that what,

(has been revealed unto you), O Muhammad,

(from your Lord) is the truth about which there is no doubt and in which there is no confusion, vagueness or contradiction. Rather, they believe that all of it is the truth, each part of it testifying to another. They believe that none of its parts contradicts the others, that all its information is true and that all its commandments and prohibitions are just,

(And the Word of your Lord has been fulfilled in truth and in justice.) (6:15) It is accurate in its information and stories and just in what it orders. Therefore, the Ayah says, those who believe in the truth that you brought, O Muhammad, are not at all similar to those who are blind and cannot find guidance to what benefits them, which they cannot even comprehend. And even if they comprehend the guidance, they will not follow it, believe in it or abide by it.' Allah said in another Ayah,

(Not equal are the dwellers of the Fire and the dwellers of the Paradise. It is the dwellers of Paradise that will be successful.) (59:20) Allah said in this honorable Ayah,

(Shall he then who knows that what has been revealed unto you from your Lord is the truth, be like him who is blind) They are not equal. Allah said next,

(But it is only the men of understanding that pay heed.) meaning, it is those who have sound minds who draw lessons, gain wisdom and understand. We ask Allah to make us among them.

Surah: 13 Ayah: 20, Ayah: 21, Ayah: 22, Ayah: 23 & Ayah: 24

﴿ ٱلَّذِينَ يُوفُونَ بِعَهْدِ ٱللَّهِ وَلَا يَنقُضُونَ ٱلْمِيثَٰقَ ﴾

20. Those who fulfill the Covenant of Allâh and break not the Mîthâq (bond, treaty, covenant).

﴿ وَٱلَّذِينَ يَصِلُونَ مَآ أَمَرَ ٱللَّهُ بِهِۦٓ أَن يُوصَلَ وَيَخْشَوْنَ رَبَّهُمْ وَيَخَافُونَ سُوٓءَ ٱلْحِسَابِ ﴾

21. Those who join that which Allâh has commanded to be joined (i.e. they are good to their relatives and do not sever the bond of kinship), and fear their Lord, and dread the terrible reckoning (i.e. abstain from all kinds of sins and evil deeds

which Allâh has forbidden and perform all kinds of good deeds which Allâh has ordained).

﴿وَٱلَّذِينَ صَبَرُواْ ٱبْتِغَآءَ وَجْهِ رَبِّهِمْ وَأَقَامُواْ ٱلصَّلَوٰةَ وَأَنفَقُواْ مِمَّا رَزَقْنَٰهُمْ سِرًّا وَعَلَانِيَةً وَيَدْرَءُونَ بِٱلْحَسَنَةِ ٱلسَّيِّئَةَ أُوْلَٰٓئِكَ لَهُمْ عُقْبَى ٱلدَّارِ ۝﴾

22. And those who remain patient, seeking their Lord's Countenance, perform As-Salât (Iqâmat-as-Salât), and spend out of that which We have bestowed on them, secretly and openly, and defend evil with good, for such there is a good end.

﴿جَنَّٰتُ عَدْنٍ يَدْخُلُونَهَا وَمَن صَلَحَ مِنْ ءَابَآئِهِمْ وَأَزْوَٰجِهِمْ وَذُرِّيَّٰتِهِمْ وَٱلْمَلَٰٓئِكَةُ يَدْخُلُونَ عَلَيْهِم مِّن كُلِّ بَابٍ ۝﴾

23. 'Adn (Eden) Paradise (everlasting Gardens), which they shall enter and (also) those who acted righteously from among their fathers, and their wives, and their offspring. And angels shall enter unto them from every gate (saying):

﴿سَلَٰمٌ عَلَيْكُم بِمَا صَبَرْتُمْ فَنِعْمَ عُقْبَى ٱلدَّارِ ۝﴾

24. "Salâmun 'Alaikum (peace be upon you) for you persevered in patience! Excellent indeed is the final home!"

Transliteration

20. Allatheena yoofoona biAAahdi Allahi wala yanqudoona almeethaqa 21. Waallatheena yasiloona ma amara Allahu bihi an yoosala wayakhshawna rabbahum wayakhafoona soo-a alhisabi 22. Waallatheena sabaroo ibtighaa wajhi rabbihim waaqamoo alssalata waanfaqoo mimma razaqnahum sirran waAAalaniyatan wayadraoona bialhasanati alssayyi-ata ola-ika lahum AAuqba alddari 23. Jannatu AAadnin yadkhuloonaha waman salaha min aba-ihim waazwajihim wathurriyyatihim waalmala-ikatu yadkhuloona AAalayhim min kulli babin 24. Salamun AAalaykum bima sabartum faniAAma AAuqba alddari

Tafsir Ibn Kathir

Qualities of the Blessed Ones, which will lead to Paradise

Allah states that those who have these good qualities, will earn the good, final home: victory and triumph in this life and the Hereafter,

(Those who fulfill the covenant of Allah and break not the trust.) They are nothing like the hypocrites who when one of them makes a covenant, he breaks it; if he disputes, he is most quarrelsome; if he speaks, he lies; and if he is entrusted, he betrays his trust. Allah said next,

(And those who join that which Allah has commanded to be joined) they are good to their relatives and do not sever the bond of kinship. They are also kind to the poor and the needy and generous in nature,

(and fear their Lord), in what they do or do not do of actions and statements. They remember that Allah is watching during all of this and are afraid of His terrifying reckoning in the Hereafter. Therefore, all their affairs are on the straight path and correct, whether they are active or idle, and in all of their affairs, including those that affect others,

(And those who remain patient, seeking their Lord's Face,) They observe patience while staying away from sins and evil deeds, doing so while dedicating themselves to the service of their Lord the Exalted and Most Honored and seeking His pleasure and generous reward,

(and perform the Salah), preserving its limits, times, bowing, prostration and humbleness, according to the established limits and rulings of the religion,

(and spend out of that which We have bestowed on them,) They spend on those whom they are obliged to spend on them, such as their spouses, relatives and the poor and needy in general,

(secretly and openly,) They spend during all conditions and times, whether during the night or the day, secretly and openly,

(and repel evil with good) they resist evil with good conduct. When the people harm them they face their harm with good patience, forbearing, forgiveness and pardon. Allah said in another Ayah,

(Repel (the evil) with one which is better, then verily he, between whom and you there was enmity, (will become) as though he was a close friend. But none is granted it except those who are patient - and none is granted it except the owner of the great portion in this world.)(41:34-35) This is why Allah states here that those who have these good qualities, the blessed ones, will earn the final home, which He explained next,

(`Adn Gardens), where, `Adn, indicates continuous residence; they will reside in the gardens of everlasting life. Allah said next,

(and (also) those who acted righteously from among their fathers, and their wives, and their offspring.) Allah will gather them with their loved ones, from among their fathers, family members and offspring, those who are righteous and deserve to enter Paradise, so that their eyes are comforted by seeing them. He will also elevate the grade of those who are lower, to the grades of those who are higher, a favor from Him out of His kindness, without decreasing the grade of those who are higher up (in Paradise). Allah said in another Ayah,

(And those who believe and whose offspring follow them in faith: to them shall We join their offspring.) (52:21) Allah said next,

(And angels shall enter unto them from every gate (saying): "Salamun `Alaykum (peace be upon you) for you persevered in patience! Excellent indeed is the final home!") The angels will enter on them from every direction congratulating them for entering Paradise. The angels will welcome them with the Islamic greeting and commend them for earning Allah's closeness and rewards, as well as, being admitted into the Dwelling of Peace, neighbors to the honorable Messengers, the Prophets and the truthful believers. Imam Ahmad recorded that `Abdullah bin `Amr bin Al-`As, may Allah be pleased with them both, narrated that the Messenger of Allah said,

《هَلْ تَدْرُونَ أَوَّلَ مَنْ يَدْخُلُ الْجَنَّةَ مِنْ خَلْقِ اللهِ؟》

(Do you know who among Allah's creation will enter Paradise first) They said, "Allah and His Messenger have more knowledge." He said,

《أَوَّلُ مَنْ يَدْخُلُ الْجَنَّةَ مِنْ خَلْقِ اللهِ الْفُقَرَاءُ الْمُهَاجِرُونَ الَّذِينَ تُسَدُّ بِهِمُ الثُّغُورُ، وَتُتَّقَى بِهِمُ الْمَكَارِهُ، وَيَمُوتُ أَحَدُهُمْ وَحَاجَتُهُ فِي صَدْرِهِ، لَا يَسْتَطِيعُ لَهَا قَضَاءً، فَيَقُولُ اللهُ تَعَالَى لِمَنْ يَشَاءُ مِنْ مَلَائِكَتِهِ: ائْتُوهُمْ فَحَيُّوهُمْ، فَتَقُولُ الْمَلَائِكَةُ: نَحْنُ سُكَّانُ سَمَائِكَ، وَخِيرَتُكَ مِنْ خَلْقِكَ، أَفَتَأْمُرُنَا أَنْ نَأْتِيَ هَؤُلَاءِ وَنُسَلِّمَ عَلَيْهِمْ؟ فَيَقُولُ: إِنَّهُمْ كَانُوا عِبَادًا يَعْبُدُونَنِي لَا يُشْرِكُونَ بِي شَيْئًا، وَتُسَدُّ بِهِمُ الثُّغُورُ، وَتُتَّقَى بِهِمُ الْمَكَارِهُ، وَيَمُوتُ أَحَدُهُمْ وَحَاجَتُهُ فِي صَدْرِهِ لَا يَسْتَطِيعُ لَهَا قَضَاءً قَالَ: فَتَأْتِيهِمُ الْمَلَائِكَةُ عِنْدَ ذَلِكَ فَيَدْخُلُونَ عَلَيْهِمْ مِنْ كُلِّ بَابٍ》

(The first among Allah's creation to enter Paradise are the poor emigrants (in Allah's cause) with whom the outposts (of the land) are secured and the various afflictions are warded off. One of them would die while his need is still in his chest, because he was unable to satisfy it himself. Allah will say to whom He will among His angels, "Go to them and welcome them with the Salam." The angels will say, "We are the residence of Your heaven and the best of Your creation, do You command us to go to them and welcome them with the Salam" Allah will say, "They are My servants who worshipped Me and did not associate anyone or anything with Me in worship. With them, the outposts were secured and the afflictions were warded off. One of them would die while his need is in his chest, unable to satisfy it." So the angels will go to them from every gate (of Paradise),) saying,

(Salamun `Alaykum (peace be upon you) for you persevered in patience! Excellent indeed is the final home!)"

Surah: 13 Ayah: 25

﴿ وَٱلَّذِينَ يَنقُضُونَ عَهْدَ ٱللَّهِ مِنۢ بَعْدِ مِيثَٰقِهِۦ وَيَقْطَعُونَ مَآ أَمَرَ ٱللَّهُ بِهِۦٓ أَن يُوصَلَ وَيُفْسِدُونَ فِى ٱلْأَرْضِ أُو۟لَٰٓئِكَ لَهُمُ ٱللَّعْنَةُ وَلَهُمْ سُوٓءُ ٱلدَّارِ ﴾

25. And those who break the Covenant of Allâh, after its ratification, and sever that which Allâh has commanded to be joined (i.e. they sever the bond of kinship and are not good to their relatives), and work mischief in the land, on them is the curse (i.e. they will be far away from Allâh's Mercy), and for them is the unhappy (evil) home (i.e. Hell).

Transliteration

25. Waallatheena yanqudoona AAahda Allahi min baAAdi meethaqihi wayaqtaAAoona ma amara Allahu bihi an yoosala wayufsidoona fee al-ardi ola-ika lahumu allaAAnatu walahum soo-o alddari

Tafsir Ibn Kathir

Characteristics of the Wretched Ones which will lead to the Curse and the Evil Home

This is the destination of the Wretched ones and these are their characteristics. Allah mentioned their end in the Hereafter, to contrast the end that the believers earned, since their characteristics were to the opposite of the believer's qualities in this life. The latter used to keep Allah's covenant and join that which Allah has ordained on them to join. As for the former, they used to,

(break the covenant of Allah, after its ratification, and sever that which Allah has commanded to be joined, and work mischief in the land,) An authentic Hadith states that,

«آيَةُ الْمُنَافِقِ ثَلَاثٌ: إِذَا حَدَّثَ كَذَبَ، وَإِذَا وَعَدَ أَخْلَفَ، وَإِذَا اؤْتُمِنَ خَانَ»

(The signs of a hypocrite are three: Whenever he speaks, he tells a lie; whenever he promises, he always breaks it (his promise); if you entrust him, he proves to be dishonest.") In another narration, the Prophet said,

«وَإِذَا عَاهَدَ غَدَرَ وَإِذَا خَاصَمَ فَجَر»

(If he enters into a covenant, he betrays it; and if he disputes, he proves to be most quarrelsome.) This is why Allah said next,

(on them is the curse,) they will be cast away from Allah's mercy, (and for them is the unhappy home.) the evil end and destination,

(Their dwelling place will be Hell; and worst indeed is that place for rest.) (13:18)

Surah: 13 Ayah: 26

﴿ ٱللَّهُ يَبْسُطُ ٱلرِّزْقَ لِمَن يَشَآءُ وَيَقْدِرُ وَفَرِحُوا۟ بِٱلْحَيَوٰةِ ٱلدُّنْيَا وَمَا ٱلْحَيَوٰةُ ٱلدُّنْيَا فِى ٱلْءَاخِرَةِ إِلَّا مَتَـٰعٌ ۝ ﴾

26. Allâh increases the provision for whom He wills, and straitens (it for whom He wills), and they rejoice in the life of the world, whereas the life of this world as compared with the Hereafter is but a brief passing enjoyment.

Transliteration

26. Allahu yabsutu alrrizqa liman yashao wayaqdiru wafarihoo bialhayati alddunya wama alhayatu alddunya fee al-akhirati illa mataAAun

Tafsir Ibn Kathir

Increase and Decrease in Provision is in Allah's Hand

Allah states that He alone increases the provisions for whom He wills and decreases it for whom He wills, according to His wisdom and perfect justice. So, when the disbelievers rejoice with the life of the present world that was given to them, they do not know that they are being tested and tried. Allah said in other Ayat,

(Do they think that in wealth and children with which We enlarge them, We hasten unto them with good things. Nay, but they perceive not.)(23:55-56) Allah belittled the life of the present world in comparison to what He has prepared for His believing servants in the Hereafter,

(whereas the life of this world compared to the Hereafter is but a brief passing enjoyment.) Allah said in other Ayat,

(Say: "Short is the enjoyment of this world. The Hereafter is (far) better for him who has Taqwa, and you shall not be dealt with unjustly even equal to the amount of a Fatila.)(4:77) and,

(Nay, you prefer the life of this world, although the Hereafter is better and more lasting.)(87:16-17) Imam Ahmad recorded that Al-Mustawrid, from Bani Fihr, said that the Messenger of Allah said,

«مَا الدُّنْيَا فِي الْآخِرَةِ إِلَّا كَمَا يَجْعَلُ أَحَدُكُمْ إِصْبَعَهُ هَذِهِ فِي الْيَمِّ، فَلْيَنْظُرْ بِمَ تَرْجِع»

(The life of the present world, compared to the Hereafter, is just like when one of you inserts his finger in the sea, so let him contemplate how much of it will it carry.) and he pointed with the index finger. Imam Muslim also collected this Hadith in his Sahih. In another Hadith, the Prophet passed by a dead sheep, whose ears were small, and said,

«وَاللهِ لَلدُّنْيَا أَهْوَنُ عَلَى اللهِ مِنْ هَذَا عَلَى أَهْلِهِ حِينَ أَلْقَوْهُ»

(By Allah! The life of this present world is as insignificant to Allah as this sheep was to its owners when they threw it away.)

Surah: 13 Ayah: 27, Ayah: 28 & Ayah: 29

﴿ وَيَقُولُ ٱلَّذِينَ كَفَرُواْ لَوْلَآ أُنزِلَ عَلَيْهِ ءَايَةٌ مِّن رَّبِّهِۦ ۗ قُلْ إِنَّ ٱللَّهَ يُضِلُّ مَن يَشَآءُ وَيَهْدِىٓ إِلَيْهِ مَنْ أَنَابَ ۝ ﴾

27. And those who disbelieve say: "Why is not a sign sent down to him (Muhammad (peace be upon him)) from his Lord?" Say: "Verily, Allâh sends astray whom He wills and guides unto Himself those who turn to Him in repentance."

﴿ ٱلَّذِينَ ءَامَنُواْ وَتَطْمَئِنُّ قُلُوبُهُم بِذِكْرِ ٱللَّهِ ۗ أَلَا بِذِكْرِ ٱللَّهِ تَطْمَئِنُّ ٱلْقُلُوبُ ۝ ﴾

28. Those who believed (in the Oneness of Allâh - Islâmic Monotheism), and whose hearts find rest in the remembrance of Allâh: Verily, in the remembrance of Allâh do hearts find rest.

﴿ ٱلَّذِينَ ءَامَنُواْ وَعَمِلُواْ ٱلصَّٰلِحَٰتِ طُوبَىٰ لَهُمْ وَحُسْنُ مَـَٔابٍ ۝ ﴾

29. Those who believed (in the Oneness of Allâh - Islâmic Monotheism), and work righteousness, Tûbâ (all kinds of happiness or name of a tree in Paradise) is for them and a beautiful place of (final) return.

Transliteration

27. Wayaqoolu allatheena kafaroo lawla onzila AAalayhi ayatun min rabbihi qul inna Allaha yudillu man yashao wayahdee ilayhi man anaba   28. Allatheena amanoo watatma-innu quloobuhum bithikri Allahi ala bithikri Allahi tatma-innu alquloobu   29. Allatheena amanoo waAAamiloo alssalihati tooba lahum wahusnu maabin

Tafsir Ibn Kathir

Disbelievers ask for Miracles, Allah's Response to Them

Allah says that the idolators said,

(Why is not), meaning, there should be,

(a sign sent down to him from his Lord) The idolators also said,

(Let him then bring us an Ayah like the ones (Prophets) that were sent before (with signs)!) (21:5) We mentioned this subject several times before and stated that Allah is able to bring them what they wanted. There is a Hadith which mentions that the idolators asked the Prophet to turn Mount As-Safa into gold and, they also asked him for a spring to gush forth for them and to remove the mountains from around Makkah and replace them with green fields and gardens. Allah revealed to His Messenger : "If You wish, O Muhammad, I will give them what they asked for. However, if they disbelieve thereafter, I will punish them with a punishment that I did not punish any among the `Alamin (mankind and the Jinns). Or, if you wish, I will open for them the door to repentance and mercy." The Prophet said,

«بَلْ تَفْتَحُ لَهُمْ بَابَ التَّوْبَةِ وَالرَّحْمَةِ»

(Rather, open for them the door to repentance and mercy.) This is why Allah said to His Messenger next,

(Say: "Verily, Allah sends astray whom He wills and guides unto Himself those who turn to Him in repentance.") Allah states that He brings misguidance or guidance whether the Messenger was given a sign (a miracle) according to their asking or not. Verily, earning the misguidance or the guidance are not connected to the miracles or the lack of them. Allah said in other Ayat, f

(But neither Ayat nor warners benefit those who believe not.) (10:101)

(Truly, those, against whom the Word of your Lord has been justified, will not believe. Even if every sign should come to them, until they see the painful torment.)(10:96-97), and,

(And even if We had sent down unto them angels, and the dead had spoken unto them, and We had gathered together all things before their very eyes, they would not have believed, unless Allah willed, but most of them behave ignorantly.) (6:111) Allah said here,

(Say: "Verily, Allah sends astray whom He wills and guides unto Himself those who turn to Him in repentance.") meaning, He guides to Him those who repent, turn to Him, beg Him, seek His help and humbly submit to Him.

The Believer's Heart finds Comfort in the Remembrance of Allah

Allah said,

(Those who believed, and whose hearts find rest in the remembrance of Allah.) for their hearts find comfort on the side of Allah, become tranquil when He is remembered and pleased to have Him as their Protector and Supporter. So Allah said,

(Verily, in the remembrance of Allah do hearts find rest.) and surely, He is worthy of it.

The Meaning of Tuba

Allah said,

(Those who believed, and work righteousness, Tuba is for them and a beautiful place of (final) return.) `Ali bin Abi Talhah reported that Ibn `Abbas said that Tuba means, "Happiness and comfort or refreshment of the eye." `Ikrimah said that Tuba means, "How excellent is what they earned," while Ad-Dahhak said, "A joy for them." Furthermore, Ibrahim An-Nakh`i said that Tuba means, "Better for them," while Qatadah said that it is an Arabic word that means, `you have earned a good thing.' In another narration, Qatadah said that `Tuba for them' means, "It is excellent for them,"

(and a beautiful place of return.) and final destination. These meanings for Tuba are all synonymous and they do not contradict one another. Imam Ahmad recorded that Abu Sa'id Al-Khudri said that a man asked, "O Allah's Messenger! Tuba for those who saw you and believed in you!" The Prophet said,

《طُوبَى لِمَنْ رَآنِي وَآمَنَ بِي، وَطُوبَى ثُمَّ طُوبَى ثُمَّ طُوبَى لِمَنْ آمَنَ بِي وَلَمْ يَرَنِي》

(Tuba is for he who saw me and believed in me. Tuba, and another Tuba, and another Tuba for he who believed in me, but did not see me.) A man asked, "What is Tuba" The Prophet said,

《شَجَرَةٌ فِي الْجَنَّةِ مَسِيرَتُهَا مِائَةُ عَامٍ ثِيَابُ أَهْلِ الْجَنَّةِ تَخْرُجُ مِنْ أَكْمَامِهَا》

(A tree in Paradise whose width is a hundred years, and the clothes of the people of Paradise are taken from its bark.) Al-Bukhari and Muslim recorded that Sahl bin Sa`d said that the Messenger of Allah said,

《إِنَّ فِي الْجَنَّةِ شَجَرَةً يَسِيرُ الرَّاكِبُ فِي ظِلِّهَا مِائَةَ عَامٍ لَا يَقْطَعُهَا》

(There is a tree in Paradise, If a rider travels in its shade for one hundred years, he would not be able to cross it.) An-Nu`man bin Abi `Ayyash Az-Zuraqi added, "Abu Sa`id Al-Khudri narrated to me that the Prophet said,

《إِنَّ فِي الْجَنَّةِ شَجَرَةً يَسِيرُ الرَّاكِبُ الْجَوَادَ الْمُضَمَّرَ السَّرِيعَ مِائَةَ عَامٍ مَا يَقْطَعُهَا》

(There is a tree in Paradise, if a rider travels in its shade on a fast, sleek horse for one hundred years, he would not be able to cross it.)" In his Sahih, Imam Muslim recorded that Abu Dharr narrated that the Messenger of Allah said that Allah the Exalted and Most Honored said,

«يَا عِبَادِي لَوْ أَنَّ أَوَّلَكُمْ وَآخِرَكُمْ وَإِنْسَكُمْ وَجِنَّكُمْ قَامُوا فِي صَعِيدٍ وَاحِدٍ فَسَأَلُونِي فَأَعْطَيْتُ كُلَّ إِنْسَانٍ مَسْأَلَتَهُ مَا نَقَصَ ذَلِكَ مِنْ مُلْكِي شَيْئًا إِلَّا كَمَا يَنْقُصُ الْمِخْيَطُ إِذَا أُدْخِلَ فِي الْبَحْرِ»

(O My slaves! If the first and the last among you, mankind and Jinns among you, stood in one spot and asked Me and I gave each person what he asked, it will not decrease from My dominion, except what the needle decreases (or carries) when entered into the sea.) Khalid bin Ma`ddan said, "There is a tree in Paradise called Tuba, that has breasts that nurse the children of the people of Paradise. Verily, the miscarriage of a woman will be swimming in one of the rivers of Paradise until the Day of Resurrection commences, when he will be gathered with people while forty years of age." Ibn Abi Hatim collected this statement.

Surah: 13 Ayah: 30

﴿كَذَلِكَ أَرْسَلْنَاكَ فِي أُمَّةٍ قَدْ خَلَتْ مِنْ قَبْلِهَا أُمَمٌ لِتَتْلُوَ عَلَيْهِمُ الَّذِي أَوْحَيْنَا إِلَيْكَ وَهُمْ يَكْفُرُونَ بِالرَّحْمَنِ قُلْ هُوَ رَبِّي لَا إِلَهَ إِلَّا هُوَ عَلَيْهِ تَوَكَّلْتُ وَإِلَيْهِ مَتَابِ ۞﴾

30. Thus have We sent you (O Muhammad (peace be upon him)) to a community before whom other communities have passed away, in order that you might recite unto them what We have revealed to you, while they disbelieve in the Most Gracious (Allâh) Say: "He is my Lord! Lâ ilâha illâ Huwa (none has the right to be worshipped but He)! In Him is my trust, and to Him will be my return with repentance."

Transliteration

30. Kathalika arsalnaka fee ommatin qad khalat min qabliha omamun litatluwa AAalayhimu allathee awhayna ilayka wahum yakfuroona bialrrahmani qul huwa rabbee la ilaha illa huwa AAalayhi tawakkaltu wa-ilayhi matabi

Tafsir Ibn Kathir

Our Prophet was sent to recite and call to Allah's Revelation

Allah says, `Just as We sent you, O Muhammad, to your Ummah,

(..in order that you might recite unto them what We have revealed to you,) so that you deliver to them Allah's Message. Likewise, We sent others to earlier nations that disbelieved in Allah. The Messengers whom We sent before you, were also denied and rejected, so you have an example in what they faced. And since We sent Our torment and revenge on those people, then let these people fear what will strike them, for their denial of you is harsher than the denial that the previous Messengers faced,'

(By Allah, We indeed sent (Messengers) to the nations before you.)(16-63) Allah said in another Ayah,

(Verily, many Messengers were denied before you, with patience they bore the denial and suffering until; till Our help reached them, and none can alter the Words (decree) of Allah. Surely, there has reached you the information (news) about the Messengers (before you).)(6-34), meaning, `How We gave them victory and granted the best end for them and their followers in this life and the Hereafter.' Allah said next,

(while they disbelieve in the Most Gracious (Allah).) Allah says, `These people, that We sent you to, disbelieve in the Most Gracious and deny Him, because they dislike describing Allah by Ar-Rahman Ar-Rahim (the Most Gracious, Most Merciful).' This is why on the day of Al-Hudaybiyyah, as Al-Bukhari narrated, they refused to write, "In the Name of Allah, Ar-Rahman Ar-Rahim," saying, "We do not know Ar-Rahman Ar-Rahim!" Qatadah narrated this words. Allah the Exalted said,

(Say: "Invoke Allah or invoke the Most Gracious (Allah), by whatever name you invoke Him, for to Him belong the Best Names.) (17:110) In his Sahih, Imam Muslim recorded that `Abdullah bin `Umar said that the Messenger of Allah said,

«إِنَّ أَحَبَّ الْأَسْمَاءِ إِلَى اللهِ تَعَالَى عَبْدُاللهِ وَعَبْدُ الرَّحْمَنِ»

(The most beloved names to Allah the Exalted are: `Abdullah and `Abdur-Rahman.)Allah said next,

(Say: "He is my Lord! None has the right to be worshipped but He!") meaning: for I believe in Allah in Whom you disbelieve and affirm His Divinity and Lordship. He is my Lord, there is no deity worthy of worship except Him,

(In Him is my trust,) in all of my affairs,

(and to Him I turn.) meaning: to Him I return and repent, for He alone is worthy of all this and none else besides Him.

Surah: 13 Ayah: 31

﴿ وَلَوْ أَنَّ قُرْءَانًا سُيِّرَتْ بِهِ ٱلْجِبَالُ أَوْ قُطِّعَتْ بِهِ ٱلْأَرْضُ أَوْ كُلِّمَ بِهِ ٱلْمَوْتَىٰ ۗ بَل لِّلَّهِ ٱلْأَمْرُ جَمِيعًا ۗ أَفَلَمْ يَا۟يْـَٔسِ ٱلَّذِينَ ءَامَنُوٓا۟ أَن لَّوْ يَشَآءُ ٱللَّهُ لَهَدَى ٱلنَّاسَ جَمِيعًا ۗ وَلَا يَزَالُ ٱلَّذِينَ كَفَرُوا۟ تُصِيبُهُم بِمَا صَنَعُوا۟ قَارِعَةٌ أَوْ تَحُلُّ قَرِيبًا مِّن دَارِهِمْ حَتَّىٰ يَأْتِىَ وَعْدُ ٱللَّهِ ۚ إِنَّ ٱللَّهَ لَا يُخْلِفُ ٱلْمِيعَادَ ﴿٣١﴾ ﴾

31. And if there had been a Qur'ân with which mountains could be moved (from their places), or the earth could be cloven asunder, or the dead could be made to speak (it would not have been other than this Qur'ân). But the decision of all things is certainly with Allâh. Have not then those who believe yet known that had Allâh willed, He could have guided all mankind? And a disaster will not cease to strike those who disbelieved because of their (evil) deeds or it (i.e. the disaster) settle close to their homes, until the Promise of Allâh comes to pass. Certainly, Allâh breaks not His Promise.

Transliteration

31. Walaw anna qur-anan suyyirat bihi aljibalu aw quttiAAat bihi al-ardu aw kullima bihi almawta bal lillahi al-amru jameeAAan afalam yay-asi allatheena amanoo an law yashao Allahu lahada alnnasa jameeAAan wala yazalu allatheena kafaroo tuseebuhum bima sanaAAoo qariAAatun aw tahullu qareeban min darihim hatta ya/tiya waAAdu Allahi inna Allaha la yukhlifu almeeAAada

Tafsir Ibn Kathir

Virtues of the Qur'an and the Denial of Disbelievers

Allah praises the Qur'an which He has revealed to Muhammad, peace be upon him, and prefers it to all other divinely revealed Books before it,

(And if there had been a Qur'an with which mountains could be moved,) Allah says, `If there were a Book among the previous Divine Books with which the mountains could be moved from their places, or the earth could be cleaved asunder, or the dead speak in their graves, it would have been this Qur'an and none else.' Or, this Qur'an is more worthy to cause all this, because of its marvelous eloquence that defies the ability of mankind and the Jinns, even if all of them gather their forces together to invent something like it or even a Surah like it. Yet, these idolators disbelieve in the Qur'an and reject it. Allah said,

(But the decision of all things is certainly with Allah.) The decision over all affairs is with Allah Alone, whatever He wills, occurs and whatever He does not will, never occurs. Certainly, he whom Allah misguides, will never find enlightenment and he whom Allah guides, will never be misled. We should state here that it is possible to call other Divine Books, `Qur'an', since this Qur'an is based on all of them. Imam Ahmad recorded that Abu Hurayrah said that the Messenger of Allah said,

«خُفِّفَتْ عَلَى دَاوُدَ الْقِرَاءَةُ فَكَانَ يَأْمُرُ بِدَابَّتِهِ أَنْ تُسْرَجَ، فَكَانَ يَقْرَأُ الْقُرْآنَ مِنْ قَبْلِ أَنْ تُسْرَجَ دَابَّتُهُ، وَكَانَ لَا يَأْكُلُ إِلَّا مِنْ عَمَلِ يَدَيْهِ»

(Reciting was made easy for (Prophet) Dawud (David) in that he used to order that his animal be prepared for him to ride and in the meantime he would read the entire Qur'an. He used to eat only from what his hand made.) Al-Bukhari collected this Hadith. The Qur'an mentioned here is refers to the Zabur. Allah said next,

Chapter 13: Ar-Rad (The Thunder), Verses 001-043

(Have not then those who believed yet known) that not all people would believe and understand and that,

(had Allah willed, He could have guided all mankind) Surely, there is not a miracle or evidence more eloquent or effective on the heart and mind than this Qur'an. Had Allah revealed it to a mountain, you would see the mountain shake and humbled from fear of Allah. The Sahih recorded that the Messenger of Allah said,

«مَا مِنْ نَبِيَ إِلَّا وَقَدْ أُوتِيَ مَا آمَنَ عَلَى مِثْلِهِ الْبَشَرُ، وَإِنَّمَا كَانَ الَّذِي أُوتِيتُهُ وَحْيًا أَوْحَاهُ اللهُ إِلَيَّ، فَأَرْجُو أَنْ أَكُونَ أَكْثَرَهُمْ تَابِعًا يَوْمَ الْقِيَامَةِ»

(Every Prophet was given (a miracle) the type of which would make (some) people believe. What I was given, however, is a revelation from Allah to me, and I hope that I will have the most following among them (Prophets) on the Day of Resurrection.) This Hadith indicates that every Prophet's miracle disappeared upon his death, but this Qur'an will remain as evidence for all times. Verily, the miracle of the Qur'an will never end, nor will it become old the more it is read, nor will scholars ever have enough of it. The Qur'an is serious and is not meant for jest; any tyrant that abandons it, Allah will destroy him; he who seeks guidance in other than the Qur'an, then Allah will misguide him. Allah said next,

(But the decision of all things is certainly with Allah.) Ibn `Abbas commented, "He will only do what He wills and He decided that He will not do that." Ibn Ishaq reported a chain for this, and Ibn Jarir At-Tabari agreed with it. Allah said next,

(And a disaster will not cease to strike those who disbelieved because of their (evil) deeds or it settles close to their homes,) because of their denial, disasters will still strike them in this life or strike those all around them, as a lesson and example for them. Allah said in other Ayat,

(And indeed We have destroyed towns round about you, and We have shown (them) the Ayat in various ways that they might return (to the truth).)(46-27), and,

(See they not that We gradually reduce the land (in their control) from its outlying borders Is it then they who will overcome) (21:44) Qatadah narrated that Al-Hasan commented on Allah's statement,

(or it settles close to their homes,) "It is in reference to the disaster." This is the apparent meaning here. Al-`Awfi reported that bin `Abbas said about,

(And a Qari`ah (disaster) strikes them because of their (evil) deeds) "A torment that descends on them from heaven,

(or it settles close to their homes,) when the Messenger of Allah camps near their area and fights them." Similar was reported from Mujahid and Qatadah. `Ikrimah said in another narration he reported from Ibn `Abbas that,

(Qari'ah) means affliction. These scholars also said that,

(until the promise of Allah comes to pass.) refers to the conquering of Makkah. Al-Hasan Al-Basri said that it refers to the Day of Resurrection. Allah said next,

(Certainly, Allah breaks not His promise.) to His Messengers to aid them and their followers in this life and the Hereafter,

(So think not that Allah will fail to keep His promise to His Messengers. Certainly, Allah is All-Mighty, All-Able of Retribution.)(14:47)

Surah: 13 Ayah: 32

﴿ وَلَقَدِ ٱسْتُهْزِئَ بِرُسُلٍ مِّن قَبْلِكَ فَأَمْلَيْتُ لِلَّذِينَ كَفَرُواْ ثُمَّ أَخَذْتُهُمْ فَكَيْفَ كَانَ عِقَابِ ﴾

32. And indeed (many) Messengers were mocked at before you (O Muhammad (peace be upon him)) but I granted respite to those who disbelieved, and finally I punished them. Then how (terrible) was My Punishment!

Transliteration

32. Walaqadi istuhzi-a birusulin min qablika faamlaytu lillatheena kafaroo thumma akhathtuhum fakayfa kana AAiqabi

Tafsir Ibn Kathir

Allah says to His Messenger, while comforting him in facing his people's denial of him,

`(And indeed (many) Messengers were mocked at before you), so you have a good example in them,

(but I granted respite to those who disbelieved,) deferred their judgment for a term appointed,

(and finally I punished them.) with encompassing punishment. How did you obtain the news of how I gave them respite and then took them with punishment' Allah said in another Ayah,

(And many a township did I give respite while it was given to wrongdoing. Then (in the end) I seized it (with punishment). And to Me is the (final) return (of all).)(22:48) It is recorded in the Two Sahihs that the Prophet said,

«إِنَّ اللهَ لَيُمْلِي لِلظَّالِمِ حَتَّى إِذَا أَخَذَهُ لَمْ يُفْلِتْهُ»

(Verily, Allah gives respite to the unjust until when He seizes him, He never lets go of him.) The Messenger next recited this Ayah,

(Such is the punishment of your Lord when He seizes the (population of) towns while they are doing wrong. Verily, His punishment is painful, (and) severe.)(11:102)

Surah: 13 Ayah: 33

﴿ أَفَمَنْ هُوَ قَآئِمٌ عَلَىٰ كُلِّ نَفْسٍ بِمَا كَسَبَتْ وَجَعَلُواْ لِلَّهِ شُرَكَآءَ قُلْ سَمُّوهُمْ أَمْ تُنَبِّئُونَهُ بِمَا لَا يَعْلَمُ فِى ٱلْأَرْضِ أَم بِظَـٰهِرٍ مِّنَ ٱلْقَوْلِ بَلْ زُيِّنَ لِلَّذِينَ كَفَرُواْ مَكْرُهُمْ وَصُدُّواْ عَنِ ٱلسَّبِيلِ وَمَن يُضْلِلِ ٱللَّهُ فَمَا لَهُ مِنْ هَادٍ ﴾

33. Is then He (Allâh) Who takes charge (guards, maintains, provides) of every person and knows all that he has earned (like any other deities who know nothing)? Yet, they ascribe partners to Allâh. Say: "Name them! Is it that you will inform Him of something He knows not in the earth or is it (just) a show of false words." Nay! To those who disbelieved, their plotting is made fairseeming, and they have been hindered from the Right Path; and whom Allâh sends astray, for him there is no guide.

Transliteration

33. Afaman huwa qa-imun AAala kulli nafsin bima kasabat wajaAAaloo lillahi shurakaa qul sammoohum am tunabbi-oonahu bima la yaAAlamu fee al-ardi am bithahirin mina alqawli bal zuyyina lillatheena kafaroo makruhum wasuddoo AAani alssabeeli waman yudlili Allahu fama lahu min hadin

Tafsir Ibn Kathir

There is no Similarity between Allah and False Deities in any Respect

Allah said,

(Is then He (Allah) Who takes charge of every person and knows all that he has earned) Allah is the guard and watcher over every living soul and knows what everyone does, whether good or evil, and nothing ever escapes His perfect observation. Allah said in other Ayat,

(Neither you do any deed nor recite any portion of the Qur'an, nor you do any deed, but we are witness thereof, when you are doing it.) (10:61) and Allah said,

(Not a leaf falls, but He knows it.) (6:59)

(And no moving creature is there on earth but its provision is due from Allah. And He knows its dwelling place and its deposits. All is in a Clear Book.)(11:6),

(It is the same (to Him) whether any of you conceals his speech or declares it openly, whether he be hid by night or goes forth freely by day.) (13:10)

(He knows the secret and that which is yet more hidden.) (20:7) and,

(And He is with you wherever you may be. And Allah is the All-Seer of what you do.) (57:4) Is He Who is like this similar to the idols, that the polytheists worship, which can neither hear nor see nor do they have a mind nor able to bring good to themselves or to their worshippers nor prevent harm from themselves or their worshippers The answer to the question in the Ayah was omitted, because it is implied, for Allah said next,

(Yet, they ascribe partners to Allah.) which they worshipped besides Him, such as idols, rivals and false deities,

(Say: "Name them!") make them known to us and uncover them so that they are known, for surely, they do not exist at all! So Allah said,

(Is it that you will inform Him of something He knows not in the earth) for had that thing existed in or on the earth, Allah would have known about it because nothing ever escapes His knowledge,

(or is it (just) a show of words) or doubts expressed in words, according to Mujahid, while Ad-Dahhak and Qatadah said, false words. Allah says, you (polytheists) worshipped the idols because you thought that they had power to bring benefit or harm, and this is why you called them gods,

(They are but names which you have named - you and your fathers - for which Allah has sent down no authority. They follow but a guess and that which they themselves desire, whereas there has surely come to them the guidance from their Lord!)(53:23) Allah said next,

(Nay! To those who disbelieved, their plotting is made fair seeming,) or their words, according to Mujahid. This Ayah refers to the misguidance of the polytheists and their propagation night and day. Allah said in another Ayah,

(And We have assigned for them (devils) intimate companions, who have made fair-seeming to them.) Allah said next,

(and they have been hindered from the right path;) Some read with Fatha over the Sad (i.e. wa Saddu), which would mean, `and they hindered from the right path, feeling fond of the misguidance they are in, thinking that it is correct, they called to it and thus hindered the people from following the path of the Messengers.' Others read it with Damma over the Sad (i.e. wa Suddu), which would mean, `and they have been hindered from the right path,' explained it this way: because they thought that their way looked fair or correct, they were hindered by it from the right path, so Allah said,

(and whom Allah sends astray, for him there is no guide.) Allah said in similar instances,

(And whomsoever Allah wants to suffer a trial, you can do nothing for him against Allah.) (5:41), and,

(If you covet for their guidance, then verily, Allah guides not those whom He makes to go astray. And they will have no helpers.)(16:37)

Surah: 13 Ayah: 34 & Ayah: 35

﴿ لَهُم عَذَابٌ فِى ٱلْحَيَوٰةِ ٱلدُّنْيَا ۖ وَلَعَذَابُ ٱلْأَخِرَةِ أَشَقُّ ۖ وَمَا لَهُم مِّنَ ٱللَّهِ مِن وَاقٍ ﴾

34. For them is a torment in the life of this world, and certainly, harder is the torment of the Hereafter. And they have no Wâq (defender or protector) against Allâh.

﴿ مَّثَلُ ٱلْجَنَّةِ ٱلَّتِى وُعِدَ ٱلْمُتَّقُونَ ۖ تَجْرِى مِن تَحْتِهَا ٱلْأَنْهَـٰرُ ۖ أُكُلُهَا دَآئِمٌ وَظِلُّهَا ۚ تِلْكَ عُقْبَى ٱلَّذِينَ ٱتَّقَواْ ۖ وَّعُقْبَى ٱلْكَـٰفِرِينَ ٱلنَّارُ ﴾

35. The description of the Paradise which the Muttaqûn (pious - see V.2:2) have been promised! Underneath it rivers flow, its provision is eternal and so is its shade; this is the end (final destination) of the Muttaqûn (the pious - see V.2:2), and the end (final destination) of the disbelievers is Fire. (See Verse 47:15)

Transliteration

34. Lahum AAathabun fee alhayati alddunya walaAAathabu al-akhirati ashaqqu wama lahum mina Allahi min waqin 35. Mathalu aljannati allatee wuAAida almuttaqoona tajree min tahtiha al-anharu okuluha da-imun wathilluha tilka AAuqba allatheena ittaqaw waAAuqba alkafireena alnnaru

Tafsir Ibn Kathir

Punishment of the Disbelievers and Reward of the Pious Believers

Here, Allah mentions the punishment of the disbelievers and the reward of the righteous believers, after describing the Kufr and Shirk that the disbelievers indulge in,

(For them is a torment in the life of this world,) by the hands of the believers, killing and capturing them,

(and certainly, the torment of the Hereafter.) which will come after they suffer humiliation in this life,

(is harder) many times harder. The Messenger of Allah said to those who agreed to Mula`anah,

«إِنَّ عَذَابَ الدُّنْيَا أَهْوَنُ مِنْ عَذَابِ الْآخِرَةِ»

(Surely, the torment of this life, is easier than the torment of the Hereafter.) Indeed, and just as the Messenger of Allah stated, the torment of this life ends but the torment of the Hereafter is everlasting in a Fire that is seventy times hot than our fire, where there are chains whose thickness and hardness are unimaginable. Allah said in other Ayat,

(So on that Day none will punish as He will punish. And none will bind as He will bind.)(89:25-26), and,

(And for those who deny the Hour, We have prepared a flaming Fire. When it (Hell) sees them from a far place, they will hear its raging and its roaring. And when they shall be thrown into a narrow place thereof, chained together, they will exclaim therein for destruction. Exclaim not today for one destruction, but exclaim for many destructions. Say: "Is that (torment) better, or the Paradise of Eternity promised for those who have Taqwa" It will be theirs as a reward and as a final destination.) (25:11-15) Similarly He said;

(The description of the Paradise which those who have Taqwa have been promised) meaning its description and qualities;

(Underneath it rivers flow,) these rivers flow in the various parts and grades of Paradise and wherever its people wish they flow and gush forth for them. Allah also said,

(The description of Paradise which those who have Taqwa have been promised (is that) in it are rivers of water the taste and smell of which are not changed, rivers of wine delicious to those who drink, and rivers of clarified honey, therein for them is every kind of fruit, and forgiveness.) (47:15) Allah said next,

(its provision is eternal and so is its shade) for Paradise has foods, fruits and drinks that never end or finish. It is recorded in the Two Sahihs that Ibn `Abbas narrated in the Hadith about the Eclipse prayer that the Companions said, "O Allah's Messenger! While you were standing (in prayer), we saw you reach for something with your hand and then you brought it back." The Messenger said,

«إِنِّي رَأَيْتُ الْجَنَّةَ أَوْ أُرِيتُ الْجَنَّةَ فَتَنَاوَلْتُ مِنْهَا عُنْقُودًا، وَلَوْ أَخَذْتُهُ لَأَكَلْتُمْ مِنْهُ مَا بَقِيَتِ الدُّنْيَا»

(I saw Paradise - or was shown Paradise - and reached for a cluster (of grapes or other fruit), and had I kept it, you would have eaten from it as long as this life remains.) iImam Muslim recorded that Jabir bin `Abdullah said that the Messenger of Allah said,

«يَأْكُلُ أَهْلُ الْجَنَّةِ وَيَشْرَبُونَ، وَلَا يَتَمَخَّطُونَ وَلَا يَتَغَوَّطُونَ، وَلَا يَبُولُونَ، طَعَامُهُمْ جُشَاءٌ كَرِيحِ الْمِسْكِ، وَيُلْهَمُونَ التَّسْبِيحَ وَالتَّقْدِيسَ كَمَا يُلْهَمُونَ النَّفَس»

(The people of Paradise eat and drink, and they do not need to blow their noses, or answer the call of nature, or urinate, for they pass the food excrements in belches, which smell like musk. They will be inspired to praise and glorify (Allah) as spontaneously as they breathe.) Imams Ahmad and An-Nasa'i recorded that Thumamah bin `Uqbah said that he heard Zayd bin Arqam say, "A man from the People of the Scriptures came and said (to the Prophet ), `O Abul-Qasim! You claim that the people of Paradise eat and drink' The Prophet said,

«نَعَمْ، وَالَّذِي نَفْسُ مُحَمَّدٍ بِيَدِهِ، إِنَّ الرَّجُلَ مِنْهُمْ لَيُعطَى قُوَّةَ مِائَةِ رَجُلٍ فِي الْأَكْلِ وَالشُّرْبِ وَالْجِمَاعِ وَالشَّهْوَة»

(Yes. By He in Whose Hand is Muhammad's life, a man among them will be given the strength of a hundred men in eating, drinking, sexual intercourse and appetite.) That man asked, `He who eats and drinks needs to relieve the call of nature, but Paradise is pure (from feces and urine)' The Prophet said,

«تَكُونُ حَاجَةُ أَحَدِهِمْ رَشْحًا يَفِيضُ مِنْ جُلُودِهِمْ كَرِيحِ الْمِسْكِ فَيَضْمُرُ بَطْنُه»

(One of them (residents of Paradise) relieves the call of nature through a sweat that emanates from the skin, with the scent of musk, and the stomach becomes empty again.) Imam Ahmad and An-Nasa'i collected this Hadith. Allah said in other Ayat,

(And fruit in plenty, whose supply is not cut off nor are they out of reach.)(56:32-33), and,

(And the shade thereof is close upon them, and the bunches of fruit thereof will hang low within their reach.)(76:14) The shade of Paradise is everlasting and never shrinks, just as Allah said,

(But those who believe and do deeds of righteousness, We shall admit them to Gardens under which rivers flow, abiding therein forever. Therein they shall have pure mates, and We shall admit them to shades wide and ever deepening.)(4:57) Allah often mentions the description of Paradise and the description of the Fire together, to make Paradise appealing and warn against the Fire. This is why, after Allah mentioned the description of Paradise here, He next said,

(this is the end (final destination) of those who have Taqwa, and the end (final destination) of the disbelievers is Fire.) Allah said in another Ayah ,

(Not equal are the dwellers of the Fire and the dwellers of the Paradise. It is the dwellers of Paradise that will be successful.) (59:20)

Surah: 13 Ayah: 36 & Ayah: 37

﴿ وَٱلَّذِينَ ءَاتَيْنَـٰهُمُ ٱلْكِتَـٰبَ يَفْرَحُونَ بِمَآ أُنزِلَ إِلَيْكَ وَمِنَ ٱلْأَحْزَابِ مَن يُنكِرُ بَعْضَهُۥ ۚ قُلْ إِنَّمَآ أُمِرْتُ أَنْ أَعْبُدَ ٱللَّهَ وَلَآ أُشْرِكَ بِهِۦٓ ۚ إِلَيْهِ أَدْعُوا۟ وَإِلَيْهِ مَتَابِ ﴾

36. Those to whom We have given the Book (such as 'Abdullâh bin Salâm and other Jews who embraced Islâm), rejoice at what has been revealed unto you (i.e. the Qur'ân), but there are among the Confederates (from the Jews and pagans) those who reject a part thereof. Say (O Muhammad (peace be upon him)) "I am commanded only to worship Allâh (Alone) and not to join partners with Him. To Him (Alone) I call and to Him is my return."

﴿ وَكَذَٰلِكَ أَنزَلْنَـٰهُ حُكْمًا عَرَبِيًّا ۚ وَلَئِنِ ٱتَّبَعْتَ أَهْوَآءَهُم بَعْدَ مَا جَآءَكَ مِنَ ٱلْعِلْمِ مَا لَكَ مِنَ ٱللَّهِ مِن وَلِيٍّ وَلَا وَاقٍ ﴾

37. And thus have We sent it (the Qur'ân) down to be a judgement of authority in Arabic. Were you (O Muhammad (peace be upon him)) to follow their (vain) desires after the knowledge which has come to you, then you will not have any Walî (protector) or Wâq (defender) against Allâh.

Transliteration

36. Waallatheena ataynahumu alkitaba yafrahoona bima onzila ilayka wamina al-ahzabi man yunkiru baAAdahu qul innama omirtu an aAAbuda Allaha wala oshrika bihi ilayhi adAAoo wa-ilayhi maabi 37. Wakathalika anzalnahu hukman AAarabiyyan wala-ini ittabaAAta ahwaahum baAAda ma jaaka mina alAAilmi ma laka mina Allahi min waliyyin wala waqin

Tafsir Ibn Kathir

The Truthful Ones from among the People of the Scriptures rejoice at what Allah has revealed to Muhammad

Allah said,

(Those to whom We have given the Book,) and they adhere by it,

(rejoice at what has been revealed unto you,) i.e. the Qur'an, because they have evidence in their Books affirming the truth of the Qur'an and conveying the good news of its imminent revelation, just as Allah said in another Ayah,

(Those to whom We gave the Book recite it as it should be recited.) (2:121) Allah said,

(Say: "Believe in it (the Qur'an) or do not believe.") (17:107), until,

(Truly, the promise of our Lord must be fulfilled.) (17:109) meaning, Allah's promise to us in our Books to send Muhammad is true. It is certain and will surely come to pass and be fulfilled, so all praise to our Lord, how truthful is His promise, all the thanks are due to Him,

(And they fall down on their faces weeping and it increases their humility.) (17:109) Allah said next,

(but there are among the Ahzab (Confederates) those who reject a part thereof.) meaning, `There are those among the sects who disbelieve in some of what was revealed to you (O Muhammad).' Mujahid said that,

(but there are among the Ahzab (Confederates)), refers to Jews and Christians,

(those who reject a part thereof), meaning, `They reject a part of the truth that came down to you - O Muhammad.' Similar was reported from Qatadah and `Abdur-Rahman bin Zayd bin Aslam. Allah said in similar Ayat,

(And there are, certainly, among the People of the Scripture, those who believe in Allah.) (3:199) Allah said next,

(Say: "I am commanded only to worship Allah and not to join partners with Him...") meaning, `I (Muhammad) was sent with the religion of worshipping Allah alone without partners, just as the Messengers before me,

(To Him (alone) I call), I call the people to His path,

(and to Him is my return.) final destination and destiny.' Allah said,

(And thus have We sent it (the Qur'an) down to be a judgement of authority in Arabic.) Allah says, `Just as We sent Messengers before you and revealed to them Divine Books from heaven, We sent down to you the Qur'an, a judgement of authority in Arabic, as an honor for you, and We preferred you among all people with this clear, plain and unequivocal Book that,

(Falsehood cannot come to it from before it or behind it: (it is) sent down by the All-Wise, Worthy of all praise.)' (41:42) Allah's statement,

(Were you to follow their (vain) desires), means, their opinions,

(after the knowledge which has come to you) from Allah, all praise to Him,

(then you will not have any Wali (protector) or defender against Allah.) This part of the Ayah warns people of know- ledge against following the paths of misguid- ance after they had gained knowledge in (and abided by) the Prophetic Sunnah and the path of Muhammad, may Allah's best peace and blessings be on him.

Surah: 13 Ayah: 38 & Ayah: 39

$$﴿ وَلَقَدْ أَرْسَلْنَا رُسُلًا مِّن قَبْلِكَ وَجَعَلْنَا لَهُمْ أَزْوَٰجًا وَذُرِّيَّةً ۚ وَمَا كَانَ لِرَسُولٍ أَن يَأْتِيَ بِـَٔايَةٍ إِلَّا بِإِذْنِ ٱللَّهِ ۗ لِكُلِّ أَجَلٍ كِتَابٌ ﴿٣٨﴾ ﴾$$

38. And indeed We sent Messengers before you (O Muhammad (peace be upon him)) and made for them wives and offspring. And it was not for a Messenger to bring a sign except by Allâh's Leave. (For) every matter there is a Decree (from Allâh). (Tafsir Al-Tabari)

$$﴿ يَمْحُوا۟ ٱللَّهُ مَا يَشَآءُ وَيُثْبِتُ ۖ وَعِندَهُۥٓ أُمُّ ٱلْكِتَٰبِ ﴿٣٩﴾ ﴾$$

39. Allâh blots out what He wills and confirms (what He wills). And with Him is the Mother of the Book (Al-Lauh Al-Mahfûz)

Transliteration

38. Walaqad arsalna rusulan min qablika wajaAAalna lahum azwajan wathurriyyatan wama kana lirasoolin an ya/tiya bi-ayatin illa bi-ithni Allahi likulli ajalin kitabun   39. Yamhoo Allahu ma yashao wayuthbitu waAAindahu ommu alkitabi

Tafsir Ibn Kathir

All Prophets and Messengers were Humans

Allah says, `Just as We have sent you O Muhammad, a Prophet and a human, We sent the Messengers before you from among mankind, that eat food, walk in the markets, and We gave them wives and offspring.' Allah said to the most honorable and Final Messenger,

(Say: "I am only a man like you. It has been revealed to me.") (18:110) It is recorded in the Two Sahihs that the Messenger of Allah said,

$$«أَمَّا أَنَا فَأَصُومُ وَأُفْطِرُ، وَأَقُومُ وَأَنَامُ، وَآكُلُ اللَّحْمَ، وَأَتَزَوَّجُ النِّسَاءَ، فَمَنْ رَغِبَ عَنْ سُنَّتِي فَلَيْسَ مِنِّي»$$

(As for me, I fast and break the fast, stand in prayer at night and sleep, eat meat and marry women; so whoever turns away from my Sunnah is not of mine.)

No Prophet can bring a Miracle except by Allah's Leave

Allah said, (And it was not for a Messenger to bring a sign except by Allah's leave.) meaning, no Prophet could have brought a miracle to his people except by Allah's permission and will, for this matter is only decided by Allah the Exalted and Most Honored, not the Prophets; surely Allah does what He wills and decides what He wills.

((For) every matter there is a decree (from Allah).) for every term appointed, there is a record (or decree) that keeps it, and everything has a specific due measure with Allah, (Know you not that Allah knows all that is in the heaven and on the earth Verily, it is (all) in the Book. Verily, that is easy for Allah.)(22:70)

Meaning of Allah blotting out what He wills and confirming what He wills of the Book

Allah said,

(Allah blots out what He wills) of the divinely revealed Books,

(and confirms), until the Qur'an, revealed from Allah to His Messenger peace be upon him, abrogated them all. Mujahid commented;

(Allah blots out what He wills and confirms (what He wills).) "Except life and death, misery and happiness (i.e., faith and disbelief), for they do not change." Mansur said that he asked Mujahid, "Some of us say in their supplication, `O Allah! If my name is with those who are happy (believers), affirm my name among them, and if my name is among the miserable ones (disbelievers), remove it from among them and place it among the happy ones." Mujahid said. "This supplication is good." I met him a year or more later and repeated the same question to him and he recited these Ayat,

(We sent it (this Qur'an) down on a blessed night.) Mujahid commented next, "During Laylatul-Qadr (Night of the Decrees), Allah decides what provisions and disasters will occur in the next year of. He then brings forward or back (or blots out) whatever He wills. As for the Book containing the records of the happy (believers) and the miserable (disbelievers), it does not change." Al-A`mash narrated that Abu Wa'il, Shaqiq bin Salamah said that he used to recite this supplication often, "O Allah, if You wrote us among the wretched ones, remove this status from us and write us among the blessed ones. If You wrote us among the blessed ones, please let us stay that way, for surely, You blot out and confirm what You will, and with You is the Mother of the Book." Ibn Jarir At-Tabari collected this. Similar statements were collected from `Umar bin Al-Khattab and `Abdullah bin Mas`ud, indicating that Allah blots out (or abrogates) and affirms what He wills in the Book of Records. What further supports this meaning is that Imam Ahmad recorded that Thawban said that the Messenger of Allah said,

«إِنَّ الرَّجُلَ لَيُحْرَمُ الرِّزْقَ بِالذَّنْبِ يُصِيبُهُ، وَلَا يَرُدُّ الْقَدَرَ إِلَّا الدُّعَاءُ، وَلَا يَزِيدُ فِي الْعُمْرِ إِلَّا الْبِرِّ»

(A man might be deprived of a provision (that was written for him) because of a sin that he commits; only supplication changes Al-Qadar (Predestination); and only Birr (righteousness) can increase the life span.") An-Nasa'i and Ibn Majah collected this Hadith. There is also a Hadith recorded in the Sahih that affirms that maintaining the ties of the womb increases the life span. Al-`Awfi reported that Ibn `Abbas said about Allah's statement,

(Allah blots out what He wills and confirms (what He wills). And with Him is the Mother of the Book.) "A man might work in Allah's obedience for a while but he reverts to the disobedience of Him and then dies while misguided. This is what Allah blots out, while what He confirms is a man who works in His disobedience, but since goodness was destined for him, he dies after reverting to the obedience of Allah. This is what Allah confirms." It was also reported that Sa`id bin Jubayr said that this Ayah is in the meaning of another Ayah,

(Then He forgives whom He wills and punishes whom He wills. And Allah is able to do all things.) (2:284)

Surah: 13 Ayah: 40 & Ayah: 41

﴿ وَإِن مَّا نُرِيَنَّكَ بَعْضَ ٱلَّذِى نَعِدُهُمْ أَوْ نَتَوَفَّيَنَّكَ فَإِنَّمَا عَلَيْكَ ٱلْبَلَـٰغُ وَعَلَيْنَا ٱلْحِسَابُ ﴾

40. Whether We show you (O Muhammad (peace be upon him)) part of what We have promised them or cause you to die, your duty is only to convey (the Message) and on Us is the reckoning.

﴿ أَوَلَمْ يَرَوْاْ أَنَّا نَأْتِى ٱلْأَرْضَ نَنقُصُهَا مِنْ أَطْرَافِهَا وَٱللَّهُ يَحْكُمُ لَا مُعَقِّبَ لِحُكْمِهِۦ وَهُوَ سَرِيعُ ٱلْحِسَابِ ﴾

41. See they not that We gradually reduce the land (of disbelievers, by giving it to the believers, in war victories) from its outlying borders. And Allâh judges, there is none to put back His Judgement and He is Swift at reckoning.

Transliteration

40. Wa-in ma nuriyannaka baAAda allathee naAAiduhum aw natawaffayannaka fa-innama AAalayka albalaghu waAAalayna alhisabu 41. Awa lam yaraw anna na/tee al-arda nanqusuha min atrafiha waAllahu yahkumu la muAAaqqiba lihukmihi wahuwa sareeAAu alhisabi

Tafsir Ibn Kathir

Punishment is by Allah, and the Messenger's Job is only to convey the Message

Allah said to His Messenger,

`(Whether We show you) O Muhammad, part of the disgrace and humiliation We have promised your enemies in this life,

(or cause you to die) before that,

(your duty is only to convey We have only sent you to convey to them Allah's Message, and by doing so, you will have fulfilled the mission that was ordained on you,

(and on Us is the reckoning), their reckoning and recompense is on Us.' Allah said in similar Ayat,

(So remind them - you are only one who reminds. You are not a dictator over them - Save the one who turns away and disbelieves. Then Allah will punish him with the greatest punishment. Verily, to Us will be their return, Then verily, for Us will be their reckoning.)(88:21-26) Allah said next,

(See they not that We gradually reduce the land from its outlying borders.) Ibn `Abbas commented, "See they not that We are granting land after land to Muhammad ()" Al-Hasan and Ad-Dahhak commented that this Ayah refers to Muslims gaining the upper hand over idolators, just as Allah said in another Ayah,

(And indeed We have destroyed towns round about you.) (46:27)

Surah: 13 Ayah: 42

﴿ وَقَدْ مَكَرَ ٱلَّذِينَ مِن قَبْلِهِمْ فَلِلَّهِ ٱلْمَكْرُ جَمِيعًا ۚ يَعْلَمُ مَا تَكْسِبُ كُلُّ نَفْسٍ ۗ وَسَيَعْلَمُ ٱلْكُفَّـٰرُ لِمَنْ عُقْبَى ٱلدَّارِ ﴾

42. And verily, those before them did devise plots, but all planning is Allâh's. He knows what every person earns, and the disbelievers will know who gets the good end (final destination).

Transliteration

42. Waqad makara allatheena min qablihim falillahi almakru jameeAAan yaAAlamu ma taksibu kullu nafsin wasayaAAlamu alkuffaru liman AAuqba alddari

Tafsir Ibn Kathir

The Disbelievers plot, but the Believers gain the Good End

Allah says,

(And verily, those before them did devise plots,) against their Messengers, they wanted to expel them from their land, but Allah devised plots against the disbelievers and gave the good end to those who fear Him. Allah said in other Ayat,

(And (remember) when the disbelievers plotted against you to imprison you, or to kill you, or to get you out; they were plotting and Allah too was plotting; and Allah is the Best of those who plot.) (8:30), and,

(So they plotted a plot, and We planned a plan, while they perceived not. Then see how was the end of their plot! Verily, We destroyed them and their nation, all together.)(27:50,51) Allah said next,

(He knows what every person earns,) meaning, He alone knows all secrets and concealed thoughts and will reckon each person according to his work, (

and the Kafir (disbeliever) will know

or the Kuffar (disbelievers) according to another way of reciting,

(who gets the good end.) who will earn the ultimate and final victory, they or the followers of the Messengers. Indeed, the followers of the Messengers will earn the good end in this life and the Hereafter, all thanks and praise is due to Allah.

Surah: 13 Ayah: 43

﴿ وَيَقُولُ ٱلَّذِينَ كَفَرُواْ لَسْتَ مُرْسَلًا قُلْ كَفَىٰ بِٱللَّهِ شَهِيدًۢا بَيْنِى وَبَيْنَكُمْ وَمَنْ عِندَهُۥ عِلْمُ ٱلْكِتَٰبِ ﴾

43. And those who disbelieved, say: "You (O Muhammad (peace be upon him)) are not a Messenger." Say: "Sufficient as a witness between me and you is Allâh and those too who have knowledge of the Scripture (such as 'Abdullâh bin Salâm and other Jews and Christians who embraced Islâm)."

Transliteration

43. Wayaqoolu allatheena kafaroo lasta mursalan qul kafa biAllahi shaheedan baynee wabaynakum waman AAindahu AAilmu alkitabi

Tafsir Ibn Kathir

Allah and those who have Knowledge of the Scripture are Sufficient as Witness to the Message of the Prophet

Allah says, the disbelievers reject you and say, (You are not a Messenger.) from Allah, (Say: "Sufficient as a witness between me and you is Allah...") meaning, say, `Allah is sufficient for me and He is the witness over me and you. He is witness that I (Muhammad) have conveyed the Message from Him and over you, O rejecters, to the falsehood that you invent.' Allah said,

(and those too who have knowledge of the Scripture.) This refers to `Abdullah bin Salam, according to Mujahid. However, this opinion is not plausible, since this Ayah was revealed in Makkah and `Abdullah bin Salam embraced Islam soon after the Prophet emigrated to Al-Madinah. A more suitable explanation is that narrated by Al-`Awfi from Ibn `Abbas that this Ayah refers to Jews and Christians. Qatadah said that among them are, `Abdullah bin Salam, Salman (Al-Farisi) and Tamim Ad-Dari. The correct view is that this Ayah,

(and those too who have. ..), refers to the scholars of the People of the Scriptures who find the description of Muhammad in their Books and the good news of his advent that were conveyed to them by their Prophets. Allah said in other Ayat,

(And My mercy embraces all things. That (mercy) I shall ordain for those who have Taqwa, and give Zakah; and those who believe in Our Ayat; Those who follow the Messenger, the Prophet who can neither read nor write whom they find written with them in the Tawrah and the Injil.) (7:156-157) and,

(It is not a sign to them that the learned scholars of the Children of Israel knew it (as true))(26:197) There are similar Ayat that affirm that the scholars of the Children of Israel know this fact from their divinely revealed Books. This is the end of Surat Ar-Ra`d, and all praise is due to Allah and all favors are from Him.

CHAPTER (SURAH) 14: IBRAHIM (ABRAHAM), VERSES 001-052

(بِسْمِ اللَّهِ الرَّحْمَنِ الرَّحِيمِ)

In the Name of Allah, the Most Gracious, the Most Merciful.

Surah: 14 Ayah: 1, Ayah: 2 & Ayah: 3

﴿ الٓرۚ كِتَٰبٌ أَنزَلْنَٰهُ إِلَيْكَ لِتُخْرِجَ ٱلنَّاسَ مِنَ ٱلظُّلُمَٰتِ إِلَى ٱلنُّورِ بِإِذْنِ رَبِّهِمْ إِلَىٰ صِرَٰطِ ٱلْعَزِيزِ ٱلْحَمِيدِ ۝ ﴾

1. Alif-Lâm-Râ. [These letters are one of the miracles of the Qur'ân, and none but Allâh (Alone) knows their meanings]. (This is) a Book which We have revealed unto you (O Muhammad SAW) in order that you might lead mankind out of darkness (of disbelief and polytheism) into light (of belief in the Oneness of Allâh and Islâmic Monotheism) by their Lord's Leave to the Path of the All-Mighty, the Owner of all Praise.

﴿ ٱللَّهِ ٱلَّذِى لَهُۥ مَا فِى ٱلسَّمَٰوَٰتِ وَمَا فِى ٱلْأَرْضِ ۗ وَوَيْلٌ لِّلْكَٰفِرِينَ مِنْ عَذَابٍ شَدِيدٍ ۝ ﴾

2. Allâh to Whom belongs all that is in the heavens and all that is in the earth! And woe unto the disbelievers from a severe torment.

﴿ ٱلَّذِينَ يَسْتَحِبُّونَ ٱلْحَيَوٰةَ ٱلدُّنْيَا عَلَى ٱلْءَاخِرَةِ وَيَصُدُّونَ عَن سَبِيلِ ٱللَّهِ وَيَبْغُونَهَا عِوَجًا ۚ أُوْلَٰٓئِكَ فِى ضَلَٰلٍ بَعِيدٍ ۝ ﴾

3. Those who prefer the life of this world to the Hereafter, and hinder (men) from the Path of Allâh (i.e. Islâm) and seek crookedness therein - they are far astray.

Transliteration

1. Alif-lam-ra kitabun anzalnahu ilayka litukhrija alnnasa mina alththulumati ila alnnoori bi-ithni rabbihim ila sirati alAAazeezi alhameedi 2. Allahi allathee lahu ma fee

alssamawati wama fee al-ardi wawaylun lilkafireena min AAathabin shadeedin 3. Allatheena yastahibboona alhayata alddunya AAala al-akhirati wayasuddoona AAan sabeeli Allahi wayabghoonaha AAiwajan ola-ika fee dalalin baAAeedin

Tafsir Ibn Kathir

Describing the Qur'an and warning Those Who defy it

Previously we discussed the meaning of the separate letters that appear in the beginnings of some Surahs.

((This is) a Book which We have revealed unto you...) Allah says, `This is a Book that We have revealed to you, O Muhammad. This `Book', is the Glorious Qur'an, the most honored Book, that Allah sent down from heaven to the most honored Messenger of Allah sent to all the people of the earth, Arabs and non-Arabs alike,

(in order that you might lead mankind out of darkness into light) We sent you, O Muhammad, with this Book in order that you might lead mankind away from misguidance and crookedness to guidance and the right way,'

(Allah is the Wali (Protector or Guardian) of those who believe. He brings them out from darkness into light. But as for those who disbelieve, their Awliya (supporters and helpers) are Taghut (false deities), they bring them out from light into darkness.) (2:257), and,

(It is He Who sends down manifest Ayat to His servant that He may bring you out from darkness into light.) (57:9) Allah said next,

(by their Lord's leave), He guides those whom He destined to be guided by the hand of His Messenger , whom He sent to guide them by His command,

(to the path of the All-Mighty,) Who can never be resisted or overpowered. Rather, Allah is Irresistible above everything and everyone else,

(the Praised.) Who is glorified and praised in all His actions, statements, legislation, commandments and prohibitions and Who only says the truth in the information He conveys. Allah's statement,

(Allah to Whom belongs all that is in the heavens and all that is in the earth!), is similar to,

(Say: "O mankind! Verily, I am sent to you all as the Messenger of Allah - to Whom belongs the dominion of the heavens and the earth.) (7:158) Allah's statement,

(And woe unto the disbelievers from a severe torment.) means, `woe to them on the Day of Judgment because they defied you, O Muhammad, and rejected you.' Allah described the disbelievers as preferring the life of the present world to the Hereafter, coveting the former life and working hard for its sake. They have forgotten the Hereafter and abandoned it behind their backs,

(and hinder (men) from the path of Allah), from following the Messengers, (and seek crookedness therein) they seek to make Allah's path crooked, even though it is straight itself and does not deviate on account of those who defy or betray it. When the disbelievers do this, they become engulfed in ignorance and misguidance far away from truth, and therefore, there is no hope that they will gain guidance and correctness while on this state.

Surah: 14 Ayah: 4

﴿ وَمَآ أَرْسَلْنَا مِن رَّسُولٍ إِلَّا بِلِسَانِ قَوْمِهِۦ لِيُبَيِّنَ لَهُمْ ۖ فَيُضِلُّ ٱللَّهُ مَن يَشَآءُ وَيَهْدِى مَن يَشَآءُ ۚ وَهُوَ ٱلْعَزِيزُ ٱلْحَكِيمُ ﴾

4. And We sent not a Messenger except with the language of his people, in order that he might make (the Message) clear for them. Then Allâh misleads whom He wills and guides whom He wills. And He is the All-Mighty, the All-Wise.

Transliteration

4. Wama arsalna min rasoolin illa bilisani qawmihi liyubayyina lahum fayudillu Allahu man yashao wayahdee man yashao wahuwa alAAazeezu alhakeemu

Tafsir Ibn Kathir

Every Prophet was sent with the Language of His People; Guidance or Misguidance follows the Explanation

Allah is Kind and Compassionate with His creation, sending Messengers to them from among them and speaking their language, so that they are able to understand the Message that the Messengers were sent with. Allah said next,

(Then Allah misleads whom He wills and guides whom He wills.) after the proof and evidence have been established for the people, Allah misguides whom He wills from the path of guidance and guides whom He wills to the truth,

(And He is the All-Mighty,) whatever He wills occurs and whatever He does not will never occurs,

(the All-Wise.) in His decisions, misleading those who deserve to be misled and guiding those who deserve guidance. This is from Allah's wisdom with His creation, every Prophet He sent to a people spoke their language and everyone of these Prophets were only sent to their people. Muhammad bin `Abdullah, Allah's Messenger, peace and blessings be upon him, was sent to all people. It is recorded in the Two Sahihs that Jabir said that the Messenger of Allah said,

«أُعْطِيتُ خَمْسًا لَمْ يُعْطَهُنَّ أَحَدٌ مِنَ الْأَنْبِيَاءِ قَبْلِي: نُصِرْتُ بِالرُّعْبِ مَسِيرَةَ شَهْرٍ، وَجُعِلَتْ لِيَ الْأَرْضُ مَسْجِدًا وَطَهُورًا، وَأُحِلَّتْ لِيَ الْغَنَائِمُ وَلَمْ تُحَلَّ لِأَحَدٍ

قَبْلِي، وَأُعْطِيتُ الشَّفَاعَةَ، وَكَانَ النَّبِيُّ يُبْعَثُ إِلَى قَوْمِهِ خَاصَّةً وَبُعِثْتُ إِلَى النَّاسِ عَامَّةً»

(I have been given five things which were not given to anyone else before me. Allah made me victorious by awe, (by His frightening my enemies) for a distance of one month's journey. The earth has been made for me (and for my followers) a place for worship and a purifier. The war booty has been made lawful for me and it was not lawful for anyone else before me. I have been given the right of Intercession (on the Day of Resurrection). Every Prophet used to be sent to his nation only, but I have been sent to all mankind.) Allah said,

(Say: "O mankind! Verily, I am sent to you all as the Messenger of Allah...) (7:158)

Surah: 14 Ayah: 5

﴿ وَلَقَدْ أَرْسَلْنَا مُوسَىٰ بِـَٔايَـٰتِنَآ أَنْ أَخْرِجْ قَوْمَكَ مِنَ ٱلظُّلُمَـٰتِ إِلَى ٱلنُّورِ وَذَكِّرْهُم بِأَيَّىٰمِ ٱللَّهِ إِنَّ فِى ذَٰلِكَ لَـَٔايَـٰتٍ لِّكُلِّ صَبَّارٍ شَكُورٍ ﴾

5. And indeed We sent Mûsa (Moses) with Our Ayât (signs, proofs, and evidences) (saying): "Bring out your people from darkness into light, and remind them of the annals of Allâh. Truly, therein are Ayât (evidences, proofs and signs) for every patient, thankful (person)."

Transliteration

5. Walaqad arsalna moosa bi-ayatina an akhrij qawmaka mina alththulumati ila alnnoori wathakkirhum bi-ayyami Allahi inna fee thalika laayatin likulli sabbarin shakoorin

Tafsir Ibn Kathir

Story of Musa and His People

Allah says here, `Just as We sent you (O, Muhammad) and sent down to you the Book, in order that you might guide and call all people out of darkness into the light, We also sent Musa to the Children of Israel with Our Ayat (signs, or miracles).' Mujahid said that this part of the Ayah refers to the nine miracles.

(Bring out your people) he is being commanded;

(Bring out your people from darkness into light,) call them to all that is good and righteous, in order that they might turn away from the darkness of ignorance and misguidance they indulged in, to the light of guidance and the enlightenment of faith,

(and remind them of the annals (or days) of Allah) remind them (O Musa) of Allah's days, meaning, favors and bounties which He bestowed on them when He delivered them from the grip of Fir`awn and his injustice, tyranny and brutality. This is when Allah delivered them from their enemy, made a passage for them through the sea, shaded them with clouds, sent down manna and quails for them, and other favors and bounties. Mujahid, Qatadah and several others said this. Allah said next,

(Truly, therein are Ayat for every patient, thankful (person).) Allah says, `Our delivering of Our loyal supporters among the Children of Israel from the grasp of Fir`awn and saving them from the disgraceful torment, provides a lesson to draw from for those who are patient in the face of affliction, and thankful in times of prosperity. Qatadah said, "Excellent is the servant who if he is tested, he observes patience, and if he is granted prosperity, he is thankful for it." It is recorded in the Sahih that the Messenger of Allah said,

«إِنَّ أَمْرَ الْمُؤْمِنِ كُلَّهُ عَجَبٌ، لَا يَقْضِي اللهُ لَهُ قَضَاءً إِلَّا كَانَ خَيْرًا لَهُ، إِنْ أَصَابَتْهُ ضَرَّاءُ صَبَرَ، فَكَانَ خَيْرًا لَهُ، وَإِنْ أَصَابَتْهُ سَرَّاءُ شَكَرَ، فَكَانَ خَيْرًا لَهُ»

(Verily, all of the matter of the believer is amazing, for every decision that Allah decrees for him is good for him. If an affliction strikes him, he is patient and this is good for him; if a bounty is give to him, he is thankful and this is good for him.)

Surah: 14 Ayah: 6, Ayah: 7 & Ayah: 8

﴿ وَإِذْ قَالَ مُوسَىٰ لِقَوْمِهِ ٱذْكُرُوا۟ نِعْمَةَ ٱللَّهِ عَلَيْكُمْ إِذْ أَنجَىٰكُم مِّنْ ءَالِ فِرْعَوْنَ يَسُومُونَكُمْ سُوٓءَ ٱلْعَذَابِ وَيُذَبِّحُونَ أَبْنَآءَكُمْ وَيَسْتَحْيُونَ نِسَآءَكُمْ ۚ وَفِى ذَٰلِكُم بَلَآءٌ مِّن رَّبِّكُمْ عَظِيمٌ ۝ ﴾

6. And (remember) when Mûsa (Moses) said to his people: "Call to mind Allâh's Favor to you, when He delivered you from Fir'aun's (Pharaoh) people who were afflicting you with horrible torment, and were slaughtering your sons and letting your women alive; and in it was a tremendous trial from your Lord."

﴿ وَإِذْ تَأَذَّنَ رَبُّكُمْ لَئِن شَكَرْتُمْ لَأَزِيدَنَّكُمْ ۖ وَلَئِن كَفَرْتُمْ إِنَّ عَذَابِى لَشَدِيدٌ ۝ ﴾

7. And (remember) when your Lord proclaimed: "If you give thanks (by accepting Faith and worshipping none but Allâh), I will give you more (of My Blessings); but if you are thankless (i.e. disbelievers), verily My Punishment is indeed severe."

﴿ وَقَالَ مُوسَىٰٓ إِن تَكْفُرُوٓا۟ أَنتُمْ وَمَن فِى ٱلْأَرْضِ جَمِيعًا فَإِنَّ ٱللَّهَ لَغَنِىٌّ حَمِيدٌ ۝ ﴾

8. And Mûsa (Moses) said: "If you disbelieve, you and all on earth together, then verily Allâh is Rich (Free of all needs), Owner of all Praise."

Transliteration

6. Wa-ith qala moosa liqawmihi othkuroo niAAmata Allahi AAalaykum ith anjakum min ali firAAawna yasoomoonakum soo-a alAAathabi wayuthabbihoona abnaakum wayastahyoona nisaakum wafee thalikum balaon min rabbikum AAatheemun 7. Wa-ith taaththana rabbukum la-in shakartum laazeedannakum wala-in kafartum inna AAathabee lashadeedun   8. Waqala moosa in takfuroo antum waman fee al-ardi jameeAAan fa-inna Allaha laghaniyyun hameedun

Tafsir Ibn Kathir

Allah states that Musa reminded his people about Allah's annals and days and of Allah's favors and bounties that He bestowed on them, when He saved them from Fir`awn and his people and the torment and disgrace they used to exert on them.

They used to slaughter whomever they could find among their sons and let their females live. Allah delivered them from all this torment, and this is a great bounty, indeed. This is why Allah described this affliction,

(and in it was a tremendous trial from your Lord.) `for He granted you (O Children of Israel) a great favor for which you are unable to perfectly thank Him.' Some scholars said that this part of the Ayah means, `what Fir`awn used to do to you was a tremendous

(trial.)' Both meanings might be considered here and Allah knows best. Allah said in another Ayah ,

(And We tried them with good and evil in order that they might turn (to Allah).) (7:168) Allah's statement next,

(And (remember) when your Lord proclaimed) means, proclaimed and made known His promise to you. It is possible that this Ayah means, your Lord has vowed and sworn by His might, grace and exaltness. Allah said in a similar Ayah,

(And (remember) when your Lord declared that He would certainly keep on sending against them (i.e. the Jews), till the Day of Resurrection.) (7:167) Allah said,

(If you give thanks, I will give you more;) meaning, `if you appreciate My favor on you, I will give you more of it,

(but if you are thankless) if you are not thankful for My favors, covering and denying, them,

(verily, My punishment is indeed severe), by depriving you of the favor and punishing you for being unappreciative of it.' A Hadith states that,

(A servant might be deprived of a provision (that was written for him) because of a sin that he commits.) Allah said,

(And Musa said: "If you disbelieve, you and all on earth together, then verily, Allah is Rich (free of all needs), Worthy of all praise.") Allah does not need the gratitude of His servants, and He is worthy of all praise even if the disbelievers disbelieve in Him,

(If you disbelieve, then verily, Allah is not in need of you) (39:7) and,

(So they disbelieved and turned away. But Allah was not in need (of them). And Allah is Rich (free of all needs), Worthy of all praise.) (64:6) In his Sahih, Muslim recorded that Abu Dharr said that the Messenger of Allah said that his Lord the Exalted and Most Honored said,

«يَا عِبَادِي لَوْ أَنَّ أَوَّلَكُمْ وَآخِرَكُمْ وَإِنْسَكُمْ وَجِنَّكُمْ كَانُوا عَلَى أَتْقَى قَلْبِ رَجُلٍ وَاحِدٍ مِنْكُمْ، مَا زَادَ ذَلِكَ فِي مُلْكِي شَيْئًا، يَا عِبَادِي لَوْ أَنَّ أَوَّلَكُمْ وَآخِرَكُمْ وَإِنْسَكُمْ وَجِنَّكُمْ كَانُوا عَلَى أَفْجَرِ قَلْبِ رَجُلٍ وَاحِدٍ مِنْكُمْ، مَا نَقَصَ ذَلِكَ فِي مُلْكِي شَيْئًا، يَا عِبَادِي لَوْ أَنَّ أَوَّلَكُمْ وَآخِرَكُمْ وَإِنْسَكُمْ وَجِنَّكُمْ قَامُوا فِي صَعِيدٍ وَاحِدٍ، فَسَأَلُونِي، فَأَعْطَيْتُ كُلَّ إِنْسَانٍ مَسْأَلَتَهُ، مَا نَقَصَ ذَلِكَ مِنْ مُلْكِي شَيْئًا إِلَّا كَمَا يَنْقُصُ الْمِخْيَطُ إِذَا أُدْخِلَ الْبَحْرَ»

(O My servants. If the first and the last among you, mankind and Jinns among you, had the heart of the most pious and righteous man among you, that will not increase my kingdom in the least. O My servants! If the first and the last among you, mankind and the Jinns among you, had the heart of the most wicked man among you, that will not decrease My kingdom in the least. O My servants! If the first and the last among you, the mankind and Jinns among you, stood in one flat area and each asked me (what they wish), and I gave each one of them what they asked, that will not decrease My kingdom except by that which the needle carries (of water) when inserted in the ocean.") Verily, all praise and glory are due to Allah, the Rich (free of need), the Worthy of all praise.

Surah: 14 Ayah: 9

﴿ أَلَمْ يَأْتِكُمْ نَبَؤُاْ ٱلَّذِينَ مِن قَبْلِكُمْ قَوْمِ نُوحٍ وَعَادٍ وَثَمُودَ ۛ وَٱلَّذِينَ مِنۢ بَعْدِهِمْ ۛ لَا يَعْلَمُهُمْ إِلَّا ٱللَّهُ ۚ جَآءَتْهُمْ رُسُلُهُم بِٱلْبَيِّنَٰتِ فَرَدُّوٓاْ أَيْدِيَهُمْ فِىٓ أَفْوَٰهِهِمْ وَقَالُوٓاْ إِنَّا كَفَرْنَا بِمَآ أُرْسِلْتُم بِهِۦ وَإِنَّا لَفِى شَكٍّۢ مِّمَّا تَدْعُونَنَآ إِلَيْهِ مُرِيبٍۢ ﴿٩﴾

9. Has not the news reached you, of those before you, the people of Nûh (Noah), and 'Ad, and Thamûd? And those after them? None knows them but Allâh. To them came their Messengers with clear proofs, but they put their hands in their mouths (biting them from anger) and said: "Verily, we disbelieve in that with which you have been sent, and we are really in grave doubt as to that to which you invite us (i.e. Islâmic Monotheism)."

Transliteration

9. Alam ya/tikum nabao allatheena min qablikum qawmi noohin waAAadin wathamooda waallatheena min baAAdihim la yaAAlamuhum illa Allahu jaat-hum rusuluhum bialbayyinati faraddoo aydiyahum fee afwahihim waqaloo inna kafarna bima orsiltum bihi wa-inna lafee shakkin mimma tadAAoonana ilayhi mureebun

Tafsir Ibn Kathir

Earlier Nations disbelieved in Their Prophets

Allah narrated to this Ummah (followers of Muhammad) the stories of the people of Prophet Nuh, `Ad and Thamud, and other ancient nations that belied their Messengers. Only Allah knows the count of these nations,

(To them came their Messengers with clear proofs,) they brought them evidences and plain, tremendous proofs and signs. Ibn Ishaq reported that `Amr bin Maymun said that `Abdullah said about Allah's statement,

(None knows them but Allah.) "The genealogists utter lies." This is why `Urwah bin Az-Zubayr said, "We did not find anyone who knows the forefathers of Ma`dd bin `Adnan."

Meaning of, "They put Their Hands in Their Mouths

Allah said next,

(but they put their hands in their mouths) It is said that they pointed to the Messengers' mouths asking them to stop calling them to Allah, the Exalted and Most Honored. It is also said that it means, they placed their hands on their mouths in denial of the Messengers. It was also said that it means that they did not answer the call of the Messengers, or they were biting their hands in rage. Mujahid, Muhammad bin Ka`b and Qatadah said that they belied the Messengers and refuted their call with their mouths. I (Ibn Kathir) say that Mujahid's Tafsir is supported by the completion of the narrative,

(and said: "Verily, we disbelieve in that with which you have been sent, and we are really in grave doubt as to that to which you invite us.") Al-`Awfi reported that Ibn `Abbas said, "When they heard Allah's Word, they were amazed and placed their hands on their mouths,"

(and said: "Verily, we disbelieve in that with which you have been sent.") They said, We do not believe what you brought us, and have strong doubt in its authenticity. '

Surah: 14 Ayah: 10, Ayah: 11 & Ayah: 12

﴿ ۞ قَالَتْ رُسُلُهُمْ أَفِي ٱللَّهِ شَكٌّ فَاطِرِ ٱلسَّمَـٰوَٰتِ وَٱلْأَرْضِ يَدْعُوكُمْ لِيَغْفِرَ لَكُم مِّن ذُنُوبِكُمْ وَيُؤَخِّرَكُمْ إِلَىٰٓ أَجَلٍ مُّسَمًّى ۚ قَالُوٓا۟ إِنْ أَنتُمْ إِلَّا بَشَرٌ مِّثْلُنَا تُرِيدُونَ أَن تَصُدُّونَا عَمَّا كَانَ يَعْبُدُ ءَابَآؤُنَا فَأْتُونَا بِسُلْطَـٰنٍ مُّبِينٍ ۞ ﴾

10. Their Messengers said: "What! Can there be a doubt about Allâh, the Creator of the heavens and the earth? He calls you (to Monotheism and to be obedient to Allâh) that He may forgive you of your sins and give you respite for a term appointed." They said: "You are no more than human beings like us! You wish to turn us away from what our fathers used to worship. Then bring us a clear authority (i.e. a clear proof of what you say)."

﴿ قَالَتْ لَهُمْ رُسُلُهُمْ إِن نَّحْنُ إِلَّا بَشَرٌ مِّثْلُكُمْ وَلَـٰكِنَّ ٱللَّهَ يَمُنُّ عَلَىٰ مَن يَشَآءُ مِنْ عِبَادِهِ ۖ وَمَا كَانَ لَنَآ أَن نَّأْتِيَكُم بِسُلْطَـٰنٍ إِلَّا بِإِذْنِ ٱللَّهِ ۚ وَعَلَى ٱللَّهِ فَلْيَتَوَكَّلِ ٱلْمُؤْمِنُونَ ۞ ﴾

11. Their Messengers said to them: "We are no more than human beings like you, but Allâh bestows His Grace to whom He wills of His slaves. It is not ours to bring you an authority (proof) except by the Permission of Allâh. And in Allâh (Alone) let the believers put their trust.

﴿ وَمَا لَنَآ أَلَّا نَتَوَكَّلَ عَلَى ٱللَّهِ وَقَدْ هَدَىٰنَا سُبُلَنَا ۚ وَلَنَصْبِرَنَّ عَلَىٰ مَآ ءَاذَيْتُمُونَا ۚ وَعَلَى ٱللَّهِ فَلْيَتَوَكَّلِ ٱلْمُتَوَكِّلُونَ ۞ ﴾

12. "And why should we not put our trust in Allâh while He indeed has guided us our ways. And we shall certainly bear with patience all the hurt you may cause us, and in Allâh (Alone) let those who trust, put their trust."

Transliteration

10. Qalat rusuluhum afee Allahi shakkun fatiri alssamawati waal-ardi yadAAookum liyaghfira lakum min thunoobikum wayu-akhkhirakum ila ajalin musamman qaloo in antum illa basharun mithluna tureedoona an tasuddoona AAamma kana yaAAbudu abaona fa/toona bisultanin mubeenin   11. Qalat lahum rusuluhum in nahnu illa basharun mithlukum walakinna Allaha yamunnu AAala man yashao min AAibadihi wama kana lana an na/tiyakum bisultanin illa bi-ithni Allahi waAAala Allahi falyatawakkali almu/minoona   12. Wama lana alla natawakkala AAala Allahi waqad hadana subulana walanasbiranna AAala ma athaytumoona waAAala Allahi falyatawakkali almutawakkiloona

Tafsir Ibn Kathir

The Argument between the Prophets and the Disbelievers

Allah narrates to us the arguments that ensued between the disbelievers and their Messengers. When their nations doubted the Message of worshipping Allah alone without partners, the Messengers said,

((What!) Can there be a doubt about Allah...) about His Lordship and having the exclusive right to be worshipped alone, being the only Creator of all creatures Verily, none besides Allah is worthy of worship, alone without partners with Him. Most nations were, and still are, affirming the existence of the Creator, but they call upon intermediaries besides Him whom they think will benefit them or bring them closer to Allah. Their Messengers said to them,

(He calls you that He may forgive you of your sins) in the Hereafter,

(and give you respite for a term appointed.), in this worldly life. Allah said in other Ayat,

(Seek the forgiveness of your Lord, and turn to Him in repentance, that He may grant you good enjoyment, for a term appointed, and bestow His abounding grace to every owner of grace.) (10:3) However, their nations went on arguing against their prophethood, after they had to submit to the first evidence (that Allah Alone created everything).

Disbelievers reject Prophethood because the Messengers were Humans!

Their nations said,

(You are no more than human beings like us!) so why should we follow you just because you say so, even though we did not witness a miracle by your hands,

(Then bring us a clear authority.), a miracle of our choice.

(Their Messengers said to them: "We are no more than human beings like you...") affirming that truly, they were only human being like their nations,

(but Allah bestows His grace to whom He wills of His servants.), with prophethood and messengership which is His choice,

(It is not ours to bring you an authority) according to your choice,

((except by the permission of Allah.), after we beg Him and He provides us with a miracle,

(And in Allah (alone) let the believers put their trust.) in all their affairs. Their Messengers said to them next,

(And why should we not put our trust in Allah), after He had guided us to the best, most clear and plain way,

(And we shall certainly bear with patience all the hurt you may cause us), such as foolish actions and abusive statements,

(and in Allah (alone) let those who trust, put their trust.)

Surah: 14 Ayah: 13, Ayah: 14, Ayah: 15, Ayah: 16 & Ayah: 17

﴿ وَقَالَ ٱلَّذِينَ كَفَرُوا۟ لِرُسُلِهِمْ لَنُخْرِجَنَّكُم مِّنْ أَرْضِنَآ أَوْ لَتَعُودُنَّ فِى مِلَّتِنَا ۖ فَأَوْحَىٰٓ إِلَيْهِمْ رَبُّهُمْ لَنُهْلِكَنَّ ٱلظَّٰلِمِينَ ۝ ﴾

13. And those who disbelieved, said to their Messengers: "Surely, we shall drive you out of our land, or you shall return to our religion." So their Lord inspired them: "Truly, We shall destroy the Zâlimûn (polytheists, disbelievers and wrong-doers).

﴿ وَلَنُسْكِنَنَّكُمُ ٱلْأَرْضَ مِنۢ بَعْدِهِمْ ۚ ذَٰلِكَ لِمَنْ خَافَ مَقَامِى وَخَافَ وَعِيدِ ۝ ﴾

14. "And indeed, We shall make you dwell in the land after them. This is for him who fears standing before Me (on the Day of Resurrection or fears My Punishment) and also fears My threat."

﴿ وَٱسْتَفْتَحُوا۟ وَخَابَ كُلُّ جَبَّارٍ عَنِيدٍ ۝ ﴾

15. But they (the Messengers) sought victory and help (from their Lord (Allâh)) and every obstinate, arrogant dictator (who refuses to believe in the Oneness of Allâh) was brought to a complete loss and destruction.

﴿ مِّن وَرَآئِهِۦ جَهَنَّمُ وَيُسْقَىٰ مِن مَّآءٍ صَدِيدٍ ۝ ﴾

16. In front of him (every obstinate, arrogant dictator) is Hell, and he will be made to drink boiling, festering water.

﴿ يَتَجَرَّعُهُۥ وَلَا يَكَادُ يُسِيغُهُۥ وَيَأْتِيهِ ٱلْمَوْتُ مِن كُلِّ مَكَانٍ وَمَا هُوَ بِمَيِّتٍ ۖ وَمِن وَرَآئِهِۦ عَذَابٌ غَلِيظٌ ۝ ﴾

17. He will sip it unwillingly, and he will find a great difficulty to swallow it down his throat; and death will come to him from every side, yet he will not die and in front of him, will be a great torment.

Transliteration

13. Waqala allatheena kafaroo lirusulihim lanukhrijannakum min ardina aw lataAAoodunna fee millatina faawha ilayhim rabbuhum lanuhlikanna alththalimeena 14. Walanuskinannakumu al-arda min baAAdihim thalika liman khafa maqamee wakhafa waAAeedi 15. Waistaftahoo wakhaba kullu jabbarin AAaneedin 16. Min

wara-ihi jahannamu wayusqa min ma-in sadeedin   17. YatajarraAAuhu wala yakadu yuseeghuhu waya/teehi almawtu min kulli makanin wama huwa bimayyitin wamin wara-ihi AAathabun ghaleethun

Tafsir Ibn Kathir

Disbelieving Nations threaten Their Messengers with Expulsion

Allah narrates to us how the disbelieving nations threatened their Messengers, that being, expulsion from their land and banshiment. For instance, the people of Prophet Shu`ayb, peace be upon him, said to him and to those who believed in him,

(We shall certainly drive you out from our town, O Shu`ayb, and those who have believed with you.) (7:88) The people of Prophet Lut, peace be upon him, said,

(Drive out the family of Lut from your city.) (27:56) Allah said about the idolators of Quraysh,

(And verily, they were about to frighten you so much as to drive you out from the land. But in that case they would not have stayed after you, except for a little while.)(17:76) and,

(And when the disbelievers plotted against you to imprison you, or to kill you, or to expel you out; they were plotting and Allah too was plotting; and Allah is the Best of those who plot.) (8:30) Allah gave victory and aid to His Messenger after he emigrated from Makkah and gathered followers, supporters, and soldiers around him, who fought in the cause of Allah, the Exalted. Allah kept granting His Messenger more dominance until He opened for him Makkah, which sought to expel him. Allah gave him dominance over it, even when his enemies from Makkah and the rest of the people of the earth disliked it. Soon after, people began embracing the religion of Allah in large crowds and in a very short time Allah's Word and religion became high over all other religions, from the eastern and western parts of the world. Hence Allah's statement,

(So their Lord revealed to them: "Truly, We shall destroy the wrongdoers. And indeed, We shall make you dwell in the land after them.") (14:13,14) Allah said in other Ayat,

(And, verily, Our Word has gone forth of old for Our servants, the Messengers, that they verily, would be made triumphant, and that Our hosts! They verily, would be the victors.) (37:171-173),

(Allah has decreed: "Verily, it is I and My Messengers who shall be the victorious. Verily, Allah is All-Powerful, All-Mighty.")(58:21)

(And indeed We have written in Az-Zabur after Adh-Dhikr.) (21:05)

(Musa said to his people: "Seek help in Allah and be patient. Verily, the earth is Allah's. He gives it as a heritage to whom He wills of His servants: and the (blessed) end is for the those who have Taqwa.")(7:128) and,

(And We made the people who were considered weak to inherit the eastern parts of the land and the western parts thereof which We have blessed. And the fair Word of your Lord was fulfilled for the Children of Israel, because of their endurance. And We destroyed completely all the great works and buildings which Fir`awn and his people erected.)(7:137) Allah said next,

(This is for him who fears standing before Me and also fears My threat.) this warning is for he who fears standing before Him on the Day of Resurrection and fears His warnings and torment. Allah said in other instances,

(Then for him who transgressed all bounds, and preferred the life of this world, verily, his abode will be Hellfire. But as for him who feared standing before his Lord, and restrained himself from impure evil desires and lusts. Verily, Paradise will be his abode.)(79:37-41) and,

(But for him who fears the standing before his Lord, there will be two Gardens.)(55:46) Allah said next,

(And they sought victory and help) refers to the Messengers who sought the help and victory of their Lord over their nations, according to `Abdullah bin `Abbas, Mujahid and Qatadah. `Abdur-Rahman bin Zayd bin Aslam said that this Ayah refers to the nations, invoking Allah's victory against themselves! Some idolators said,

(O Allah ! If this (Qur'an) is indeed the truth (revealed) from You, then rain down stones on us from the sky or bring on us a painful torment.) (8:32) It is possible that both meanings are desired here, for the idolators (of Quraysh) invoked Allah against themselves on the day of Badr, and the Messenger of Allah invoked Him for victory and support. Allah said to the idolators then,

((O disbelievers) if you ask for a judgment, now has the judgment come unto you; and if you cease (to do wrong), it will be better for you.) (8:19) Allah knows best. Allah said next,

(and every obstinate, arrogant dictator was brought to a complete loss and destruction.) those who were arrogant and rebelled against the truth. Allah said in other Ayat,

((Allah will say to the angels): "Both of you throw into Hell every stubborn disbeliever - hinderer of good, transgressor, doubter, who set up another deity with Allah. Then both of you cast him in the severe torment.") (50:24-26) The Prophet said,

«إِنَّهُ يُؤْتَى بِجَهَنَّمَ يَوْمَ الْقِيَامَةِ، فَتُنَادِي الْخَلَائِقَ، فَتَقُولُ: إِنِّي وُكِّلْتُ بِكُلِّ جَبَّارٍ عَنِيدٍ»

(On the Day of Resurrection, Jahannam (Hellfire) will be brought and it will call the creatures, saying, "I was given the responsibility of every rebellious tyrant.")

Therefore, every tyrant has earned utter demise and loss when the Prophets invoked Allah, the Mighty, the Able for victory. Allah said next,

(In front of him is Hell,) Allah says that Jahannam is in front of every obstinate tyrant, awaiting him, and he will reside in it forever on the Day of Return. He will be brought to it in the morning and the afternoon until the Day of the Call,

(and he will be made to drink boiling, festering water.) in the Fire, his only drink will be from Hamim and Ghassaq, the former is very hot and the latter is very cold and rotten. Allah said in another instance,

(This is so! Then let them taste it - Hamim and Ghassaq. And other (torments) of similar kind all together!)(38:57-58) Mujahid and `Ikrimah said that this festering water is made of puss and blood. Allah said in other Ayat,

(And be given to drink boiling water so that it cuts up their bowels.) (47:15) and,

(And if they ask for help, they will be granted water like boiling oil, that will scald their faces.) (18:29) Allah's statement,

(He will sip it unwillingly), indicates that he will hate to drink this water, but he will be forced to sip it; he will refuse until the angel strikes him with an iron bar,

(And for them are hooked rods of iron.)(22:21) Allah said next,

(and he will find great difficulty in swallowing it down his throat,) meaning, he will hate to swallow it because of its awful taste, color and unbearable heat or coldness,

(and death will come to him from every side,) his organs, limbs and entire body will suffer pain because of this drink. `Amr bin Maymun bin Mahran commented, "Every bone, nerve and blood vessel." Ad-Dahhak reported that Ibn `Abbas commented on Allah's statement,

(and death will come to him from every side,) "All types of torment that Allah will punish him with on the Day of Resurrection in the fire of Jahannam will come to him carrying death, if he were to die. However, he will not die because Allah the Exalted said,

(Neither will it affect them that they die nor shall its torment be lightened for them)(35:36)." Therefore, according to Ibn `Abbas, may Allah be pleased with him and his father, every type of punishment will come to him (the obstinate, rebellious tyrant) carrying death with it, if he will ever die there. Yet, he will not die, he will instead receive eternal punishment and torment. Hence Allah's statement here,

(and death will come to him from every side, yet he will not die,) Allah said,

(and in front of him, will be a great torment.) even in this condition, he will still suffer another severe type of torment, more severe and painful from the one before it, harsher more bitter. Allah described the tree of Zaqqum,

(Verily, it is a tree that springs out of the bottom of Hellfire, the shoots of its fruits stalks are like the heads of Shayatin; Truly, they will eat thereof and fill their bellies therewith. Then on top of that they will be given boiling water to drink so that it becomes a mixture. Then thereafter, verily, their return is to the flaming fire of Hell.)(37:64-68) Allah states that they will either be eating from the Zaqqum, drinking the Hamim, or being tormented in the Fire, again and again; we seek refuge with Allah from all of this. Allah also said,

(This is the Hell which the criminals denied. They will go between it (Hell) and the fierce boiling water!)(55:43-44),

(Verily, the tree of Zaqqum will be the food of the sinners. Like boiling oil, it will boil in the bellies, like the boiling of scalding water. (It will be said) "Seize him and drag him into the midst of blazing Fire, then pour over his head the torment of boiling water. Taste you (this)! Verily, you were the mighty, the generous! Verily, this is that whereof you used to doubt!")(44:43-50),

(And those on the Left Hand - how (unfortunate) will be those on the Left Hand In fierce hot wind and boiling water, and shadow of black smoke, neither cool nor pleasant.)(56:41-44), and, r

(This is so! And for the Taghun will be an evil final return. Hell! Where they will burn, and worst is that place to rest! This is so! Then let them taste it Hamim and Ghassaq. And other (torments) of similar kind all together!)(38:55-58) There are many other similar Ayat that indicate that the punishment they will receive is of different kinds, and that it is repeated in various types and forms that only Allah the Exalted knows, as just recompense,

(And your Lord is not at all unjust to (His) slaves.) (41:46)

Surah: 14 Ayah: 18

﴿مَّثَلُ ٱلَّذِينَ كَفَرُواْ بِرَبِّهِمْ أَعْمَٰلُهُمْ كَرَمَادٍ ٱشْتَدَّتْ بِهِ ٱلرِّيحُ فِى يَوْمٍ عَاصِفٍ لَّا يَقْدِرُونَ مِمَّا كَسَبُواْ عَلَىٰ شَىْءٍ ذَٰلِكَ هُوَ ٱلضَّلَٰلُ ٱلْبَعِيدُ ۞﴾

18. The parable of those who disbelieved in their Lord is that their works are as ashes, on which the wind blows furiously on a stormy day, they shall not be able to get aught of what they have earned. That is the straying, far away (from the Right Path).

Transliteration

18. Mathalu allatheena kafaroo birabbihim aAAmaluhum karamadin ishtaddat bihi alrreehu fee yawmin AAasifin la yaqdiroona mimma kasaboo AAala shay-in thalika huwa alddalalu albaAAeedu

Tafsir Ibn Kathir

A Parable for the Deeds of the Disbelievers

This is a parable that Allah has given for the deeds and actions of the disbelievers who worshipped others besides Him and rejected His Messengers, thus building their acts on groundless basis. Their actions vanished from them when they were most in need of their rewards. Allah said,

(The parable of those who disbelieved in their Lord is that their works) on the Day of Judgment, when they will seek their rewards from Allah the Exalted. They used to think that they had something, but they will find nothing, except what remains of ashes when a strong wind blows on it,

(on a stormy day;) They will not earn rewards for any of the good works they performed during this life, except what they can preserve of ashes during a day of strong wind. Allah said in other Ayat,

(And We shall turn to whatever deeds they did, and We shall make such deeds as scattered floating particles of dust.)(25:23),

(The parable of what they spend in this world is that of a wind which is extremely cold; it struck the harvest of a people who did wrong against themselves and destroyed it. Allah wronged them not, but they wronged themselves.)(3:117),and,

(O you who believe! Do not render in vain your Sadaqah (charity) by reminders of your generosity or by injury, like him who spends his wealth to be seen of men, and he does not believe in Allah, nor in the Last Day. His parable is that of a smooth rock on which is a little dust; on it falls heavy rain which leaves it bare. They are not able to do anything with what they have earned. And Allah does not guide the disbelieving people.)(2:264) Allah said in this Ayah,

(That is the straying, far away from the right path) meaning, their work and deeds were not based on firm, correct grounds, and thus, they lost their rewards when they needed them the most,

(That is the straying, far away from the right path.)

Surah: 14 Ayah: 19 & Ayah: 20

﴿ أَلَمْ تَرَ أَنَّ اللَّهَ خَلَقَ السَّمَاوَاتِ وَالْأَرْضَ بِالْحَقِّ إِن يَشَأْ يُذْهِبْكُمْ وَيَأْتِ بِخَلْقٍ جَدِيدٍ ﴾

19. Do you not see that Allâh has created the heavens and the earth with truth? If He wills, He can remove you and bring (in your place) a new creation!

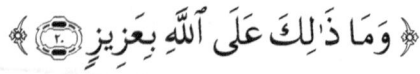

20. And for Allâh that is not hard or difficult.

Transliteration

19. Alam tara anna Allaha khalaqa alssamawati waal-arda bialhaqqi in yasha/ yuthhibkum waya/ti bikhalqin jadeedin   20. Wama thalika AAala Allahi biAAazeezin

Tafsir Ibn Kathir

Proof that Resurrection occurs after Death

Allah affirms His ability to resurrect the bodies on the Day of Resurrection, stating that He has created the heavens and earth which are stronger than the creation of man. Is it not He Who is able to create the heavens, high, wide and strongly built, which include in them the planets and stars and the various heavenly objects and clear signs. Is it not He Who created this earth with all what it contains of land, valleys, mountains, deserts, green fields, barren lands, seas and various shapes, benefits, species and colors of trees, plants and animals

(Do they not see that Allah, Who created the heavens and the earth, and was not wearied by their creation, is able to give life to the dead. Yes, He surely, is able to do all things.)(46:33),

(Does not man see that We have created him from Nutfah (drop of sperm). Yet behold he (stands forth) as an open opponent. And he puts forth for Us a parable, and forgets his own creation. He says: "Who will give life to these bones after they are rotten and have become dust" Say: "He will give life to them Who created them for the first time! And He is the All-Knower of every creation!" He Who produces for you fire out of the green tree, when behold you kindle therewith. Is not He Who created the heavens and the earth, able to create the like of them. Yes, indeed! He is the All-Knowing Supreme Creator. Verily, His command, when He intends a thing, is only that He says to it, "Be!" - and it is! So glorified is He and exalted above all that they associate with Him, and in Whose Hands is the dominion of all things: and to Him you shall be returned.)(36:77-83) Allah's statement,

(If He wills, He can remove you and bring (in your place) a new creation! And for Allah that is not hard or difficult.) means, it is not hard or impossible for Allah to do that. Rather, it is easy for Him, that if you defy His order, He takes you away and brings in your place another creation who is unlike you. Allah said in other Ayat,

(O mankind! It is you who stand in need of Allah. But Allah is Rich, Worthy of all praise. If He willed, He could destroy you and bring about a new creation. And that is not hard for Allah.)(35:15-17),

(And if you turn away, He will exchange you for some other people and they will not be your likes.) (47:38)

(O you who believe! Whoever from among you turns back from his religion, Allah will bring a people whom He will love and they will love Him.)(5:54) and,

(If He wills, He can take you away, O people, and bring others. And Allah is Ever All-Potent over that.)(4:133)

Surah: 14 Ayah: 21

﴿ وَبَرَزُواْ لِلَّهِ جَمِيعًا فَقَالَ ٱلضُّعَفَٰٓؤُاْ لِلَّذِينَ ٱسْتَكْبَرُوٓاْ إِنَّا كُنَّا لَكُمْ تَبَعًا فَهَلْ أَنتُم مُّغْنُونَ عَنَّا مِنْ عَذَابِ ٱللَّهِ مِن شَىْءٍ ۚ قَالُواْ لَوْ هَدَىٰنَا ٱللَّهُ لَهَدَيْنَٰكُمْ ۖ سَوَآءٌ عَلَيْنَآ أَجَزِعْنَآ أَمْ صَبَرْنَا مَا لَنَا مِن مَّحِيصٍ ﴾

21. And they all shall appear before Allâh (on the Day of Resurrection); then the weak will say to those who were arrogant (chiefs): "Verily, we were following you; can you avail us anything from Allâh's Torment?" They will say: "Had Allâh guided us, we would have guided you. It makes no difference to us (now) whether we rage, or bear (these torments) with patience; there is no place of refuge for us."

Transliteration

21. Wabarazoo lillahi jameeAAan faqala algguAAafao lillatheena istakbaroo inna kunna lakum tabaAAan fahal antum mughnoona AAanna min AAathabi Allahi min shay-in qaloo law hadana Allahu lahadaynakum sawaon AAalayna ajaziAAna am sabarna ma lana min maheesin

Tafsir Ibn Kathir

Disbelieving Chiefs and Their Followers will dispute in the Fire

Allah said,

(And they shall appear) meaning, all the creatures, the wicked and the righteous among them, will appear before Allah the One, the Irresistible. They will be gathered on a flat plain that does not have anything those present could use for cover,

(then the weak will say) the followers who used to obey their chiefs, leaders and notables will say,

(to those who were arrogant) who rebelled against worshipping Allah alone without partners and obeying the Messengers,

(Verily, we were following you,), we obeyed your orders and implemented them,

(can you avail us anything against Allah's torment) They will ask, 'can you prevent any of Allah's torment from striking us as you used to promise and vow to us' The leaders will say in response,

`(Had Allah guided us, we would have guided you.) but the statement of our Lord shall come to pass concerning us, and the destiny that He has appointed for us and you shall come true; the word of punishment shall befall the disbelievers,

(It makes no difference to us (now) whether we rage, or bear (these torments) with patience; there is no place of refuge for us.) we have no means of escape from what we are in, whether we face it with patience or grief.' I (Ibn Kathir) say that it appears that this conversation will occur in the Fire after they enter it, just as Allah said in other Ayat,

(And, when they will dispute in the Fire, the weak will say to those who were arrogant: "Verily, we followed you, can you then take from us some portion of the Fire" Those who were arrogant will say: "We are all (together) in this (Fire)! Verily, Allah has judged between (His) servants!")(40:47-48),

((Allah) will say: "Enter you in the company of nations who passed away before you, of men and Jinn, into the Fire." Every time a new nation enters, it curses its sister nation (that went before) until they will be gathered all together in the Fire. The last of them will say to the first of them: "Our Lord! These misled us, so give them a double torment of the Fire." He will say: "For each one there is double (torment), but you know not." The first of them will say to the last of them: "You were not better than us, so taste the torment for what you used to earn.")(7:38-39), and,

(Our Lord! Verily, we obeyed our chiefs and our great ones, and they misled us from the (right) way. Our Lord! Give them a double torment and curse them with a mighty curse!)(33:67-68) Disbelievers will also dispute on the Day of Gathering,

(But if you could see when the wrongdoers will be made to stand before their Lord, how they will cast the (blaming) word one to another! Those who were deemed weak will say to those who were arrogant: "Had it not been for you, we certainly have been believers!" And those who were arrogant will say to those who were deemed weak: "Did we keep you back from guidance after it had come to you. Nay, but you were wrongdoers." Those who were deemed weak will say to those who were arrogant: "Nay, but it was your plotting by night and day: when you ordered us to disbelieve in Allah and set up rivals to Him!" And We shall put iron collars round the necks of those who disbelieved. Are they requited aught except what they used to do)(34:31-33)

Surah: 14 Ayah: 22 & Ayah: 23

﴿ وَقَالَ ٱلشَّيْطَٰنُ لَمَّا قُضِيَ ٱلْأَمْرُ إِنَّ ٱللَّهَ وَعَدَكُمْ وَعْدَ ٱلْحَقِّ وَوَعَدتُّكُمْ فَأَخْلَفْتُكُمْ ۖ وَمَا كَانَ لِىَ عَلَيْكُم مِّن سُلْطَٰنٍ إِلَّآ أَن دَعَوْتُكُمْ فَٱسْتَجَبْتُمْ لِى ۖ فَلَا تَلُومُونِى وَلُومُوٓا۟ أَنفُسَكُم ۖ مَّآ أَنَا۠ بِمُصْرِخِكُمْ وَمَآ أَنتُم بِمُصْرِخِىَّ ۖ إِنِّى كَفَرْتُ بِمَآ أَشْرَكْتُمُونِ مِن قَبْلُ ۗ إِنَّ ٱلظَّٰلِمِينَ لَهُمْ عَذَابٌ أَلِيمٌ ۝ ﴾

22. And Shaitân (Satan) will say when the matter has been decided: "Verily, Allâh promised you a promise of truth. And I too promised you, but I betrayed you. I had no authority over you except that I called you and, you responded to me. So blame me not, but blame yourselves. I cannot help you, nor can you help me. I deny your former act in associating me (Satan) as a partner with Allâh (by obeying me in the life of the world). Verily, there is a painful torment for the Zâlimûn (polytheists and wrong-doers)."

$$\left\{ \text{وَأُدْخِلَ ٱلَّذِينَ ءَامَنُوا۟ وَعَمِلُوا۟ ٱلصَّٰلِحَٰتِ جَنَّٰتٍ تَجْرِى مِن تَحْتِهَا ٱلْأَنْهَٰرُ خَٰلِدِينَ فِيهَا بِإِذْنِ رَبِّهِمْ ۖ تَحِيَّتُهُمْ فِيهَا سَلَٰمٌ } \right\}$$

23. And those who believed (in the Oneness of Allâh and His Messengers and whatever they brought) and did righteous deeds, will be made to enter Gardens under which rivers flow, - to dwell therein for ever (i.e. in Paradise), with the Permission of their Lord. Their greeting therein will be: Salâm (peace!).

Transliteration

22. Waqala alshshaytanu lamma qudiya al-amru inna Allaha waAAadakum waAAda alhaqqi wawaAAadtukum faakhlaftukum wama kana liya AAalaykum min sultanin illa an daAAawtukum faistajabtum lee fala taloomoonee waloomoo anfusakum ma ana bimusrikhikum wama antum bimusrikhiyya innee kafartu bima ashraktumooni min qablu inna alththalimeena lahum AAathabun aleemun 23. Waodkhila allatheena amanoo waAAamiloo alssalihati jannatin tajree min tahtiha al-anharu khalideena feeha bi-ithni rabbihim tahiyyatuhum feeha salamun

Tafsir Ibn Kathir

Shaytan disowns His Followers on the Day of Resurrection

Allah narrates to us what Iblis will say to his followers after Allah finishes with the judgement between His servants, sending the believers to the gardens of Paradise and the disbelievers to the lows (of the Fire). Iblis, may Allah curse him, will stand and address the latter, in order to add depression to their depression, sorrow to their sorrow and grief to their grief. He will declare,

`(Verily, Allah promised you a promise of truth.) by the words of His Messengers that if you follow them, you will gain safety and deliverance. Truly, Allah's promise was true and correct news, while I promised you then betrayed you.' Allah said in another Ayah,

(He (Shaytan) makes promises to them, and arouses in them false desires; and Shaytan's promises are nothing but deceptions.) (4:120)

(I had no authority over you) Shaytan will say, `I had no proof for what I called you to, nor evidence for what I promised you,

(except that I called you, and you responded to me.) even though the Messengers establish the proof and unequivocal evidences against you and affirmed the truth of what they were sent to you with. But you disobeyed the Messengers and ended up earning this fate,

(So blame me not,) today,

(but blame yourselves.), because it is your fault for defying the proofs and following me in the falsehood that I called you to.' Shaytan will say next,

(I cannot help you), I cannot benefit, save, or deliver you from what you are suffering,

(nor can you help me.), nor can you save me and deliver me from the torment and punishment I am suffering,

(I deny your former act of associating me (Shaytan) as a partner with Allah.) or because you associated me with Allah before,' according to Qatadah. Ibn Jarir commented; "I deny being a partner with Allah, the Exalted and Most Honored." This opinion is the most plausible, for Allah said in other Ayat,

(And who is more astray than one who calls on others besides Allah, such as will not answer him till the Day of Resurrection, and who are (even) unaware of their calls to them And when mankind are gathered, they will become their enemies and will deny their worshipping.)(46:5-6) and,

(Nay, but they (the so-called gods) will deny their worship of them, and become opponents to them.)(19:82) Allah said next,

(Verily, the wrongdoers), who deviate from truth and follow falsehood, will earn a painful torment. It appears that this part of the Ayah narrates the speech that Shaytan will deliver to the people of the Fire after they enter it, as we stated. `Amir Ash-Sha`bi said, "On the Day of Resurrection, two speakers will address the people. Allah the Exalted will say to `Isa, son of Maryam,

(Did you say unto men: "Worship me and my mother as two gods besides Allah") (5:116) until,

(Allah will say: "This is a Day on which the truthful will profit from their truth.")(5:119) Shaytan, may Allah curse him, will stand and address the people,

(I had no authority over you except that I called you, and you responded to me.) Allah next mentioned the final destination of the miserable ones, who earned the disgrace and torment and having to listen to Shaytan address them, then He mentioned the final destination of the happy ones,

(And those who believed and did righteous deeds, will be made to enter Gardens under which rivers flow,) wherever they wish them to flow and wherever they may be,

(to dwell therein for ever,) and will never transfer or be transferred from it, (with the permission of their Lord. Their greeting therein will be: "Salam (peace!). ") Allah said in other Ayat,

(Till, when they reach it, and its gates will be opened and its keepers will say: "Salamun `Alaykum (peace be upon you!)") (39:73)

(And angels shall enter unto them from every gate (saying): "Salamun `Alaykum (peace be upon you!).") (13:23-24)

(Therein they shall be met with greetings and the word of peace and respect.) (25:75)

(Their way of request therein will be Subhanaka Allahumma (glory to you, O Allah) and Salam (peace!) will be their greetings therein (Paradise)! And the close of their request will be: Al-Hamdu Lillahi Rabbil-'Alamin (all praise to Allah the Lord of that exists).)(10:10)

Surah: 14 Ayah: 24, Ayah: 25 & Ayah: 26

﴿ أَلَمْ تَرَ كَيْفَ ضَرَبَ ٱللَّهُ مَثَلًا كَلِمَةً طَيِّبَةً كَشَجَرَةٍ طَيِّبَةٍ أَصْلُهَا ثَابِتٌ وَفَرْعُهَا فِى ٱلسَّمَآءِ ﴾

24. See you not how Allâh sets forth a parable? A goodly word as a goodly tree, whose root is firmly fixed, and its branches (reach) to the sky (i.e. very high).

﴿ تُؤْتِى أُكُلَهَا كُلَّ حِينٍ بِإِذْنِ رَبِّهَا ۗ وَيَضْرِبُ ٱللَّهُ ٱلْأَمْثَالَ لِلنَّاسِ لَعَلَّهُمْ يَتَذَكَّرُونَ ﴾

25. Giving its fruit at all times, by the Leave of its Lord, and Allâh sets forth parables for mankind in order that they may remember.

﴿ وَمَثَلُ كَلِمَةٍ خَبِيثَةٍ كَشَجَرَةٍ خَبِيثَةٍ ٱجْتُثَّتْ مِن فَوْقِ ٱلْأَرْضِ مَا لَهَا مِن قَرَارٍ ﴾

26. And the parable of an evil word is that of an evil tree uprooted from the surface of earth having no stability.

Transliteration

24. Alam tara kayfa daraba Allahu mathalan kalimatan tayyibatan kashajaratin tayyibatin asluha thabitun wafarAAuha fee alssama/-i 25. Tu/tee okulaha kulla heenin bi-ithni rabbiha wayadribu Allahu al-amthala lilnnasi laAAallahum yatathakkaroona 26. Wamathalu kalimatin khabeethatin kashajaratin khabeethatin ijtuththat min fawqi al-ardi ma laha min qararin

Tafsir Ibn Kathir

The Parable of the Word of Islam and the Word of Kufr

`Ali bin Abi Talhah reported that `Abdullah bin `Abbas commented that Allah's statement,

(a parable: a goodly word), refers to testifying to La ilaha illallah, (none has the right to be worshipped but Allah) while,

(as a goodly tree), refers to the believer, and that,

Chapter 14: Ibrahim (Abraham), Verses 001-052

(whose root is firmly fixed), indicates that La ilaha illallah, (none has the right to be worshipped but Allah) is firm in the believers' heart,

(and its branches (reach) to the sky.) with which the believer's works are ascended to heaven. Similar is said by Ad-Dahhak, Sa'id bin Jubayr, `Ikrimah, Mujahid and several others. They stated that this parable describes the believer's deeds, good statements and good actions. The believer is just like the beneficial date tree, always having good actions ascending at all times, by day and by night. Al-Bukhari recorded that `Abdullah bin `Umar said, "We were with the Messenger of Allah when he asked,

«أَخْبِرُونِي عَنْ شَجَرَةٍ تُشْبِهُ أَوْ كَالرَّجُلِ الْمُسْلِمِ لَا يَتَحَاتُّ وَرَقُهَا صَيْفًا وَلَا شِتَاءً، وَتُؤْتِي أُكُلَهَا كُلَّ حِينٍ بِإِذْنِ رَبِّهَا»

(Tell me about a tree that resembles the Muslim, the leaves of which do not fall in summer or winter and gives its fruit at all times by the leave of its Lord.)" Ibn `Umar said, "I thought of the date palm tree, but felt shy to answer when I saw that Abu Bakr and `Umar did not talk. When they did not give an answer, the Messenger of Allah said,

«هِيَ النَّخْلَة»

(It is the date palm tree.) When we departed, I said to `Umar, `My father, by Allah! I thought that it was the date tree.' He said, `Why did you not speak then' I said, `I saw you were silent and I felt shy to say anything.' `Umar said, `Had you said it, it would have been more precious to me than such things (i.e., would have been very precious to me).'" `Abdullah bin `Abbas said that,

(as a goodly tree), is a tree in Paradise. Allah said next,

(Giving its fruit at all times,) It is said that it means by day and by night. And they say that describes the believer as a tree that always has fruits during summer and winter, by night and by day. This is the parable of the believer whose good works ascend to heaven by day and by night and at all times,

(by the leave of its Lord,) thus earning perfection and becoming beneficial, plentiful, pure and blessed,

(and Allah sets forth parables for mankind in order that they may remember.) Allah said next,

(And the parable of an evil word is that of an evil tree) describing the disbelief of the disbeliever, for it has no basis or stability. It is similar to the colocynth tree (a very bitter, unscented plant) which is also called, `Ash-Shiryan'. Shu`bah narrated that Mu`awiyah bin Abi Qurrah narrated that Anas bin Malik said that it is the colocynth tree. Allah said, (uprooted), meaning, was cutoff from the root,

(from the surface of earth, having no stability.) therefore, existing without basis or stabililty, just like Kufr (disbelief), for it does not have a basis or roots. Surely, the works of the disbelievers will never ascend nor will any of them be accepted.

Surah: 14 Ayah: 27

﴿ يُثَبِّتُ ٱللَّهُ ٱلَّذِينَ ءَامَنُوا۟ بِٱلْقَوْلِ ٱلثَّابِتِ فِى ٱلْحَيَوٰةِ ٱلدُّنْيَا وَفِى ٱلْءَاخِرَةِ وَيُضِلُّ ٱللَّهُ ٱلظَّـٰلِمِينَ ۚ وَيَفْعَلُ ٱللَّهُ مَا يَشَآءُ ﴾

27. Allâh will keep firm those who believe, with the word that stands firm in this world (i.e. they will keep on worshipping Allâh Alone and none else), and in the Hereafter. And Allâh will cause to go astray those who are Zâlimûn (polytheists and wrong-doers), and Allâh does what He wills.

Transliteration

27. Yuthabbitu Allahu allatheena amanoo bialqawli aththabiti fee alhayati alddunya wafee al-akhirati wayudillu Allahu aththalimeena wayafAAalu Allahu ma yasha/o

Tafsir Ibn Kathir

Allah keeps the Believers Firm in This Life and in the Hereafter with a Word that stands Firm

Al-Bukhari recorded that Al-Bara bin `Azib, may Allah be pleased with him, said that the Messenger of Allah said,

(When the Muslim is questioned in the grave, he will testify that, `La ilaha illallah', and that Muhammad is Allah's Messenger, hence Allah's statement, (Allah will keep firm those who believe, with word that stands firm in this world, and in the Hereafter.) Muslim and the rest of the Group recorded it. Imam Ahmad recorded that Al-Bara bin `Azib said, "We went with the Messenger of Allah to attend a funeral procession of an Ansari man. We reached the grave site when it had not yet been completed. The Messenger of Allah sat, and we sat all around him, as if there were birds hovering above our heads. The Prophet was holding a piece of wood in his hand, poking the ground with it. He next raised his head and said twice or thrice,

«اسْتَعِيذُوا بِاللهِ مِنْ عَذَابِ الْقَبْرِ»

(Seek refuge with Allah from the punishment of the grave.) He said next,

(When a believing slave is reaching the end of his term in the life of this world and the beginning of his term in the Hereafter, a group of angels, whose faces are white and as radiant as the sun, will descend onto him from heaven. They will carry with them white shroud from Paradise, and fragrance for enshrouding from Paradise. They will sit as far from him as the sight goes. Then, the angel of death, will come until he sits

Chapter 14: Ibrahim (Abraham), Verses 001-052   123

right next to his head, saying, "O, good and pure soul! Depart (your body) to Allah's forgiveness and pleasure." So the soul flows (out of its body), just as the drop flows out from the tip of the jug, and the angel of death captures it. When he captures the soul, they (the group of angels) will not leave it with him for more than an instance, and they will seize it and wrap it in that shroud, and in that fragrance. A most pleasant musk scent ever found on the earth, will flow out of the soul, and the angels will ascend it (to heaven). They will not pass by, but they will say, "Whose is this Tayyib (good) soul" They (the angels who are ascending the soul) will reply, "Such person, the son of such and such person," -- calling him by the best names that he used to be called in the world. They will reach the lower heaven and will ask that its door be opened for him, and it will be opened for them. The best residents of every heaven will then see him to the next heaven, until he is brought to the seventh heaven. Allah, the Exalted and Ever High, will say, "List my servants record in `Illiyyin and send him back to earth, for I have created them from it, and into it I shall return them, and from it I shall bring them out once again." The soul will be joined with its body, and two angels will come to him, sit him up and ask him, "Who is your Lord" He will say, "Allah is my Lord." They will ask him, "What is your religion" He will say, "My religion is Islam." They will say to him, "What do you say about this man (Prophet Muhammad) who was sent to you" He will say, "He is the Messenger of Allah." They will ask him, "And what proof do you have about it" He will say, "I read the Book of Allah (the Qur'an), and had faith and belief in him." Then, a caller (Allah) will herald from heaven, "My servant has said the truth. Therefore, furnish him from Paradise, and let him wear from (the clothes of) Paradise, and open a door for him to Paradise." So he is given from Paradise's tranquillity and good scent, and his grave will be expanded for him as far as his sight can reach. Then, a man, with a handsome face and handsome clothes and whose scent is pleasant, will come to him, saying, "Receive the glad tidings with that which pleases you. This is the Day which you were promised." He will ask him, "Who are you; for yours is the face that carries the good news" He will reply, "I am your good works." He will say, "O Lord! Hurry up with the commencement of the Hour, hurry up with the commencement of the Hour, so I can return to my family and my wealth.")

(And when the disbelieving person is reaching the end of his term in the world and the beginning of his term in the Hereafter, there will descend onto him from heaven angels with dark faces. They will bring with them Musuh, and will sit as far from him as the sight reaches. Then the angel of death will come forward and sit right next to his head, saying, "O impure, evil soul! Depart (your body) to the anger of Allah and a wrath from Him." The soul will scatter throughout his body, and the angel of death will seize it as when the thorny branch is removed from wet wool. The angel of death will seize the soul, and when he does, they (the group of angels) will not let it stay in his hand for more than an instance, and they will wrap it in the Musuh. The most putrid smell a dead corpse can ever have on earth will emit from the soul, and the angels will ascend with it. Whenever they pass by a group of angels, they will ask, "Whose is this evil soul" The angels will respond, "He is such person son of such person," -- calling him by the worst names he was known by in the world. When they reach the lowest heaven, they will request that its door be opened for him, and their request will be denied. "For them the gates of heaven will not be opened, and they will not enter Paradise until the camel goes through the eye of the needle." (7:40)

Allah will declare, "List his record in Sijjin in the lowest earth." The wicked soul will then be thrown (from heaven). "And whoever assigns partners to Allah, it is as if he had fallen from the sky, and the birds had snatched him, or the wind had thrown him to a far off place."(22:31) His soul will be returned to his body, and two angels will come to him, sit him up and ask him, "Who is your Lord" He will say, "Oh, oh! I do not know." They will ask him, "What is your religion", and he will say, "Oh, oh! I do not know." They will ask him, "What do you say about this man (Prophet Muhammad) who was sent to you" He will say, "Oh, oh, I do not know!" A caller (Allah) will herald from heaven, "My servant has lied, so furnish him with the Fire and open a door for him to the Fire." He will find its heat and fierce hot wind. And his grave will be reduced in size, until his bones crush each other. Then, a man with a dreadful face, wearing dreadful clothes and with a disgusting smell emitting from him will come to him, saying, "Receive the glad tidings with that which will displease you! This is the Day that you have been promised." He will ask that man, "And who are you, for yours is the face that brings about evil" He will say, "I am your evil work." He will therefore cry, "O, my Lord! Do not commence the Hour!") Abu Dawud and Ibn Majah collected this Hadith. In his Musnad, Imam `Abd bin Humayd recorded that Anas bin Malik said that the Messenger of Allah said,

(Verily, when the servant is placed in his grave and his friends (or family) depart, as he hears the sound of their shoes, two angels will come to him. They will sit him up and ask him, `What do you say about this man (Muhammad)' As for the believer, he will say, `I bear witness that He is Allah's servant and Messenger.' He will be told, `Look at your seat in the Fire, Allah has replaced it for you with a seat in Paradise.') The Prophet said next,

(So he will see both seats.) Qatadah added, "We were told that his grave will be enlarged up to seventy forearms length and will be filled with greenery for him until the Day of Judgement." Muslim collected this Hadith also from `Abd bin Humayd, while An-Nasa'i collected it from Yunus bin Muhammad bin Al-Mu'addah. Al-Hafiz Abu `Isa At-Tirmidhi, may Allah grant him mercy, recorded that Abu Hurayrah said that the Messenger of Allah said,

(When the dead - or one of you - is buried, two dark and blue angels will come to him; one is called `Munkir' and the other is called `Nakir'. They will ask him, `What did you say about this man (Muhammad)' He will reply, `What he used to say, that he is Allah's servant and Messenger. I bear witness that there is no true deity except Allah and that Muhammad is His servant and Messenger.' They will say, `We know that you used to say that,' and his grave will be made larger for him to seventy forearms length by seventy forearms length and will be filled with light for him. He will be told, `Sleep,' but he will reply, `Let me go back to my family in order that I tell them.' They will say, `Sleep, just like the bridegroom who is awakened by the dearest of his family, until Allah resurrects him from that sleep.' If he was a hypocrite, his answer will be, `I do not know! I heard people say something, so I used to repeat what they were saying.' They will say, `We know that you used to say that.' The earth will be commanded, `Come closer all around him,' and it will come closer to him until his ribs cross each other. He will remain in this torment, until Allah resurrects him

Chapter 14: Ibrahim (Abraham), Verses 001-052   *125*

from his sleep.) At-Tirmidhi said, "This Hadith is Hasan, Gharib." Abu Hurayrah narrated that the Messenger of Allah said,

(Allah will keep firm those who believe, with the word that stands firm in this world, and in the Hereafter.)

(When he will be asked in the grave, `Who is your Lord What is your religion Who is your Prophet' He will reply, `Allah is my Lord, Islam is my religion and Muhammad is my Prophet who brought the clear proofs from Allah. I believed in him and had faith in him.' He will be told, `You have said the truth; you have lived on this, died on it and will be resurrected on it.') Ibn Jarir At-Tabari recorded that Abu Hurayrah said that the Prophet said,

(By He Who owns my life! The dead person hears the sound of your slippers (or shoes) when you depart and leave him. If he is a believer, the prayer will stand by his head, Zakah to his right and the fast by his left; the righteous deeds, such as charity, keeping relations with kith and kin and acts of kindness to people will stand by his feet. He will be approached from his head, and the prayer will declare, `No entrance from my side.' He will be approached from his right, and Zakah will declare, `There is no entrance from my side.' He will be approached from his left, and the fast will declare, `There is no entrance from my side.' He will be approached from his feet, and the acts of righteousness will declare, `There is no entrance from our side.' He will be commanded to sit up, and he will sit up while the sun appears to him just like when it is about to set. He will be told, `Tell us about what we are going to ask you.' He will say, `Leave me until I pray.' He will be told, `You will pray, but first tell us what we want to know.' He will ask, `What are your questions' He will be told, `This man who was sent among you, what do you say about him and what is your testimony about him' He will ask, `Muhammad' He will be answered in the positive and he will reply, `I bear witness that he is the Messenger of Allah and that he has brought us the proofs from our Lord. We believed in him.' He will be told, `This is the way you lived and died and Allah willing, you will be resurrected on it.' His grave will be made wider for him seventy forearms length, and it will be filled with light. A door will also be opened for him to Paradise. He will be told, `Look at what Allah has prepared for you in it.' He will increase in joy and delight and then his soul will be placed with the pure souls, inside green birds eating from the trees of Paradise. The body will be returned to its origin, dust. So Allah said,

(Allah will keep firm those who believe, with the word that stands firm in this world, and in the Hereafter.)) Ibn Hibban collected this Hadith, and his narration added the disbeliever's answer and his torment. `Abdur-Razzaq recorded that Tawus said,

(Allah will keep firm those who believe, with the word that stands firm in this world,) is in reference to La ilaha ilallah, while,

(and in the Hereafter) is in reference to the questioning in the grave. Qatadah commented, "As for this life, Allah will make them firm on the way of righteousness and good deeds,

(and in the Hereafter.) in the grave." Several others among the Salaf said the same.

Surah: 14 Ayah: 28, Ayah: 29 & Ayah: 30

﴿ ● أَلَمْ تَرَ إِلَى ٱلَّذِينَ بَدَّلُواْ نِعْمَتَ ٱللَّهِ كُفْرًا وَأَحَلُّواْ قَوْمَهُمْ دَارَ ٱلْبَوَارِ ﴿٢٨﴾ ﴾

28. Have you not seen those who have changed the Blessings of Allâh into disbelief (by denying Prophet Muhammad (peace be upon him) and his Message of Islâm), and caused their people to dwell in the house of destruction?

﴿ جَهَنَّمَ يَصْلَوْنَهَا وَبِئْسَ ٱلْقَرَارُ ﴿٢٩﴾ ﴾

29. Hell, in which they will burn, - and what an evil place to settle in!

﴿ وَجَعَلُواْ لِلَّهِ أَندَادًا لِّيُضِلُّواْ عَن سَبِيلِهِۦ قُلْ تَمَتَّعُواْ فَإِنَّ مَصِيرَكُمْ إِلَى ٱلنَّارِ ﴿٣٠﴾ ﴾

30. And they set up rivals to Allâh, to mislead (men) from His Path! Say: "Enjoy (your brief life)! But certainly, your destination is the (Hell) Fire!"

Transliteration

28. Alam tara ila allatheena baddaloo niAAmata Allahi kufran waahalloo qawmahum dara albawari 29. Jahannama yaslawnaha wabi/sa alqararu 30. WajaAAaloo lillahi andadan liyudilloo AAan sabeelihi qul tamattaAAoo fa-inna maseerakum ila alnnari

Tafsir Ibn Kathir

The Recompense of Those Who have changed the Blessings of Allah into Disbelief

Al-Bukhari said, "Allah's statement,

Have you not seen those who have changed the blessings of Allâh into disbelief..., means, do you have knowledge in. Allâh said in other Ayât,

(Saw you not how.) and,

(Did you not think of those who went forth.)

(A lost people) (25:18) Ali bin `Abdullah narrated that Sufyan said that `Amr said that `Ata said that he heard Ibn `Abbas saying that,

"(Have you not seen those who have changed the blessings of Allah into disbelief), is in reference to the people of Makkah." Ibn Abi Hatim recorded that Abu At-Tufayl said that Ibn Al-Kawwa' asked `Ali about Allah's statement,

(those who have changed the blessings of Allah into disbelief, and caused their people to dwell in the house of destruction) and `Ali said that it refers to the disbelievers of Quraysh on the day of Badr. He also said that the blessing of Allah was faith that came to the polytheists of Quraysh, and they changed this blessing into disbelief and led their people to utter destruction. This includes all disbelievers, for Allah sent Muhammad as a mercy and a blessing to all mankind. Those who accepted this blessing and were thankful for it, will enter Paradise, while those who denied it and disbelieved in it, will enter the Fire. Allah said next,

(And they set up rivals to Allah, to mislead from His path!) meaning, they set up partners to Allah whom they worship besides Him and called the people to worship them. Allah threatened them and warned them by the words of His Prophet ,

(Say: "Enjoy (your brief life)! But certainly, your destination is the (Hell) Fire!") `Whatever you are able to do in this life, then do it, for no matter what will happen,

(But certainly, your destination is the (Hell) Fire!) for to Us will be your destination and end.' Allah said in other Ayat,

(We let them enjoy for a little while, then in the end We shall force them to (enter) a great torment.)(31:24) and,

((A brief) enjoyment in this world! And then unto Us will be their return, then We shall make them taste the severest torment because they used to disbelieve.)(10:70)

Surah: 14 Ayah: 31

﴿ قُل لِّعِبَادِىَ ٱلَّذِينَ ءَامَنُوا۟ يُقِيمُوا۟ ٱلصَّلَوٰةَ وَيُنفِقُوا۟ مِمَّا رَزَقْنَٰهُمْ سِرًّا وَعَلَانِيَةً مِّن قَبْلِ أَن يَأْتِىَ يَوْمٌ لَّا بَيْعٌ فِيهِ وَلَا خِلَٰلٌ ﴾

31. Say (O Muhammad (peace be upon him)) to 'Ibâdî (My slaves) who have believed, that they should perform As-Salât (Iqâmat-as-Salât), and spend in charity out of the sustenance We have given them, secretly and openly, before the coming of a Day on which there will be neither mutual bargaining nor befriending.

Transliteration

31. Qul liAAibadiya allatheena amanoo yuqeemoo alssalata wayunfiqoo mimma razaqnahum sirran waAAalaniyatan min qabli an ya/tiya yawmun la bayAAun feehi wala khilalun

Tafsir Ibn Kathir

The Command for Prayer and Charity

Allah orders His servants to obey Him, fulfill His rights and be kind to His creatures. He ordained the prayer, which affirms the worship of Allah alone, without partners, and to spend from the provisions that He has granted them, by paying the due Zakah, spending on relatives and being kind to all others. Establishing the prayer requires performing it on time, perfectly, preserving its act of bowing having humility during it, and preserving its prostrations. Allah has ordained spending from what He granted, in secret and public, so that the people save themselves, (before the coming of a Day), the Day of Resurrection,

(on which there will be neither mutual bargaining nor befriending.) on which no ransom will be accepted from anyone, if he seeks to buy himself. Allah said in another Ayah,

(So this Day no ransom shall be taken from you, nor of those who disbelieved.) (57:15) Allah said here,

(nor befriending.) Ibn Jarir commented, "Allah says that on that Day, there will be no friendship between friends that might save those deserving punishment from it. Rather, on that Day, there will be fairness and justice." Qatadah said, "Allah knows that in this life, there is mutual bargaining and there are friendships which people benefit from. A man chooses his friends and the reasons behind befriending them; if it was for Allah's sake, their friendship should be maintained, but if it was for other than Allah, their friendship is bound to be cutoff." I say that the meaning of this, is that Allah the Exalted is declaring that on that Day, no mutual bargaining or ransom will avail anyone, even if he ransoms himself with the earth's fill of gold if he could find that amount! No friendship or intercession shall avail one if he meets Allah while a disbeliever. Allah the Exalted said,

(And fear the Day when no person shall avail another, nor shall compensation be accepted from him, nor shall intercession be of use to him, nor shall they be helped.)(2:123) and,

(O you believe! Spend of that with which We have provided for you, before a Day comes when there will be no bargaining, nor friendship, nor intercession. And it is the disbelievers who are the wrongdoers.)(2:254)

Surah: 14 Ayah: 32, Ayah: 33 & Ayah: 34

﴿ ٱللَّهُ ٱلَّذِى خَلَقَ ٱلسَّمَٰوَٰتِ وَٱلْأَرْضَ وَأَنزَلَ مِنَ ٱلسَّمَآءِ مَآءً فَأَخْرَجَ بِهِۦ مِنَ ٱلثَّمَرَٰتِ رِزْقًا لَّكُمْ ۖ وَسَخَّرَ لَكُمُ ٱلْفُلْكَ لِتَجْرِىَ فِى ٱلْبَحْرِ بِأَمْرِهِۦ ۖ وَسَخَّرَ لَكُمُ ٱلْأَنْهَٰرَ ﴿٣٢﴾ ﴾

32. Allâh is He Who has created the heavens and the earth and sends down water (rain) from the sky, and thereby brought forth fruits as provision for you; and He has made the ships to be of service to you, that they may sail through the sea by His Command; and He has made rivers (also) to be of service to you.

﴿ وَسَخَّرَ لَكُمُ ٱلشَّمْسَ وَٱلْقَمَرَ دَآئِبَيْنِ ۖ وَسَخَّرَ لَكُمُ ٱلَّيْلَ وَٱلنَّهَارَ ﴿٣٣﴾ ﴾

33. And He has made the sun and the moon, both constantly pursuing their courses, to be of service to you; and He has made the night and the day, to be of service to you.

﴿ وَءَاتَىٰكُم مِّن كُلِّ مَا سَأَلْتُمُوهُ ۚ وَإِن تَعُدُّواْ نِعْمَتَ ٱللَّهِ لَا تُحْصُوهَآ ۗ إِنَّ ٱلْإِنسَـٰنَ لَظَلُومٌ كَفَّارٌ ﴾

34. And He gave you of all that you asked for, and if you count the Blessings of Allâh, never will you be able to count them. Verily! Man is indeed an extreme wrong-doer, a disbeliever (an extreme ingrate, who denies Allâh's Blessings by disbelief, and by worshipping others besides Allâh, and by disobeying Allâh and His Prophet Muhammad (peace be upon him))

Transliteration

32. Allahu allathee khalaqa alssamawati waal-arda waanzala mina alssama-i maan faakhraja bihi mina alththamarati rizqan lakum wasakhkhara lakumu alfulka litajriya fee albahri bi-amrihi wasakhkhara lakumu al-anhara 33. Wasakhkhara lakumu alshshamsa waalqamara da-ibayni wasakhkhara lakumu allayla waalnnahara 34. Waatakum min kulli ma saaltumoohu wa-in taAAuddoo niAAmata Allahi la tuhsooha inna alinsana lathaloomun kaffarun

Tafsir Ibn Kathir

Describing Some of Allah's Tremendous Favors

Allah mentions some of the favors He has done for His creatures, such as creating the heavens as a protective ceiling and the earth as a bed. He also sends down rain from the sky and, in its aftermath brings forth a variety of vegetation, fruits and plants of different colors, shapes, tastes, scents and uses. Allah also made the ships sail on the surface of the water by His command and He made the sea able to carry these ships in order that travelers can transfer from one area to another to transport goods. Allah also created the rivers that flow through the earth from one area to another as provision for the servants which they use to drink and irrigate, and for other benefits,

(And He has made the sun and the moon, both constantly pursuing their courses), rotating by night and by day,

(It is not for the sun to overtake the moon, nor does the night outstrip the day. They all float, each in an orbit.)(36:40) and,

(He brings the night as a cover over the day, seeking it rapidly, and (He created) the sun, the moon, the stars subjected to His command. His is the creation and commandment. Blessed is Allah, the Lord of all that exists!) (7:54) The sun and the moon rotate in succession, and the night and the day are opposites, each taking from the length of the other or giving up some of its length,

((Allah) merges the night into day, and merges the day into night.) (35:13) and,

(And He has subjected the sun and the moon. Each running (on a fixed course) for an appointed term. Verily, He is the Almighty, the Oft-Forgiving.) (39:5) Allah said next,

(And He gave you of all that you asked for), He has prepared for you all that you need in all conditions, and what you ask Him to provide for you,

(and if you (try to) count the blessings of Allah, never will you be able to count them.) Allah states that the servants are never able to count His blessings, let alone thank Him duly for them. In Sahih Al-Bukhari it is recorded that the Messenger of Allah used to supplicate;

»اللَّهُمَّ لَكَ الْحَمْدُ غَيْرَ مَكْفِيٍّ وَلَا مُوَدَّعٍ وَلَا مُسْتَغْنًى عَنْهُ رَبَّنَا«

(O Allah! All praise is due to You, without being able to sufficiently thank You, nor ever wish to be cutoff from You, nor ever feeling rich from relying on You; our Lord!) It was reported that Prophet Dawud, peace be upon him, used to say in his supplication, "O Lord! How can I ever duly thank You, when my thanking You is also a favor from You to me" Allah the Exalted answered him, "Now, you have thanked Me sufficiently, O Dawud," meaning, `when you admitted that you will never be able to duly thank Me.'

Surah: 14 Ayah: 35 & Ayah: 36

﴿ وَإِذْ قَالَ إِبْرَاهِيمُ رَبِّ اجْعَلْ هَذَا الْبَلَدَ ءَامِنًا وَاجْنُبْنِي وَبَنِيَّ أَن نَّعْبُدَ الْأَصْنَامَ ﴿٣٥﴾

35. And (remember) when Ibrâhim (Abraham) said: "O my Lord! Make this city (Makkah) one of peace and security, and keep me and my sons away from worshipping idols.

﴿ رَبِّ إِنَّهُنَّ أَضْلَلْنَ كَثِيرًا مِّنَ النَّاسِ ۖ فَمَن تَبِعَنِي فَإِنَّهُ مِنِّي ۖ وَمَنْ عَصَانِي فَإِنَّكَ غَفُورٌ رَّحِيمٌ ﴿٦﴾

36. "O my Lord! They have indeed led astray many among mankind. But whoso follows me, he verily is of me. And whoso disobeys me, still You are indeed Oft-Forgiving, Most Merciful.

Transliteration

35. Wa-ith qala ibraheemu rabbi ijAAal hatha albalada aminan waojnubnee wabaniyya an naAAbuda al-asnama 36. Rabbi innahunna adlalna katheeran mina alnnasi faman tabiAAanee fa-innahu minnee waman AAasanee fa-innaka ghafoorun raheemun

Tafsir Ibn Kathir

Ibrahim's Supplication to Allah when He brought Isma`il to Makkah

Allah mentions here, while bringing forth more evidences against Arab polytheists, that the Sacred House in Makkah was established on the worship of Allah alone,

Chapter 14: Ibrahim (Abraham), Verses 001-052

without partners. He also states that Ibrahim, who establsihed the city, has disowned those who worship others besides Allah, and that he begged Allah to make Makkah peaceful and secure,

(O my Lord! Make this city (Makkah) of peace and security,) and Allah accepted his supplication. Allah said in other Ayat,

(Have they not seen that We have made (Makkah) a secure sanctuary.) (29:67) and,

(Verily, the first House (of worship) appointed for mankind was that at Bakkah (Makkah), full of blessing, and a guidance for Al-'Alamin. In it are manifest signs, the Maqam of Ibrahim; whosoever enters it, he attains security.)(3:96) Allah said here that Ibrahim supplicated,

(O my Lord! Make this city (Makkah) a of peace and security,) saying, "this city", after he established it, and this is why he said afterwards,

(All praise is due to Allah, Who has given me in old age Isma`il and Ishaq.) (14:39) It is well-known that Isma`il was thirteen years older than Ishaq. When Ibrahim took Isma`il and his mother to Makkah, while Isma`il was still young enough to nurse, he supplicated to Allah,

(O my Lord! Make this city (Makkah) a place of peace and security.) (2:126) as we in explained in Surat Al-Baqarah. Ibrahim then said,

(and keep me and my sons away from worshipping idols.) It is proper for whoever supplicates to Allah to also ask for the benefit of his parents and offspring, as well as himself. Ibrahim next mentioned that many among mankind were led astray because of idols, and he disowned those who worship them and referred their matter to Allah; if Allah wills, He will punish them, and if He wills, He will forgive them. `Isa, peace be upon him, said similar words,

(If You punish them, they are Your servants, and if You forgive them, verily, You, only You are the Almighty, the All-Wise.)(5:118) This supplication refers this and all matters to Allah, not that it is actually going to happen. `Abdullah bin `Amr narrated that the Messenger of Allah recited Ibrahim's supplication,

(O my Lord! They have indeed led astray many among mankind.), and the supplication of `Isa,

(If You punish them, they are Your servants.) (5:118) then raised his hands and said,

«اللَّهُمَّ أُمَّتِي، اللَّهُمَّ أُمَّتِي، اللَّهُمَّ أُمَّتِي»

(O Allah, Save my Ummah! O, Allah, Save my Ummah! O, Allah, Save my Ummah!) and cried. Allah said to the angel Jibril, "O Jibril, go to Muhammad, and Your Lord has more knowledge, and ask him what makes him cry." Jibril came to the Prophet and asked him, and he repeated to him what he said (in his supplication). Allah said, "Go to Muhammad and tell him this; 'We will make you pleased with your Ummah, O Muhammad, and will not treat them in a way you dislike.'"

Surah: 14 Ayah: 37

﴿ رَبَّنَآ إِنِّى أَسْكَنتُ مِن ذُرِّيَّتِى بِوَادٍ غَيْرِ ذِى زَرْعٍ عِندَ بَيْتِكَ ٱلْمُحَرَّمِ رَبَّنَا لِيُقِيمُوا۟ ٱلصَّلَوٰةَ فَٱجْعَلْ أَفْـِٔدَةً مِّنَ ٱلنَّاسِ تَهْوِىٓ إِلَيْهِمْ وَٱرْزُقْهُم مِّنَ ٱلثَّمَرَٰتِ لَعَلَّهُمْ يَشْكُرُونَ ﴾

37. "O our Lord! I have made some of my offspring to dwell in an uncultivable valley by Your Sacred House (the Ka'bah at Makkah) in order, O our Lord, that they may perform As-Salât (Iqâmat-as-Salât). So fill some hearts among men with love towards them, and (O Allâh) provide them with fruits so that they may give thanks.

Transliteration

37. Rabbana innee askantu min thurriyyatee biwadin ghayri thee zarAAin AAinda baytika almuharrami rabbana liyuqeemoo alssalata faijAAal af-idatan mina alnnasi tahwee ilayhim waorzuqhum mina aththamarati laAAallahum yashkuroona

Tafsir Ibn Kathir

This Ayah indicates that this was different supplication than the first one that Ibrahim said when he left Hajar and her son Isma`il in Makkah, before the Sacred House was built. This prayer, it appears, was said after the House was built, begging Allah and seeking His favor, and He is the Exalted and Most Honored. Ibrahim said here,

(by Your Sacred House...) then he,

(O our Lord, that they may perform Salah.) Ibn Jarir At-Tabari commented that this, "Refers to his earlier statement,

(the Sacred...)," meaning, `You have made this House Sacred so that people establish the prayer next to it,'

(So fill some hearts among men with love towards them,) Ibn `Abbas, Mujahid and Sa'id bin Jubayr said, "Had Ibrahim said, `The hearts of mankind', Persians, Romans, the Jews, the Christians and all other people would have gathered around it." However, Ibrahim said,

(among men), thus making it exclusive to Muslims only. He said next,

(and (O Allah) provide them with fruits) in order that they may be helped in obeying You, and because this is a barren valley; bring to them fruits that they might eat. Allah accepted Ibrahim's supplication,

(Have We not established for them a secure sanctuary (Makkah), to which are brought fruits of all kinds, a provision from Ourselves.) (28:57) This only indicates Allah's compassion, kindness, mercy and blessing, in that there are no fruit producing trees in the Sacred City, Makkah, yet all kinds of fruits are being brought to it from all around; this is how Allah accepted the supplication of the Khalil - Allah's intimate friend, Prophet Ibrahim, peace be upon him.

Surah: 14 Ayah: 38, Ayah: 39, Ayah: 40 & Ayah: 41

﴿ رَبَّنَآ إِنَّكَ تَعْلَمُ مَا نُخْفِى وَمَا نُعْلِنُ ۗ وَمَا يَخْفَىٰ عَلَى ٱللَّهِ مِن شَىْءٍ فِى ٱلْأَرْضِ وَلَا فِى ٱلسَّمَآءِ ﴾ ﴿٣٨﴾

38. "O our Lord! Certainly, You know what we conceal and what we reveal. Nothing on the earth or in the heaven is hidden from Allâh.

﴿ ٱلْحَمْدُ لِلَّهِ ٱلَّذِى وَهَبَ لِى عَلَى ٱلْكِبَرِ إِسْمَـٰعِيلَ وَإِسْحَـٰقَ ۚ إِنَّ رَبِّى لَسَمِيعُ ٱلدُّعَآءِ ﴾ ﴿٣٩﴾

39. "All the praises and thanks are to Allâh, Who has given me in old age Ismâ'îl (Ishmael) and Ishâq (Isaac). Verily! My Lord is indeed the All-Hearer of invocations.

﴿ رَبِّ ٱجْعَلْنِى مُقِيمَ ٱلصَّلَوٰةِ وَمِن ذُرِّيَّتِى ۚ رَبَّنَا وَتَقَبَّلْ دُعَآءِ ﴾ ﴿٤٠﴾

40. "O my Lord! Make me one who performs As-Salât (Iqâmat-as-Salât), and (also) from my offspring, our Lord! And accept my invocation.

﴿ رَبَّنَا ٱغْفِرْ لِى وَلِوَٰلِدَىَّ وَلِلْمُؤْمِنِينَ يَوْمَ يَقُومُ ٱلْحِسَابُ ﴾ ﴿٤١﴾

41. "Our Lord! Forgive me and my parents, and (all) the believers on the Day when the reckoning will be established."

Transliteration

38. Rabbana innaka taAAlamu ma nukhfee wama nuAAlinu wama yakhfa AAala Allahi min shay-in fee al-ardi wala fee alssama/-i 39. Alhamdu lillahi allathee wahaba lee AAala alkibari ismaAAeela wa-ishaqa inna rabbee lasameeAAu aldduAAa/-i 40. Rabbi ijAAalnee muqeema alssalati wamin thurriyyatee rabbana wtaqabbal duAAa/-i 41. Rabbana ighfir lee waliwalidayya walilmu/mineena yawma yaqoomu alhisabu

Tafsir Ibn Kathir

Ibn Jarir At-Tabari said, "Allah said that Ibrahim, His Khalil, said,

(O our Lord! Certainly, You know what we conceal and what we reveal.) meaning, `You know the intention behind my supplication for the people of this town, seeking Your pleasure in sincerity to You. You know all things, apparent and hidden, and nothing escapes Your knowledge on the earth or in heaven.'" He next praised and thanked his Lord the Exalted and Most Honored for granting him offspring after he became old,

(All praise is due to Allah, Who has given me in old age Isma'il (Ishmael) and Ishaq (Isaac). Verily, my Lord is indeed the All-Hearer of invocations.) `He accepts the supplication of those who invoke Him, and has accepted my invocation when I asked Him to grant me offspring. ' Ibrahim said next,

(O my Lord! Make me one who performs Salah,), preserving its obligations and limits,

(and (also) from my offspring,), make them among those who establish the prayer, as well,

(our Lord! And accept my invocation.), all of my invocation which I invoked You with herein,

(Our Lord! Forgive me and my parents,) Ibrahim said this before he declared himself innocent from his father, after he became sure that he was an enemy of Allah,

(and the believers), all of them,

(on the Day when the reckoning will be established.) on the Day when You will reckon Your servants and recompense or reward them for their deeds - good for good and evil for evil.

Surah: 14 Ayah: 42 & Ayah: 43

﴿ وَلَا تَحْسَبَنَّ ٱللَّهَ غَافِلاً عَمَّا يَعْمَلُ ٱلظَّالِمُونَ ۚ إِنَّمَا يُؤَخِّرُهُمْ لِيَوْمٍ تَشْخَصُ فِيهِ ٱلْأَبْصَـٰرُ ﴿٤٢﴾

42. Consider not that Allâh is unaware of that which the Zâlimûn (polytheists, wrong-doers) do, but He gives them respite up to a Day when the eyes will stare in horror.

﴿ مُهْطِعِينَ مُقْنِعِى رُءُوسِهِمْ لَا يَرْتَدُّ إِلَيْهِمْ طَرْفُهُمْ وَأَفْـِٔدَتُهُمْ هَوَآءٌ ﴿٤٣﴾

43. (They will be) hastening forward with necks outstretched, their heads raised up (towards the sky), their gaze returning not towards them and their hearts empty (from thinking because of extreme fear).

Transliteration

42. Wala tahsabanna Allaha ghafilan AAamma yaAAmalu aththalimoona innama yu-akhkhiruhum liyawmin tashkhasu feehi al-absaru   43. MuhtiAAeena muqniAAee ruoosihim la yartaddu ilayhim tarfuhum waaf-idatuhum hawa/on

Chapter 14: Ibrahim (Abraham), Verses 001-052 135

Tafsir Ibn Kathir

Allah gives Respite to the Disbelievers and is never unaware of what They do

Allah says, `O Muhammad, do not think that Allah is unaware of what the unjust disbelievers do. Do not think because Allah gave them respite and delayed their punishment that He is unaware or ignoring punishing them for what they do. Rather, Allah keeps full account of this for them and keeps it on record against them,

(but He gives them respite up to a Day when the eyes will stare in horror.) from the horror of the Day of Resurrection.' Allah next mentions how they will all be raised up from their graves and hurriedly gathered for the Day of Gathering,

(hastening forward), in a hurry. Allah said in other Ayat,

(Hastening towards the caller.) (54:8)

(On that Day mankind will follow strictly Allah's caller, no crookedness will they show him.) (20:108) until,

(And (all) faces shall be humbled before the Ever Living, the Sustainer.) (20:111) Allah said: another Ayah,

(The Day when they will come out of the graves quickly.) (70:43) Allah said next,

(with necks outstretched) meaning, raising their heads up, according to Ibn `Abbas, Mujahid and several others. Allah said next,

(their gaze returning not towards them) meaning, their eyes are staring in confusion, trying not to blink because of the horror and tremendous insights they are experiencing, and fear of what is going to strike them, we seek refuge with Allah from this end. This is why Allah said,

(and their hearts empty.) meaning, their hearts are empty due to extreme fear and fright. Qatadah and several others said that the places of their hearts are empty then, because the hearts will ascend to the throats due to extreme fear. Allah said next to His Messenger ,

Surah: 14 Ayah: 44, Ayah: 45 & Ayah: 46

﴿ وَأَنذِرِ ٱلنَّاسَ يَوْمَ يَأْتِيهِمُ ٱلْعَذَابُ فَيَقُولُ ٱلَّذِينَ ظَلَمُوا۟ رَبَّنَآ أَخِّرْنَآ إِلَىٰٓ أَجَلٍ قَرِيبٍ نُّجِبْ دَعْوَتَكَ وَنَتَّبِعِ ٱلرُّسُلَ ۗ أَوَلَمْ تَكُونُوٓا۟ أَقْسَمْتُم مِّن قَبْلُ مَا لَكُم مِّن زَوَالٍ ﴿٤٤﴾ ﴾

44. And warn (O Muhammad (peace be upon him)) mankind of the Day when the torment will come unto them; then the wrong-doers will say: "Our Lord! Respite us for a little while, we will answer Your Call and follow the Messengers!" (It will

be said): "Had you not sworn aforetime that you would not leave (the world for the Hereafter).

﴿ وَسَكَنتُمْ فِى مَسَـٰكِنِ ٱلَّذِينَ ظَلَمُوٓاْ أَنفُسَهُمْ وَتَبَيَّنَ لَكُمْ كَيْفَ فَعَلْنَا بِهِمْ وَضَرَبْنَا لَكُمُ ٱلْأَمْثَالَ ﴾

45. "And you dwelt in the dwellings of men who wronged themselves, and it was clear to you how We had dealt with them. And We put forth (many) parables for you."

﴿ وَقَدْ مَكَرُواْ مَكْرَهُمْ وَعِندَ ٱللَّهِ مَكْرُهُمْ وَإِن كَانَ مَكْرُهُمْ لِتَزُولَ مِنْهُ ٱلْجِبَالُ ﴾

46. Indeed, they planned their plot, and their plot was with Allâh, though their plot was not such as to remove the mountains (real mountains or the Islâmic law) from their places (as it is of no importance) (Tafsir Ibn Kathir).

Transliteration

44. Waanthiri alnnasa yawma ya/teehimu alAAathabu fayaqoolu allatheena thalamoo rabbana akhkhirna ila ajalin qareebin nujib daAAwataka wanattabiAAi alrrusula awa lam takoonoo aqsamtum min qablu ma lakum min zawalin 45. Wasakantum fee masakini allatheena thalamoo anfusahum watabayyana lakum kayfa faAAalna bihim wadarabna lakumu al-amthala 46. Waqad makaroo makrahum waAAinda Allahi makruhum wa-in kana makruhum litazoola minhu aljibalu

Tafsir Ibn Kathir

There will be no Respite after the Coming of the Torment

Allah mentions what those who committed injustice against themselves will say when they witness the torment,

(Our Lord! Respite us for a little while, we will answer Your call and follow the Messengers!) Allah said in other Ayat,

(Until, when death comes to one of them, he says: "My Lord! Send me back.")(23:99) and,

(O you who believe! Let not your properties divert you.) (63:9-10) Allah described the condition of the wrongdoers on the Day of Gathering, when He said,

(And if you only could see when the criminals shall hang their heads.) (32:12),

(If you could but see when they will be held over the Fire! They will say: "Would that we were but sent back (to the world)! Then we would not deny the Ayat of Our Lord...."!) (6:27) and,

(Therein they will cry.) (35:27) Allah refuted their statement here,

(Had you not sworn aforetime that you would not leave.) Allah says, `Had you not vowed before, that your previous state will not change, that there will be no Resurrection or Reckoning Therefore, taste this torment because of what you vowed before.' Mujahid commented that,

(that you would not leave.) refers to leaving this worldly life to the Hereafter. Allah also said,

(And they swear by Allah with their strongest oaths, that Allah will not raise up him who dies.) (16:38) Allah said next,

(And you dwelt in the dwellings of men who wronged themselves, and it was clear to you how We had dealt with them. And We put forth (many) parables for you.) Allah says, `you have witnessed or heard of the news of what happened to the earlier disbelieving nations, but you did not draw a lesson from their end, nor did what We punished them with provide an example for you,'

(Perfect wisdom but the warners benefit then not.)(54:5) Shu`bah narrated that Abu Ishaq said that `Abdur-Rahman bin Dabil said that `Ali bin Abi Talib commented on Allah's statement,

(though their plot was not such as to remove the mountains from their places.) "He who disputed with Ibrahim about his Lord, took two eaglets and raised them until they became adult eagles. Then he tied each eagle's leg to a wooden box with ropes and left them go hungry. He and another man sat inside the wooden box and raised a staff with a piece of meat on its tip. So, the two eagles started flying. The king asked his companion to tell him what he was seeing, and he described the scenes to him, until he said that he saw the earth as a fly. So, the king brought the staff closer to the eagles and they started landing slowly. This is why Allah said, `though their plot was hardly one to remove the mountains from their places."' Mujahid also mentioned that this story was about Nebuchadnezzar, and that when the king's sight was far away from earth and its people, he was called, `O tyrant one! Where are you headed to' He became afraid and brought the staff closer to the eagles, which flew faster with such haste that the mountains almost shook from the noise they made. The mountains were almost moved from their places, so Allah said,

(though their plot was not such as to remove the mountains from their places.)" Ibn Jurayj narrated that Mujahid recited this Ayah in a way that means, "though their plot was such as to remove the mountains from their places." However, Al-`Awfi reported that Ibn `Abbas said that,

(though their plot was not such as to remove the mountains from their places.) indicates that their plot was not such as to remove the mountains from their places. Similar was said by Al-Hasan Al-Basri. Ibn Jarir reasoned that, "Associating others with Allah and disbelieving in Him, which they brought upon themselves, did not bother the mountains nor other creatures. Rather, the harm of their actions came to haunt them." I (Ibn Kathir) said, this meaning is similar to Allah's statement,

(And walk not on the earth with conceit and arrogance. Verily, you can neither rend nor penetrate the earth, nor can you attain a stature like the mountains in height.)(17:37) There is another way of explaining this Ayah; `Ali bin Abi Talhah reported that Ibn `Abbas said that,

(though their plot was not such as to remove the mountains from their places.) refers to their Shirk, for Allah said in another Ayah,

(Whereby the heavens are almost torn.) (19:90) Ad-Dahhak and Qatadah said similarly.

Surah: 14 Ayah: 47 & Ayah: 48

﴿ فَلَا تَحْسَبَنَّ ٱللَّهَ مُخْلِفَ وَعْدِهِۦ رُسُلَهُۥٓ إِنَّ ٱللَّهَ عَزِيزٌ ذُو ٱنتِقَامٍ ۞ ﴾

47. So think not that Allâh will fail to keep His Promise to His Messengers. Certainly, Allâh is All-Mighty, All-Able of Retribution.

﴿ يَوْمَ تُبَدَّلُ ٱلْأَرْضُ غَيْرَ ٱلْأَرْضِ وَٱلسَّمَـٰوَٰتُ وَبَرَزُوا۟ لِلَّهِ ٱلْوَٰحِدِ ٱلْقَهَّارِ ۞ ﴾

48. On the Day when the earth will be changed to another earth and so will be the heavens, and they (all creatures) will appear before Allâh, the One, the Irresistible.

Transliteration

47. Fala tahsabanna Allaha mukhlifa waAAdihi rusulahu inna Allaha AAazeezun thoo intiqamin 48. Yawma tubaddalu al-ardu ghayra al-ardi waalssamawatu wabarazoo lillahi alwahidi alqahhari

Tafsir Ibn Kathir

Allah never breaks a Promise

Allah affirms His promise,

(So think not that Allah will fail to keep His promise to His Messengers.) His promise to grant them victory in this life and on the Day when the Witnesses shall come forth. Allah affirms that He is All-Able and that nothing He wills escapes His power and none can resist Him. Allah affirms that He is Able to exact retribution from those who disbelieve in Him and deny Him,

(Woe that Day to the deniers!)(77:15) Allah said here,

(On the Day when the earth will be changed to another earth and so will be the heavens,) meaning, His promise shall come to pass on the Day when the earth will be changed to an earth other than this earth that we know and recognize. It is recorded in the Two Sahihs that Sahl bin Sa`d said that the Messenger of Allah said,

Chapter 14: Ibrahim (Abraham), Verses 001-052

«يُحْشَرُ النَّاسُ يَوْمَ الْقِيَامَةِ عَلَى أَرْضٍ بَيْضَاءَ عَفْرَاءَ كَقُرْصَةِ النَّقِيِّ لَيْسَ فِيهَا مَعْلَمٌ لِأَحَدٍ»

(On the Day of Resurrection, the people will be gathered on a white (barren), flat earth just like the wheat bread, it has no recognizable features for anyone.) Imam Ahmad recorded that `A'ishah said, "I was the first among all people who asked the Messenger of Allah about this Ayah,

(On the Day when the earth will be changed to another earth and so will be the heavens,) saying, `O Allah's Messenger! Where will the people be then' He said,

«عَلَى الصِّرَاطِ»

(On the Sirat.)" Muslim, but not Al-Bukhari, collected this Hadith. At-Tirmidhi and Ibn Majah also recorded it, and At-Tirmidhi said "Hasan Sahih". Imam Muslim bin Al-Hajjaj recorded in his Sahih that Thawban the servant of the Messenger of Allah said, "I was standing next to the Messenger of Allah when a Jewish rabbi came to him and said, `Peace be to you, O Muhammad.' I pushed him with such a force that almost caused him to fall down and he asked me why I did that. I said, `Why did you not say, `O Messenger of Allah' The Jew said, `We call him by the name which his family gave him.' The Messenger of Allah said,

«إِنَّ اسْمِي مُحَمَّدٌ الَّذِي سَمَّانِي بِهِ أَهْلِي»

(Muhammad is indeed the name which my family gave me.) The Jew said, `I came to ask you about something.' The Messenger of Allah replied,

«أَيَنْفَعُكَ شَيْئًا إِنْ حَدَّثْتُكَ؟»

(Would it benefit you if I replied to your question) He said, `I will hear it with my ear.' The Messenger of Allah poked the ground with a staff he had and said,

«سَلْ»

(Ask.) The Jew said, `Where will the people be when the earth will be changed to another earth and so will the heavens' The Messenger of Allah said,

«هُمْ فِي الظُّلْمَةِ دُونَ الْجِسْرِ»

(In the darkness before the Bridge (Jasr).) He asked, `Who will be the first to pass it' He said, (The poor emigrants (Muhajirin).) He asked, `What will their (refreshment) be when they enter Paradise' He said, (The caul of fish liver.) He asked, `What will they have after that' He said, (A bull of Paradise which grazed through its pathways will be slaughtered for them.) He asked, `From what will they drink' He said, (From a fountain whose name is Salsabil.) He said, `You have said the truth. I have come to ask you something about which none of the inhabitants of the earth knows, with the exception of a Prophet or one or two other men.' He said, (Would you benefit by me informing you about it) He replied, `I would listen. I have come to ask you about the child.' He said, (The fluid of the man is white, and the woman's is yellow. When they meet, if the discharge of the man is greater than that of the woman, then it becomes a male, by Allah's permission. When the womans discharge is greater than the man's, it becomes a female by Allah's permission.) The Jew said, `You have told the truth and are indeed a Prophet.' Then he left. So Allah's Messenger said; (He asked me such things that I had no knowledge of it until Allah gave it to me.) Allah said next,

(and they will appear before Allah), describing when the creatures will be resurrected before Allah from their graves,

(the One, the Irresisti- ble.) Who has full power and control over all things and to Whom the necks and minds are subservient.

Surah: 14 Ayah: 49, Ayah: 50 & Ayah: 51

﴿ وَتَرَى ٱلۡمُجۡرِمِينَ يَوۡمَئِذٍ مُّقَرَّنِينَ فِى ٱلۡأَصۡفَادِ ۝ ﴾

49. And you will see the Mujrimûn (criminals, disbelievers in the Oneness of Allâh - Islâmic Monotheism, polytheists) that Day Muqarranûn (bound together) in fetters.

﴿ سَرَابِيلُهُم مِّن قَطِرَانٍ وَتَغۡشَىٰ وُجُوهَهُمُ ٱلنَّارُ ۝ ﴾

50. Their garments will be of pitch, and fire will cover their faces.

﴿ لِيَجۡزِىَ ٱللَّهُ كُلَّ نَفۡسٍ مَّا كَسَبَتۡ إِنَّ ٱللَّهَ سَرِيعُ ٱلۡحِسَابِ ۝ ﴾

51. That Allâh may requite each person according to what he has earned. Truly, Allâh is Swift at reckoning.

Transliteration

49. Watara almujrimeena yawma-ithin muqarraneena fee al-asfadi 50. Sarabeeluhum min qatranin wataghsha wujoohahumu alnnaru 51. Liyajziya Allahu kulla nafsin ma kasabat inna Allaha sareeAAu alhisabi

Tafsir Ibn Kathir

The Condition of the criminals on the Day of Resurrection

Allah said,

(On the Day when the earth will be changed to another earth and so will be the heavens) 'and the creations will be brought before their Lord, and you, O Muhammad, will witness the criminals who committed the crimes of Kufr and mischief,'

(Muqarranin) bound together, each with his or her like, just as Allah said,

(Assemble those who did wrong, together with their companions.) (37:22)

(And when the souls are joined with their bodies.)(81:7),

(And when they shall be thrown into a narrow place thereof, chained together, they will exclaim therein for destruction.) (25:13) and,

(And also the Shayatin from the Jinn (including) every kind of builder and diver, and also others bound in fetters.)(38:37-38) Allah said next,

(Their garments will be of Qatiran (pitch),) that is used to coat camels. Qatadah commented that Qatiran (tar) is one of the fastest objects to catch fire. Ibn `Abbas used to say that the Qatiran, mentioned in the Ayah, is dissolved lead. It is possible that this Ayah reads as: (قِطْرآنٍ مِنْ سَرَابِيلُهُمْ) refering to heated lead that has reached tremendous heat, according to Mujahid, Ikrimah, Sa'id bin Jubayr Al-Hasan and Qatadah. Allah said next,

(and fire will cover their faces), which is similar to His other statement,

(The Fire will burn their faces, and therein they will grin, with displaced lips.)(23:104) Imam Ahmad recorded that Yahya bin Abi Ishaq said that Aban bin Yazid said that Yahya bin Abi Kathir said that Zayd bin Abi Salam said that Abu Malik Al-Ash`ari said that the Messenger of Allah said,

«أَرْبَعٌ فِي أُمَّتِي مِنْ أَمْرِ الْجَاهِلِيَّةِ لَا يَتْرُكُونَهُنَّ: الْفَخْرُ بِالْأَحْسَابِ، وَالطَّعْنُ فِي الْأَنْسَابِ، وَالِاسْتِسْقَاءُ بِالنُّجُومِ، وَالنِّيَاحَةُ عَلَى الْمَيِّتِ، وَالنَّائِحَةُ إِذَا لَمْ تَتُبْ قَبْلَ مَوْتِهَا، تُقَامُ يَوْمَ الْقِيَامَةِ وَعَلَيْهَا سِرْبَالٌ مِنْ قَطِرَانٍ وَدِرْعٌ مِنْ جَرَبٍ»

(Four characteristics from the time of Jahiliyyah will remain in my Ummah, since they will not abandon them: boasting about their family lineage, discrediting family ties, seeking rain through the stars, and wailing for their dead. Verily, if she who wails, dies before she repents from her behavior, she will be resurrected on the Day of Resurrection while wearing a dress of Qatiran and a cloak of mange.) Muslim collected this Hadith. Allah said next,

(That Allah may requite each person according to what he has earned.) meaning, on the Day of Resurrection. Allah said in another Ayah,

(That He may requite those who do evil with that which they have done.) (53:31) Allah said here,

(Truly, Allah is swift at reckoning.) when He wills to reckon a servants of His, for He knows everything and nothing ever escapes His observation. Verily, His power over all of His creation is the same as His power over one creature,

(The creation of you all and the resurrection of you all are only as a single person.)(31:28) And this is why Mujahid said,

(swift at reckoning), means "keeping count."

Surah: 14 Ayah: 52

﴿ هَـٰذَا بَلَـٰغٌ لِّلنَّاسِ وَلِيُنذَرُواْ بِهِۦ وَلِيَعْلَمُوٓاْ أَنَّمَا هُوَ إِلَـٰهٌ وَٰحِدٌ وَلِيَذَّكَّرَ أُوْلُواْ ٱلْأَلْبَـٰبِ ۝ ﴾

52. This (Qur'ân) is a Message for mankind (and a clear proof against them), in order that they may be warned thereby, and that they may know that He is the only One Ilâh (God - Allâh) - (none has the right to be worshipped but Allâh) - and that men of understanding may take heed.

Transliteration

52. Hatha balaghun lilnnasi waliyuntharoo bihi waliyaAAlamoo annama huwa ilahun wahidun waliyaththakkara oloo al-albabi

Tafsir Ibn Kathir

Allah states that this Qur'an is a Message for mankind,

((So) that I may therewith warn you and whomsoever it may reach.) (6:19) This Qur'an is for all mankind and the Jinns, just as Allah said in the beginning of this Surah,

(Alif-Lam-Ra. (This is) a Book which We have revealed unto you in order that you might lead mankind out of darkness into light.) (14:1) Allah said next,

(in order that they may be warned thereby), or to receive and draw lessons from it,

(and that they may know that He is the only One God) using its proofs and evidences that testify that there is no true deity except Allah,

(and that men of understanding may take heed.) meaning those who have good minds. aThis is the end of the Tafsir of Surah Ibrahim, and all praise is due to Allah.

www.ingramcontent.com/pod-product-compliance
Lightning Source LLC
Chambersburg PA
CBHW081112080526
44587CB00021B/3564